FIDDLER
OF THE OPRY

FIDDLER
OF THE OPRY

The Howdy Forrester Story

Gayel Pitchford

VIEWPOINT PRESS
TEHACHAPI, CALIFORNIA

Excerpts from *Roy Acuff: The Smoky Mountain Boys* by Elizabeth Schlappi © 1978, 1993, used by permission of the licenser, Pelican Publishing Company, Inc.

Although the author and publisher have made every effort to ensure the accuracy and completeness of information contained in this book, we assume no responsibility for errors, inaccuracies, omissions, or any inconsistency herein. Any slighting of people, places, or organizations is unintentional.

First printing 2007
ISBN-13: 978-0-943962-06-1
LCCN 2007921384

ATTENTION CORPORATIONS, UNIVERSITIES, COLLEGES, AND PROFESSIONAL ORGANIZATIONS: Quantity discounts are available on bulk purchases of this book for educational, gift purposes, or as premiums for increasing magazine subscriptions or renewals. Special books or book excerpts can also be created to fit specific needs. For information, please contact Viewpoint Press.

This book is lovingly dedicated

to the memory

of

Howard Wilson ("Big Howdy") Forrester

who forever changed the face of fiddling…

and to

brothers Clyde and Joe

and son Bob Forrester

who lived Howard's story with him.

Contents

Acknowledgments

This book would not have been possible without the intense cooperation of Howard's brothers, Joe and Clyde, and Howard's son, Bob Forrester, who know firsthand just how important Howdy Forrester was (and is) to the world of fiddling. They each gave up three weeks of their lives to share with me stories, facts, documents, pictures, recordings, videos, notebooks, and even a visit to their old homestead in Hickman County. Consummate southern gentlemen all, they provided me with reams of information and even held several jam sessions so I could play Howdy's tunes (on Howdy's fiddle, no less!) along with them and Charlie Collins, the last remaining Smoky Mountain Boy. They also helped proof the manuscript to make sure there were no factual errors, and they continue to answer my endless questions even now, as this book goes to press. To them I am most grateful. Unfortunately, Clyde passed away (at 92) in July of 2006 and did not get to see this book in its published form.

I also offer heartfelt thanks to my dear friend and fellow author, Dr. B. J. Mitchell, who encouraged me to write this book in the first place, and who helped me with research and traveled many miles to assist me with picture taking, interviews, document copying, and carrying fiddles and guitars around.

In addition, the following people all helped me, in ways large and small. Without them, this book would not have happened: Robert Cogswell, Director of Folk Life Division, Tennessee Arts Commission; Librarian Dawn Oberg, Historian John Rumble, Audio-visual Curator Alan Stoker, and Photography Curator Denny Adcock of the Country Music Foundation Library; Photographer Rick Gardner of Houston, TX; Banjoist and fellow writer Murphy Henry; Artist

Ethel M. (Dee) Chastain; Neil V. Rosenberg; Smoky Mountain Boy Charlie Collins; Jean Thomas, Howard's longtime assistant; my Internet friend Stewart Evans, who led me to Murphy Henry; fiddlers Stacey Phillips, Johnny Gimble, Ron Eldridge, and Craig Duncan; violinist Mischa Lefkowitz of the Los Angeles Philharmonic; Jeff Porterfield at Buckaroo Records and Don Jones at Misty Records; Kris Duke of the Kern County Library in Tehachapi, CA; Garland County Library in Hot Springs, AK; Public Library of Nashville & Dickson County, TN; Kansas State University Library at Emporia, KS; the kind ladies at Post-Net in Tehachapi, CA; Paige Woodward, who got me started fiddling; Rick Greene at Spring Hill Funeral Home and Cemetery in Nashville, TN; Lyn Neal, Ed Enderle, and Wayne and Cathy Agnew of California State Old Time Fiddlers Association; Lee White of Lee's House of Music in Tehachapi, CA; Writer and Musician Tom Ewing; WSM Photographer Les Leverett; Eddie Stubbs, the voice of the Opry on WSM; Ted Kitsmiller at Radio Shack in Tehachapi, CA; the late Dr. Charles K. Wolfe at Middle Tennessee State University; Gene Lowinger; BMI; Dr. Patricia Kelley; Roscoe and Ossie White; Paul Rawls and Justine Perry-Duke of the Isaac Litton High School Alumni Association; Librarian Barbara Hoffman at the Nashville Symphony; Wilson Library at the University of North Carolina at Chapel Hill; George Gruhn of Gruhn Guitars in Nashville, TN; Mark and Sally Wingate; Anton Ullrich; Peggy Lamb at SONY/ATV (formerly Acuff-Rose); Mike Armistead at RME, Inc.; Jo Stone, Guy Martin, and Maria Weir, members of the Friends of Hattie Band; Lorraine O'Driscoll at Family Travel; the staff of Best Western-Music Row Hotel in Nashville, TN; and all my music students and friends who listened and offered support.

I apologize to anyone I might have missed. So many wonderful people have stepped forward to help me learn and write about Howdy Forrester and to offer words of encouragement when I needed them most. To all of you I say, "Thank you, thank you, thank you!"

Foreword

Howdy Forrester (L) and Georgia Slim Rutland (R), Radio KRLD, Dallas, c. 1947. Notice how they are bowing on each other's fiddle! This photo was used as the basis for the drawing on the cover (pen and ink with watercolor overlay). The artist is Ethel M. "Dee" Chastain of Pasadena, CA.

Howard "Howdy" Forrester was one of Tennessee's most extraordinary native musical figures—a fiddler's fiddler, and, as Gayel Pitchford suggests, perhaps a violinist's fiddler as well. He took to the instrument in the Hickman County folk culture of his boyhood, and it took him to a lengthy career in Nashville's commercial country music industry. For an instrumentalist of Howdy's generation, there was no more prestigious or stable job than being featured player with Roy Acuff's Smoky Mountain Boys.

It was a support role to one of the most famous American celebrities of the era. Although some of Acuff's fame inevitably rubbed off, Howdy's career generated notoriety of a different character. His core following was not made up of mainstream fans, but rather of musicians and others with particular appreciation for good fiddling. His principal career rewards weren't measured in terms of money or name recognition, but were instead reflected in the currency of respect, admiration, and influence within those rarified circles. There Howdy certainly established himself as one of the most highly regarded fiddlers of the twentieth century.

The other qualifying aspect of Howdy's fame is that it has, unfortunately, also faded quite a bit since his passing in 1987. There are several reasons why. First, very little of his playing can be easily heard by contemporary listeners, even the most diehard fiddle enthusiasts. Just as all great players excel "in the moment," in his heyday, Howdy's genius perhaps pulsed strongest through impermanent radio airwaves and live concert sound systems. He did do his share of recording, but, as detailed in chapters that follow, it was often as an unacknowledged accompanist or under circumstances that did not best show off his talents as a featured performer. The two albums generally regarded as his masterpieces have been sadly out of print for decades. Surprisingly few recorded sides graced by Howdy have even made it to reissue on digital CD format.

Until now, the written record, as well, has failed to adequately document Howdy's life and music. It speaks to the magnetism of his playing that a posthumous admirer from across the country should come forward to correct this neglect, and fiddle enthusiasts owe a debt of gratitude to Gayel Pitchford for doing so. Her labor of love was inspired by the chance hearing of a Forrester tune on a fiddle anthology, fueled by her curiosity that questions about the player could not be easily answered, and sustained by the enthusiasm of surviving family and other associates and admirers for seeing to it that Howdy's story would at last be told. The character of her book—part classic country music biography, part recollective oral history, part discographic commentary, and part musical annotation—reflects that she had a lot of poorly charted ground to cover and scattered resources to draw on. I share her hope that this dedicated effort will reclaim recognition for Howdy's genius.

It may not have helped Howdy's legacy that his career and music can't be neatly categorized under a single genre of fiddling. Nowadays old-time, western swing, commercial country, bluegrass, and contest styles, not to mention regional variations, all represent particular fiddling camps with constituencies who sometimes fiercely idolize musical fine points and forebears. As Pitchford contends, Howdy was indeed a "bridge" player, not just spanning styles, but also exerting seminal influences on some of them while remaining exclusive to none. Even the roughest outline of his career and his collaborations with other fiddle masters discloses this breadth and versatility. A year's mentoring from Arthur Smith broadened Howdy's command of the Middle Tennessee vernacular as a beginning professional. His western stint with "Georgia Slim" Rutland placed him in the middle of the emergent Texas swing and contest fiddle movements. His time with Bill Monroe implicated Howdy in the birth of bluegrass, and later appearances on the festival circuit and collaborations with Chubby Wise and Kenny Baker reflected continued associations with that style. His high profile as a Grand Ole Opry sideman brought constant interaction with the likes of square dance and session great Tommy Jackson, for many years keeping Howdy active in the upper echelon of mainstream country music as well.

Howdy Forrester is surely hard to pigeonhole. A folk musician by nature, he played by ear, as did most of his Nashville peers, and he built his skills in the traditional manner—tune by tune, acquiring a huge repertory and trading these pieces like treasured currency with other fiddlers throughout his career. Yet broad experience, love of his instrument, open-mindedness, and pure curiosity also led him in extremely eclectic directions. Even as a youngster, he closely observed classical players and took elements of their technique to heart. As his professional contacts and travels exposed him to other musical streams, he drew from them as well, such as the deep tune repertories of Canadian fiddling and the tempos and structures of East European music that crept into some of his original pieces. As he matured, Howdy became a true individualist. He loved the hoedowns and other old standards, but he took ownership of them in ways that conveyed his own genius, with unique deliveries and arrangements. More than other fiddlers of his time, he also composed tunes, many inventively drawing on nontraditional influences and non-folk fiddle techniques.

Howdy was proud of his abilities and of his music. Those of us who had the privilege of hearing him firsthand will recall the enthusiasm and intensity he exuded onstage. Featured numbers usually ended with a blistering flourish, as he thrust both bow and fiddle aloft in a gesture of triumph above a flushed and beaming face. There was something very personable and childlike about that. It told the audience that this was an approachable virtuoso, just as excited about what he could do as they were.

It's been said among musicians who've tried to emulate him that Howdy's playing, arrangements, and original compositions were impossibly difficult by design, so that nobody could successfully copy him. He certainly did hold high standards, but not just as a point of arrogance. Howdy always enjoyed the company of other fiddlers and was kind, respectful, and positive toward those of lesser ability. I think fiddling to him was a like a set of puzzles or an elusive quest for perfection, and the challenges his mastery might set for others who pursued it only mirrored challenges he'd set for himself. In that spirit, I know Howdy would be pleased that this book will help keep his music alive and keep the bar high for fiddlers yet to come.

Robert Cogswell
Folklife Program Director
Tennessee Arts Commission

Introduction

Once in a blue moon someone comes along in a particular field who is so advanced, so "out of the box," so innovative and creative in approach to a chosen specialty, that the particular field of endeavor is forever changed. In the case of old-time fiddling, that special person who changed the genre so dramatically was Howard Wilson "Big Howdy" Forrester.

Forrester was truly *the* "Fiddler of the Opry," as he spent more continuous years playing on the Grand Ole Opry than any other fiddler through history—thirty-six years with Roy Acuff, plus short stints with Bill Monroe and the Bluegrass Boys (twice), Herald Goodman and the Tennessee Valley Boys, and Cowboy Copas— which adds up to some thirty-eight or more years. But his music is so much more powerful than just the number of years he spent on the Opry.

Forrester, who was one of the greatest fiddlers of all time, has been the inspiration for most of our modern-day fiddlers. Many books of fiddle tune transcriptions attribute various licks in the tunes to the way Howdy played the pieces. And his recordings on both the MGM and United Artist labels are collector's items (*if* you can find a copy) and are some of the most important recordings of the time.

Forrester was the quintessential "bridge" fiddler, spanning the years between the old-time, shuffling hoedown playing of the past and the more modern fiddlers of today, who play with great intonation and lots of technique, often built up during years of Suzuki-style violin lessons. The really good fiddlers of today know how to draw a big, beautiful tone out of their fiddle and how to execute the many flashy bow strokes, sliding double stops, harmonics, improvisational techniques, and clean playing style that Forrester perfected and made famous, although Forrester never had a violin—or fiddle—lesson in his life!

Howdy didn't just *play* the fiddle, either; he was an avid composer and arranger of music as well. His "Memory Waltz" was an instant hit when it was published on the United Artist album *Big Howdy—Fiddlin' Country Style* (1963), which sold hundreds of copies. The tune is still played today by the very finest fiddlers in contests around the country. Both "Memory Waltz" and his "Wild Fiddler's Rag" are included in several current anthologies of fiddle tunes available on the market today, although Howdy is not always credited as the composer!

Forrester is also known for his fine improvisations and for taking very old fiddle tunes and turning them into more modern hoedowns, such as his "Brilliancy," which is a pastiche of old Scottish and Irish hornpipes. Texas fiddler Johnny Gimble called Howdy "the best breakdown fiddler I was ever around," high praise from one of the virtuosos of the business. His hoedowns are quite fast and have such a strong dance beat that they are hypnotic. And his waltzes and other tunes are filled with the most beautiful slid double stops, reminiscent of the finest classical violinists of his day, such as Fritz Kreisler and Isaac Stern.

For many years Forrester played on the Grand Ole Opry with such notables as Bill Monroe and the Bluegrass Boys and Roy Acuff and the Smoky Mountain Boys. Both Monroe and Acuff were elected to the Hall of Fame, but despite the fact that Howdy's sweet and innovative fiddle was one of the reasons for their success, Forrester never was accorded the same honor as they were. Sideman were rarely recognized by the Country Music Association, and Howdy was the consummate sideman, always making his bosses look and sound good while never showing them up.

Yet Howdy remains a legend far beyond his own time and an inspiration to all the fiddlers of today. Children and adults alike are playing his tunes and listening to his records, seeking to make the same sweet sounds on their own fiddles for which Howdy was famous. Old-time fiddling has, in part, been kept alive by the way Forrester "modernized" it and made it relevant to a whole generation of fiddlers who have grown up playing the violin and reading music.

I am definitely one of those fiddlers. As a child, I learned to sing many "fiddle (folk) tunes" in school. I promptly came home and played those tunes—"Arkansas Traveler," "Red River Valley," "Little Liza Jane," "Turkey in the Straw," "Cindy," and others—by ear on the piano and later the violin, adding notes and licks as I went along, which I thought definitely improved the music. My piano teacher did not agree and used to rap my knuckles with a ruler every time I put an improvisation into a tune or song. (That is actually how I ended up playing the violin, as a way to escape a cruel piano teacher.)

I did not know there was a musical genre called fiddling and that I was actually doing fiddling. It wasn't until I was an adult and teaching others to play the violin that I came to understand this.

By then, several of my forty+ violin students were engaged in fiddling, and I bought a CD, *30 Greatest Fiddlers Hits* (Highland Music Company, Deluxe DCD 7823), so I could listen to the sound of fiddling and help my students with their tunes. The second tune on the CD was called "Still on the Hill" and was played with such a beautiful tone and such style that I looked to see who the artist was. It was someone named Howdy Forrester. I learned to play and love that tune, and thus began my search for all the music of Forrester I could find. I have since listened to dozens of recordings of other fiddlers, but few have the sweetness and beauty that Forrester projects in his tunes. His improvisations are done with the greatest of skill, and there is none of this "sharp the fourth just because I can, even though it makes no musical sense" attitude that so many fiddlers have. Howdy had an excellent ear, and his playing is clean, clear, and always in tune—clearly a model to follow. In fact, at the annual Grand Master Fiddler Championship in Nashville, they would often ask Howdy to play a tune or two before the contest started, so that the Judges had a "gold standard" to use as they evaluated the contestants!

As a result of Howdy's influence on my own playing, I have taught all of my students to fiddle, and most of them now know and love the tunes and arrangements of Forrester. And they and I have become proficient contest fiddlers, with shelves full of the trophies we have won.

Unfortunately, there is not a lot in print about this giant among fiddlers, and what *is* out there is not entirely accurate. So I have set out to capture for the future as much of the essence and music of Howdy Forrester as I can.

I hope this book inspires you to take up your fiddle and play like Howdy! And I hope some day soon the Country Music Association will elect Howdy Forrester posthumously to the honor he so richly deserves—membership in the Hall of Fame.

CHAPTER 1

Howdy in
Hickman County

The rain beat a heavy tattoo on the roof, as the young boy lay in bed gazing at the window. Water ran down the pane in rivulets, turning this way and that, and for a while the boy was lost in thought, imagining himself running through the woods haphazardly, in much the same fashion as the rain was running. Soon, however, he began to fidget.

"Mama," he called, "I want to get up now. I can't stand this any longer."

His mother came into the room and placed a cool hand on his feverish brow.

"Now, Howard," she intoned. "You heard what the doctor said. You're very sick, and you must stay in bed and rest. I'll get a cold cloth for your face; you're burning up with fever."

As she left the room, the boy gnashed his teeth and spit out these words: "Rheumatic fever. The doctor says I have rheumatic fever and I probably won't ever walk again. But I'll show that son of a bitch. I *will* walk again, and I'll go squirrel hunting in the woods with Clyde again, too."[1]

His mother returned with a cold cloth, which she put on his face, and after a time, the boy fell back to sleep. Emmie Totty shook her head. "Such a bright boy," she mused. "Why did this have to happen to him?"

Emmie was used to tragedy. Born in 1895, in a Scotch-Irish family with two children—her brother William and her—she had grown up fairly poor. The family lived on a farm, and she spent her youth doing chores, helping with crops, taking care of chickens and livestock, cooking for the men, and canning summer crops for the winter months. The family had a sorghum cane patch and a mule-powered mill to grind the cane.[2]

One of the few "fun things" in the Totty's life was that they always made time to play music. Emmie played piano and pump organ and had taught herself to play the banjo and to fingerpick the guitar. Her son Joe says: "She could pick the guitar better than Maybelle Carter could!"[3] Her dad was a fiddler, and her brother William played the guitar. Her Uncle Bob Cates (her mother's brother) played the fiddle and was one of the best-known fiddlers in Hickman County, playing for dances and parties and in an oc-casional fiddle contest. Emmie definitely had music in her blood and may even have played guitar for a few dances.

By the time she was seventeen, she had fallen in love with and married Stephen Allen Forrester, whom everyone called Allen.[4] They lived in a small house on his brother William's one-hundred-acre farm up on the ridge, between his parents (the Forresters) who lived in Possum Hollow and her parents (the Tottys) who lived on Pretty Creek. Her parents' farm was the better one, as the Possum Hollow farm was full of stones.

The closest town was Vernon, just 2.5 miles down the road from their farm. Vernon is about sixty-five miles southwest of Nash-ville, in the heart of Hickman County. This is Middle Tennessee, a place of rolling, wooded hills and small towns, a place that has produced many great fiddlers such as Fiddlin' Arthur Smith, Paul Warren, Grady Stringer, Bob Cates, and of course, Howdy Forrester.[5]

Allen and Emmie's house is still standing on the ridge, but the woods are all cleared away up to the house now, and the house has definitely been remodeled.[6] When Allen and Emmie lived there, they had no plumbing and had to draw their water from a well. They had an outhouse, which son Clyde described as "hot and smelly in summer and cold in winter."[7]

Allen came from a bigger family than Emmie. He had four brothers: Albert, Hickman, Odom, and Willie, and two half-brothers with the last name of Reeves. The Forrester side of the family liked to talk and would have free-ranging discussions about all sorts of things. Allen was a fiddler and once won the fiddle contest at the fair in Centerville.

In addition to farming, Emmie's husband, Allen, was a good carpenter, handy with tools, and clever at making things out of wood. During World War I, he actually helped build the DuPont Powder Plant near Nashville.

Over a period of eight years, Emmie gave birth to four boys: Clyde, born in 1914; Clayton, born in 1916; Joe, born in 1919; and Howard, born at 2:00 a.m. on March 31, 1922.[8] Life was tough on the farm. Their house lacked electricity, and the boys did their homework by the light of a coal oil lamp.[9]

During the 1920s, Allen worked at Old Hickory, making rayon. One day the plant manager asked him to do a job that required him to work suspended over the vats where they cooked the chemicals that made up the rayon. There was no safety net or harness, and men had actually been killed when they had inadvertently fallen into the vats. Allen refused to work up there without a safety net, and the manager fired him. Unable to find other suitable work, Allen worked on the farm, did occasional odd jobs for others, and played the fiddle for dances.[10]

In 1927, life on the farm became much harder for the young farm wife, Emmie Totty Forrester. Her husband Allen was out driving with friends when the car they were in was struck by a train at an unmarked railroad crossing. Allen died instantly, leaving Emmie with four young sons to raise.[11]

And now the youngest son, Howard, was seriously ill with rheumatic fever and the prognosis was that he would have heart and joint damage and would probably always be an invalid.

Howard was a good child, obedient, amiable, and interesting. He did well academically at the little one-room schoolhouse Emmie's sons all attended, Pretty Creek School (grades one to eight), which was located on Pretty Creek, a 2.5 mile walk from their house. Howard had become a proficient reader and seemed to have inherited some of the family's musical talent, as he had taught himself to pick out a number of tunes on an old banjo his mother had. Emmie knew she needed to have a plan to keep Howard engaged and doing something productive, even though he was very sick.

Later that day when the boy awakened and had finished his dinner, his mother said, "You know, Howard. I saw how carefully you paid attention to Uncle Bob's fiddling when we were over at Only. Maybe you would like to learn to play the fiddle?"

She could see the light start to shine in Howard's feverish eyes. He had heard Uncle Bob (his *Great*-uncle Bob) play the fiddle and had been quite taken by it. Uncle Bob knew hundreds of tunes, some of which had already begun rattling around in Howard's brain and which he had tried to pick out on his banjo.

"Oh, Mama, could I? Could I really?" His chest was suddenly so tight that, in addition to his fever, he could now hardly breathe, and he was so choked up with emotion that he couldn't speak, either. That he might someday learn to play the fiddle had been his biggest dream and desire ever since he had heard Uncle Bob play—his impossible dream. And to think that now it might come true. It was almost too much for his nine-year-old mind to comprehend.

His mother ran her fingers through his curly hair and softly said, "Now you be a good boy and get some rest. When you feel a little better, I'll try to help you get started with the fiddle."

"Oh, Mama. Thank you, Mama," was all he could manage to choke out. His mother was the best, the most wonderful woman in the world. He had always known that, even when he and the older boys had done bad things and she had whipped them for it. He rolled over, clutching his arms to his chest, his eyes closed, as he started to imagine himself standing up in front of people and playing the fiddle.

"Sleep tight," Emmie whispered, as she left the room.

As the days went by, Howard began to feel a little better. Buoyed by the fact that he was going to learn the fiddle, his spirits improved and his fever actually subsided. It was almost as if he were willing himself to get well. In Howard's own words: "Everyone tried to make an invalid out of me and, you know, I thought to myself—why, I'm not going to lay [sic] here in this bed. I'm going to get up and do something…let's get up and play the fiddle."[12] Soon he could sit up for short periods of time, and Emmie felt it was time for the instruction to begin.

"This is it, Howard. Fiddle lessons start today," Emmie said, as she reached up and took the old fiddle off the wall. "This was your Grandfather Forrester's fiddle. You know, he traded somebody for it just after the Civil War."[13] She wiped the dust off the fiddle and plucked the strings. "Ugh," she grumbled. "It's way out of tune," and she began turning the squeaky old pegs to bring the strings up to pitch.

This was how their daily fiddle sessions would begin, with Emmie tuning up the fiddle for her son. Unfortunately, Emmie was a guitar picker and not a fiddle player, so she inadvertently tuned the fiddle to an open A chord, the kind of alternate tuning used in tunes like "Black Mountain Rag" and "Pretty Polly Ann."[14] Howard, of course, didn't know any better, and each day he would tune up his fiddle in the way his mother had instructed him.

Emmie showed Howard how to pull the bow across the strings and roughly how to hold the instrument. Then she began singing songs to him, one note at a time. She would sing a pitch, and Howard would move his fingers around on the fingerboard until he had found that pitch. Then they would move on to the next note. The first tune Howard tried to learn was "Tennessee Wagoner," a fairly difficult tune normally played in the key of C. With a fiddle tuned to an A chord, Howard admitted, "I scratched with this tune, and it was very hard to master." It was a tune he remembered his father playing for him when he had been a small boy.

Howard had a good ear for the music, and as the days went by, it took him less and less time to find the pitches his mother sang, despite his strangely tuned instrument.[15]

Sometimes, just to avoid any hint of monotony, Emmie would play the tunes on her banjo or whistle them, instead of singing. She could see that not only was Howard making progress on the fiddle, but also that his health was improving, which pleased her greatly.

As for Howard, he was so excited, he could hardly think straight. After a time, his thoughts were filled with music, the notes of a tune running through his head and mixing in with words in a book, arithmetic problems on a page, or whatever else he was supposed to be working on. He went to sleep at night with tunes running in his head and awoke in the morning with the music still playing. And for the rest of his life, the music never stopped playing in his head.

One day his Uncle William Totty, his mother's brother, came to the valley to visit them and was quite amused to hear Howard sawing away on a fiddle not conventionally tuned. He insisted on tuning it properly and showed Howard how to tune it for himself. Suddenly, the tunes became much easier for Howard to learn, and his playing really started improving rapidly. "[Once] I got the fiddle tuned, why I had no trouble at all learning 'Tennessee Wagoner,'" Howard reported.[16]

Later in life, Howard would always carry a tuning fork with him and insist on tuning his fiddle perfectly before going out on stage to play, the result of the good habits his mother and Uncle William had taught him.[17]

Howard spent eight months recuperating from the rheumatic fever, which meant he missed an entire school year and had to be held back a grade. But it didn't seem to bother him, and he used the year to learn dozens of tunes on the fiddle. In the learning process, he also figured out some of the mysteries of the fiddle, such as how the notes are arranged in order on the fingerboard and how to make loud sounds—or soft ones—by using the bow in different ways and drawing it across the strings in different places. And he learned to play fast, which all children like to do and which he knew was a requisite for fiddle players from hearing Uncle Bob play. He also stopped playing the banjo entirely, as his entire musical world now revolved around the fiddle. He had discovered his *métier*, his true calling in life, which was to be a fiddle player. His love affair with the fiddle would last him his whole life. Unlike other fiddlers he came to know, he did not play the mandolin, banjo, guitar, or piano. The fiddle was it for him.

By the end of that year, 1931, he was sitting outside on the porch fiddling away, with brother Joe by his side playing strong rhythmic chords on the guitar. Suddenly, fiddling became easier, as Howard learned to listen to the chord changes Joe made and to keep a really steady rhythm to his playing, which the guitar forced him to do. Joe knew the melodies to lots of tunes himself, as he had started making music by blowing tunes on an old harmonica. He later rigged up a harmonica holder made from a baking powder can and a piece of baling wire, so he could play the harmonica and accompany himself on the guitar at the same time, a sort of early-days Bob Dylan.[18]

Howard could hardly wait for Christmas to come, as they would go to visit their Uncle Bob down at Only, ten to twelve miles away from their farm. Howard was excited to show Uncle Bob that now he, too, could play the fiddle and perhaps to get Uncle Bob to teach him some more tunes and some advanced technique.

Howard was very precise about his fiddling, playing each note exactly as he learned it. He would always be very proud of the fact that, even though he knew hundreds of tunes, he really *knew* them; that is, he could play them exactly as they were and not just sort of correctly. Later in life he would tell his son Bob how important it was to set up the tune properly by starting out with the exact melody.[19]

In September 1932 Howard went back to Pretty Creek School, where he excelled in his school work. Suddenly, Howard was forced to become more disciplined about his life, because in addition to chores and homework, he had to fit in time for fiddle practice, the most important thing in his life.

There were fine poplar trees on their farm, really tall ones, and it took a good shotgun and a good shooter to get a squirrel out of the tree. The Forrester boys had a dog named Old Mac that would tree the squirrels for them. The older boys, Clayton and Clyde, were pretty good shots, but Howard wasn't nearly so interested in such things. He and Joe would sit on the porch and play music, while Clayton and Clyde would hunt or play baseball and try to keep up with the old Philadelphia Athletics.[20]

Within a short time, Howard knew enough tunes to be considered a credible fiddler, and the four Forrester boys formed a band: Clayton, who had the best personality of any of them but didn't play music, danced; Clyde played guitar; Joe played bass; and Howard played the fiddle. They began playing for house parties and dances and were paid "a dime on the square." Each man dancing the set (three tunes) paid a dime. The boys could make two to three dollars apiece for playing an evening's dance.[21]

The Forresters didn't go to church very often, as the closest church, the Church of Christ, was some distance away. It must have been a very fundamentalist type of church, however, as when they did go to church, Howard reported being "fearful of all that hell and damnation."[22] Howard's uncle held Sunday school at the school house and, once in a while, they would go to hear some traveling preacher of whatever denomination deliver a sermon. Even without much church, though, the Forresters were good, respectful boys who learned old-fashioned values from their mother.

They raised chickens and cows, grew corn and hay, and had a big vegetable garden, where they grew beans, cabbage, onions, potatoes, and sweet potatoes. They also had a strawberry patch on one side. They all worked hard on the farm. Howard reported, "I started hoeing corn when I was six or seven years old. Everybody went to the fields in those days, and we had double shovels, bull tongues and mules and horses—and that was it. Sassafras roots—we dug 'em."[23]

While they didn't go hungry, there was no money for extras. Whatever odd jobs the boys could get or dances they could play, they took. When jobs on the farm were too large for the boys to do, some of their uncles would come and help out.

Howard's oldest brother, Clyde, went to junior high (ninth and tenth grades) at Nunelly, which was five miles from the Forresters' house. Clyde would walk to school, but often local farmers would see him trudging along with his books and give him a lift. For senior high (grades eleven and twelve), Clyde went to school in Centerville, which was so far away that he had to board with a local family there. Since he was eight years older than Howard, Clyde was staying in Centerville by the time Howard was nine. Of all the boys in the family, only Clyde actually graduated from high school.[24]

Clayton followed Clyde through junior high at Nunelly, but then left home and enlisted in the U.S. Navy, which meant that by the time Howard was about eleven, both Clyde and Clayton were gone from the family home. Notwithstanding that, the family had bonded very tightly, and the four brothers remained the closest of friends for the rest of their lives. They also loved and revered their mother very much. They may not have had many material things, but there was lots of love—and no dysfunction—in that home. Later in life, Howard would tell his son Bob, "Family and friends— that's what is really important in life. I've had both, and I wouldn't trade either one of them to be a rich man."[25]

Howard and Joe continued to practice music together, and at Christmas time, they got to play for some dances in Only, where Uncle Bob lived. One snowy night, they were playing for a square dance at a private home. They had been playing for quite some time and were really "in the groove." Pretty soon, several of Uncle Bob's friends showed up at the party. It was cold, and the men had drunk a little whiskey to help stay warm. As they climbed out of their car, they could hear the music coming through the walls of the house. "Ol' Bob Cates is really ripe tonight," one of the men said. As they reached the house, he wiped the frost from one of the window panes and peered inside. "Well, I'll be damned. That ain't Bob playin'. It's that little Forrester kid!"

But actually it was two little Forrester kids: Howard on fiddle and Joe on guitar, turning out one tune after another. They were sitting in chairs, as these types of house parties tended to go on for hours, sometimes all night. Howard, who was only eleven or twelve at the time, was so small sitting in his chair, his feet didn't even touch the floor![26]

Howard and Joe were in big demand to play for home dances and parties, and they accepted most all gigs that came their way. Howard had become a good dance fiddler, playing with a very strong, steady beat and fast enough that the music had that hypnotic quality associated with the finest fiddlers. He had learned to "set up" the tunes in dance style (AABB), playing each section twice, which coincided with what the caller did. And he had developed a fiddler's ear, working hard to play every pitch in tune. He and Joe also began singing duets together, accompanying themselves as they sang, with Howard singing the high part and Joe the low one.

They especially loved Christmas break each year, as they got to spend at least a week at Uncle Bob's house in Only, during which time they were able to play for at least three dances and sometimes more.

Some years later, Howard told his good friend, Dr. Perry Harris, "One of my and Joe's fondest memories was when we played for Mr. Will McClanahan. After we performed, he indicated that he wanted us to come stay with him permanently because 'You are as welcome here as the flowers in May time.'"[27]

By now the country was in the grip of the Great Depression, and jobs and money were really hard to come by. According to Harris, Howard and Joe still got dance jobs, however, because "they were not only fine musicians, but fine gentlemen as well."[28]

Country boys learn to drink at an early age, and Howard was no exception. Lester Harris, a barber friend of the Forresters out in Hickman County, actually gave Howard his first taste of whiskey. It may have been "moonshine" (bootleg whiskey), but in any event, Howard liked it, and he drank a lot of it over his lifetime. But ever the gentleman and ever the professional, he never let his drinking get in the way of his music.[29]

The boys continued to expand their repertoire of music, learning a number of tunes and styles from their Grandfather Totty, who was also a reputable fiddler. Once in a while they got to hear a tune or two on the Grand Ole Opry broadcast. Only a couple of families in their area had radios, and Howard and Joe would walk five to ten miles to someone's house just to listen to the Opry.[30]

Farms were far apart, and there were no mass communication media in those days, so learning even one new tune was a momentous event, as their access to new tunes was extremely limited.

They also learned tunes from Great Uncle Bob, who taught them a number of tunes that must have originated in Hickman County, as Howard later said he had never heard many of them played anywhere else. Uncle Bob also taught the boys good values: play fair, be honest, and be a person of integrity. To his dying day, Howard always told his own son, "Whatever you do, son, don't lie to me," an adage that he, no doubt, learned himself from Uncle Bob.[31]

By the time Howard was twelve, his family had recognized that he and Joe were quite musically gifted and had become credible musicians despite their tender ages. One day their Aunt Nell Totty, who listened to country music over radio station WSM out of Nashville, called the station and spoke to someone about her nephews and their fine playing. As a result, Howard and Joe were invited to Nashville to play on a WSM show called "Friends and Neighbors." It was a variety show, featuring numerous performers. The boys got to play several hoedowns live on the show, their first time ever to play on the radio. Joe Forrester must have had an inkling that this was important, as seventy years later, he still has the little certificate WSM Radio gave him for playing on the show![32]

In 1935, Howard came to Nashville to see the State Fair. While he was there, he saw an orchestra of school children playing, and he watched in rapt attention, especially the violin section. The student musicians were playing difficult music, and the violinists were playing up and down the fingerboards of their violins. At first Howard was puzzled, wondering how they could get up to those high notes on the top of the fiddle, but then he realized that they all held their violins (fiddles) differently than he did. They all played with their left arms held straight, from their elbows to their hands. In other words, their wrists were down. Howard had always "palmed" his fiddle and played with a bent left wrist, like so many of the old-time fiddlers did. He suddenly saw that he could play up on top of his fiddle where the highest notes were if he changed his grip on the instrument. He went right home and started practicing his new fiddle hold. (He would one day be famous for his ability to find all those high notes and play them in tune!)[33]

Throughout his life, Howard was quick to spot when someone was doing something that he needed to learn to do—and just as quick to go home and work through whatever it was. He always told people, "I think you can pick up a little bit from every musician you see or ever play with. You can learn something from every fiddler. He'll have something you haven't seen or heard before. So that's how you learn it. They don't even have to be good musicians. You can learn a tune, a lick, a new way to think about something, a different way to do something, or even how *not* to do something."[34] As a sideman, he became an astute observer of people, and he put his observations to work to improve his own playing.

Also in 1935, Howard's brother Clayton left home to enlist in the Navy. Following initial training, he was detailed to the *USS Tennessee*, where he served as a Gunner's Mate, doing telemetry for the Naval Gunfire Support System. Clayton liked to travel, so Navy life fit him well. Some of the highlights of his four-year hitch were riding his ship through the Panama Canal, attending the 1939 World's Fair, seeing the New York Yankees play, and witnessing the opening of the Golden Gate and Oakland Bay Bridges, and he sent cards and letters home regularly about his adventures, fueling the imagination of the young and impressionable Howard Forrester.[35]

CHAPTER 2

Strictly Forrester

In 1935, Emmie moved her smaller family to Nashville, where they lived on the east side of town, first in a little house on Maplewood Lane owned by William Totty, and later in a house on Elvira Avenue. The boys worked at odd jobs, and Emmie did housework and took in ironing. She also had a small insurance settlement from her husband's death, which she used very frugally.[36] Howard enrolled at Jerry Baxter Grammar School for seventh and eighth grade, while brother Joe enrolled at Isaac Litton High School in the tenth grade. Howard, who was an avid reader and good student, was having trouble paying attention in class, as his mind was always playing—and by now, arranging—fiddle tunes. His doodles in his school notebooks from that time reflect a definite preoccupation with music.[37]

In the eighth grade, Howard won an award for outstanding penmanship. His fine small motor coordination and attention to detail would later be hallmarks of his fiddle playing.[38] Smoky Mountain Boy Charlie Collins eventually called him "a perfectionist kind of guy."[39]

After two years at Jerry Baxter, Howard transferred to Isaac Litton High School for the ninth grade. Part way through the school year, he was required to purchase a book for his English class, *Rime of the Ancient Mariner*, but the Forrester family had no money to pay for it. Howard also had no money for fancy clothes, so he wore his overalls to school. The other students made fun of his attire and picked fights with him over it. As a result of these two things, Howard was asked to leave school before the end of the school year in 1938, which he did.[40]

In those days, the city fathers of Nashville were in a state of denial about country music. They did not want Nashville looked down upon and associated with what they called "hillbilly music." And they certainly did not want anyone to think they were backward in any way. As a result, they poured money into cultural attractions such as a symphony and opera and ballet companies. They insisted on calling Nashville "The Athens of the South" and worked hard to live up to the moniker. Yet it was country music that defined the town and brought in the money—and to which most people listened—albeit often clandestinely.

Paul Rawls, Isaac Litton High School alumnus of 1951, remembers how he loved listening to the Grand Ole Opry over radio station WSM in Nashville. But he never told his friends at school about it, as they all made fun of "that hillbilly music." One Saturday evening, someone gave Paul four tickets—front row center—to the Grand Ole Opry, and he asked three friends to go with him to see the live show at the Ryman Theater. He was astounded as each eagerly accepted his invitation and even more shocked as he scanned the audience to see dozens of his high school classmates there, the same classmates who had mocked the Opry's music![41]

The city's fathers were not the only ones in denial, but it is easy to see why a country boy in overalls—particularly one who played the fiddle instead of football—would have trouble fitting in at school. (Mark O'Connor would later have a similar problem at his Seattle high school.) Howard was born to fiddle, however. He had an ambition to get on the Grand Ole Opry, and he would not be deterred from his destiny.

Howard and Joe, of course, were still playing music every chance they got. On Saturday afternoons they would play in the Merchant's Hotel in downtown Nashville, hoping to earn enough money (fifteen to twenty cents each) to go to the Rex Theater and see a western movie.[42]

As a result of this, Howard developed a love for western movies that continued throughout his life; he would often say, "Quick, turn on the TV and get some damn cowboys on there!"[43] Interestingly enough, however, his love of westerns did not lead him in the direction of playing cowboy music.

Busking at the Merchant's Hotel raised the boys' confidence level, and soon Howard and Joe were playing for free on WSIX radio in Nashville, on a little show called "Country Store." The show was broadcast on Saturday afternoons and featured a band made up of Howard playing fiddle, Joe playing bass, the Gregory boys on guitar and steel guitar, and James and Billy Byrd on guitar and fiddle. Joe Forrester said they called themselves the Tennessee Playboys; however, Howard told interviewer Doug Green that they were the Rhythm Ramblers.[44]

James Byrd, the other fiddle player in their group, had actually taken some Suzuki-style violin lessons. Howard could see that James "knew stuff," and he watched and asked questions. Pretty soon, James had taught him a better way to hold his bow.[45] Many years later when Howard sent his son Bob for violin lessons with a member of the Nashville Symphony, Bob's teacher told him, "If you want to see how to hold your bow properly, just watch your father play. He has a perfect bow hold—curved thumb, fingers all on the stick, little finger curved up on top."[46]

One day the WSIX manager, Joe Calloway, received a call from a thirty-eight-year-old promoter named Herald Goodman, who had heard various groups play on WSIX. Goodman had been on the Grand Ole Opry with a band called the Vagabonds, which was just splitting up. He was looking for something new, and he asked Calloway if he had anyone playing there who was good enough to play on the professional side. Calloway replied, "Yes, there's two boys here that I would highly recommend." Those two boys, of course, were Howard and Joe Forrester. Goodman called them; they went for an audition and soon began working for him.[47]

According to Howard, the band now consisted of Howard, Joe, Bill and James Byrd, Hubert Gregory (later of the Fruit Jar Drinkers), and Golden Stewart, the bass player from the Crook Brothers.[48] "We had a pretty good fiddle team," Howard told Doug Green, "even though we were quite young and inexperienced."[49]

They began playing on the Opry, and on April 5, using the name of Goodman's now-defunct band, the Vagabonds, they played their first "out-of-town gig" in Adairville, Kentucky. Joe Forrester, who started a meticulous ledger of their travels, recorded that they were each paid $3.00 for this performance. On April 6, they played in Russellsville, Alabama; and on April 12, they were in Burns, Tennessee, followed by an April 13 gig in Minor Hill, Tennessee. They each made $3.00 for each of these performances as well.

On April 21, they played in Bowling Green, Kentucky, but Joe's ledger shows they received no compensation for their efforts. People liked their music, though, and they always played to a good crowd.[50]

By April 26, 1938, Herald Goodman, who loved making up names for things, had changed their name to the Tennessee Valley Boys. And, instead of being just a band, they were "entertainment." They didn't just play music; they put on a show. "Cousin Herald" Goodman was the emcee and did the comedy. Howard played fiddle, and Joe Forrester played bass on a funny-looking, "home made" bass that actually was made in a cabinet shop on Shelby Street. Billy Byrd played guitar, and "Huckleberry" Buck Fulton played guitar and sang. They played a mixture of southeastern fiddle band music and western swing, what Charles Wolfe, in his book *The Devil's Box*, referred to as "Southeastern swing."[51]

Goodman was a shrewd promoter, who figured he needed someone famous to play with the band, in order to build up a good following. At that time, the two best fiddlers around were Clayton McMichen and Fiddlin' Arthur Smith. Clayton was probably the better fiddler, but Arthur was already one of the biggest stars on the Grand Ole Opry, so Goodman asked Arthur to join his group.[52]

By now, the school year had ended, and Joe Forrester had finished the eleventh grade, which was all the formal schooling he was to receive. The Forrester family had no money, so Joe quit school and began looking for a job to help support the family. Luckily, he didn't find one right away, because Herald Goodman had booked the band to go on a tour of east Kentucky, West Virginia, Virginia, and North Carolina.[53]

Howard and Joe's mother did not want them to go on the road. Howard was only sixteen, and Emmie feared for his safety, his sanity, and his health. She knew there would be many temptations out on the road, alcohol and loose women among them. But Herald Goodman reassured her, saying, "I will take good care of your boys for you, as if they were my own sons." And according to Joe, Herald made good on that promise, keeping them out of trouble and gainfully employed. For years after, he would introduce them to people as "his sons."[54]

They were in mining country for much of this tour, and John L. Lewis, the President of the United Mine Workers, was king—or God, as the locals said. Lewis had just forced the mine owners to shore up the mines, which saved many miners' lives. Herald Goodman was a big jokester and was always threatening to lampoon Lewis at one of their performances. This gave Arthur Smith fits, as he was sure Goodman was going to get them all killed! Fortunately, Goodman never carried out his threat.[55]

In any event, Arthur Smith was the "featured performer" in their group, doing the solo work. Howard played backup to Arthur. By this time, Herald Goodman, with his penchant for naming things and people, had changed Howard's name to Howdy and, more specifically, Big Howdy. Howard never liked his new name much, but it stuck to him. Howard's family continued to call him Howard, but to audiences across the country, he would become Big Howdy Forrester.[56]

The band traveled in a four-door 1937 black Chrysler Royal, with their name, Tennessee Valley Boys, painted on each door. Sometimes, when they stopped along the road to ask for directions, people seemed afraid to talk to them. The Tennessee Valley Authority (TVA) was young in those days, and Joe Forrester opined, "Maybe they thought that we were government men!" In any event, most of the time there were seven people plus instruments in the car, not very comfortable for a long trip.[57]

The schedule Goodman worked out for them was daunting, and probably only their youth and their dreams of fame and fortune kept them going. According to Joe Forrester's journal he kept, their itinerary for May was as follows:

DATE	LOCATION	EARNINGS
May 5	Ritz Theatre, Livingston, TN	$2.00
May 6	High School, Waynesboro, TN	Expenses Only
May 7	Grand Ole Opry, Nashville, TN	$3.00
May 8	Allen Theatre, Liberty, KY	$2.00
May 12	Highland Theatre, Kingsport, TN	$3.00
May 13	Star Theatre, Salyersville, KY	Expenses Only
May 14	Grand Ole Opry	$3.00
May 15	Strand Theatre, Dawson Springs, KY	$3.00
May 16	Northcuts Core School, McMinnville	$2.00
May 19	High School, Red Boiling Springs	$2.50
May 20	School, Pelham, TN	$0
May 21	Grand Ole Opry, Nashville, TN	$1.00
May 22	Gate City Theatre, Catlettsburg	$1.50
May 23	Gate City Theatre	$1.50
May 27	Grande Theatre, Ironton, OH	$0
May 28	Grand Ole Opry, Nashville, TN	
Monthly Total		$24.50[58]

As Joe's ledger book shows, the Tennessee Valley Boys could wander far from Nashville during the week, but they had to be back in town each Saturday night to play the Opry. The great entertainer Roy Acuff once said of the Opry: "I mean, once you got on [the Opry], you stayed. It was that simple. And you played every Saturday night, no matter where you went during the week; you got back to Nashville on Saturday night, and only a death in the family—say, your own—would excuse an absence."[59]

The Opry was—and still is—a live performance, which was broadcast over radio station WSM in Nashville. WSM (We Shield Millions) was actually owned by the National Life & Accident Insurance Company. Under their auspices, some Opry performers were actually hired as station staff. (This was the case with Curt

Poulton—formerly of the Vagabonds—who played briefly with the Tennessee Valley Boys in 1939.)[60]

Unfortunately, that was *not* the case for Howard and Joe and the rest of the band, who just received a small gratuity each time they appeared on the broadcast. What *they* got from the Opry was simply exposure—to a very wide-ranging audience—as WSM was not only a "clear channel" station, but also a member of NBC's national network.

As soon as the Opry show closed on Saturday night, the Tennessee Valley Boys were back in the car and headed for their next performance. It was a tough way to make a living, and Joe Forrester kept wondering if he should return home and look for a real job. Howard, of course, was lost in the music, making up tunes and improvisations and learning by watching and listening to Arthur Smith. It was heady stuff for a sixteen-year-old country boy! Howard and Arthur would occasionally sip a little whiskey together, and Howard would ask him all sorts of questions about fiddling: why this, and how do you do that?[61]

Joe's journal shows June was an equally daunting month:

DATE	LOCATION	EARNINGS
June 4	Grand Ole Opry, Nashville, TN	$3.00
June 11	" "	$3.50
June 12	National Theatre, Louisville, KY	$3.00
June 14	Garden Theatre, Louisa, KY	$3.00
June 15	Temple Theatre, Middleport, OH	$2.00
June 16	New Arcade Theatre, Paintsville, KY	$5.00
June 17	Virginia Theatre, Welston, OH	Unknown
June 18	Grand Ole Opry, Nashville, TN	Sold candy
June 19	Fiddler's Contest, Huntington, WV	$5.00
June 20	Liberty Theatre, Oak Hill, OH	$2.00
June 21	Greenup Theatre, Greenup, KY	$2.20
June 22	Hall's Theatre, Catlettsburg, KY	$0
June 23	Margaret Theatre, Huntington, WV	$3.00

June 24	Galipolis Theatre, Galipolis, OH	Unknown
June 25	Grand Ole Opry, Nashville, TN	$1.00
June 27	Cook's School, Mt. Pilot, NC	$2.67
June 28	Flat Rock H.S., Mt. Airy, NC	$2.00
June 29	Francisco H.S.	$2.00
June 30	Shoals H.S.	$2.00
Monthly Total		$41.37[62]

The Tennessee Valley Boys were an invited band at the Fiddler's Contest on June 19, but neither Arthur Smith nor Howard played in the actual contest, although either of them could probably have won it had they entered.

July opened in similar fashion to June:

DATE	LOCATION	EARNINGS
July 1	Dobson H.S.	Unknown
July 2	Grand Ole Opry, Nashville, TN	$1.00
July 4	Camden Park, Huntington, WV	$5.00
July 5	Dixie Theatre, Olive Hill, KY	$3.00
July 6	Tabb Theatre, Mt. Sterling	$3.00
July 7	Trail Theatre, Morehead	$3.00
July 8	Strand Theatre, Irvin	$2.10
July 9	Grand Ole Opry, Nashville, TN	$1.00
July 11	Martin Theatre, Martin, KY $3.00	
July 12	Garrett Theatre, Garrett, KY	
	Wayland Theatre, Wayland, KY	$3.00
July 13	Henry Clay Theatre, Lookout, KY	$2.00
July 14	Weddington Theatre, Pikeville, KY	$3.00
July 15	Praise Theatre, Praise, KY	$2.00
July 16	Grand Ole Opry, Nashville, TN	$1.00
July 18	Lyric Theatre, New Boston, OH	$3.00

July 19	Theatre, Barbersville, WV	$2.00
July 20	Memorial Bldg., Williamson, WV	$0
July 21	Jenkins Theatre, Jenkins, KY	$3.00
July 22	Lynnwood Theatre, Grundy, VA	$3.00
July 23	Grand Ole Opry, Nashville, TN	$1.00
July 27	Oak Hill Theatre, Oak Hill, WV	$2.00
July 29	Royal Theatre, Princeton, WV	$5.00
July 30	Grand Ole Opry, Nashville, TN	Unknown
Monthly Total		$51.10

On Saturday, July 2, Huckleberry (Buck Fulton) left their group. Their July 4 concert was outdoors, where they were joined by the singer Juanita, whom Goodman dubbed the "Queen of the Mountains." Juanita sang with them until August 1, when she left the group. On July 20, Virgil "Speedy" Adkins joined the Tennessee Valley Boys on banjo.[63]

Their total take apiece for the month of July was only $51.10, which didn't leave much after all the expenses were paid. For the two Forrester boys, however, who hadn't been away from home much, all of this touring was quite an adventure, seeing all the little towns in neighboring states and a few in their own. As for Howard, the traveling fever got in his blood, and later he would make countless trips all over the world, both with Roy Acuff and on his own as a private citizen. Still, he and Joe never forgot home and their sweet mother, and they were always grateful when it was time to go home.[64]

August's schedule was equally grueling:

DATE	LOCATION	EARNINGS
August 1	Alban Theatre, St. Alban, WV	$3.00
August 2	Pine Theatre, Pineville, WV	$3.00
August 3	Community Theatre, Keystone, WV	$3.00
August 4	Man Theatre, Man, WV	$3.00
August 5	Star Theatre, Richlands, VA	$10.00

August 6	Grand Ole Opry, Nashville, TN	Unknown
August 7	Hollywood Theatre, Morgantown, KY	$3.00
August 10	Star Theatre, Jamestown, TN	$0
August 11	High School, Alexandria, TN	$0
August 12	Churchwell Pictures, Savannah, TN	$0
August 13	Grand Ole Opry, Nashville, TN	Unknown
August 14	Rialto Theatre, Bluefield, WV	$3.00
August 15	Radford Theatre, Radford, VA	$5.00
August 16	State Theatre, Damascus, VA	$3.00
August 17	Dixie Theatre, Glade Springs, VA	$3.00
August 18	Roanoke Theatre, Roanoke, VA	$3.00
August 19	" "	$3.00
August 20	" "	$3.00 + 9.00 bonus
August 23	Clinch Theatre & Square Dance, Tazwell, VA	$5.00
August 24	Royal Theatre, Mount Hope, WV	$3.00
August 25	Palace Theatre, Christiansburg, VA	$3.00
August 26	" "	$0
August 27	Grand Ole Opry, Nashville, TN	Unknown
August 28	Grand Theatre, Ashland, KY	$3.00
August 29	" "	$3.00
August 30	Virginia Theatre, Parkersburg, WV	$3.00
August 31	" "	$3.00
Monthly Total		$80.00

On Sunday, August 14, singer Mary Margaret Helton started working with the Tennessee Valley Boys, joining them for their gig at the Rialto Theatre in Bluefield, West Virginia. With their $9.00 bonus, their total take for the month was $80.00 apiece, not a bad income for two self-taught young musicians.[65]

September found them still on the road, as Joe's ledger shows:

DATE	LOCATION	EARNINGS
Sept. 1	Alpine Theatre, Pt. Pleasant, WV	$2.00
Sept. 2	Bentley Theatre, Neon, KY	$3.00
Sept. 3	Grand Ole Opry, Nashville, TN	Unknown
Sept. 4	Fiddler's Contest, Bluefield, WV	$5.00
Sept. 5	Norton Theatre, Norton, VA	$4.00
Sept. 6	St. Paul Theatre, St. Paul, VA	$3.00
Sept. 7	Wallens Theatre, Wallens Creek, KY	$3.00
Sept. 8	Appalachian Theatre, Appalachia, VA	$3.00
Sept. 9	Gate City Theatre, Gate City, VA	Unknown
Sept. 10	Grand Ole Opry, Nashville, TN	Unknown
Sept. 12	Manring Theatre, Middlesboro, KY	$3.00
Sept. 13	Lee Theatre, Pennington Gap, KY	$3.00
Sept. 14	Kentucky Theatre, Whitesburg, KY	$3.00
Sept. 15	Novo Theatre, Cumberland, KY	$3.00
Sept. 16	New Harlen Theatre, Harlen, KY	Unknown
Sept. 17	Grand Ole Opry, Nashville, TN	Unknown
Sept. 19	Elk Theatre, Elkin, NC	$3.00
Sept. 20	Parkway Theatre, W. Jefferson, NC	$1.00
Sept. 21	Moor Theatre, Moorsville, NC	Unknown
Sept. 22	Spartan Theatre, Sparta, NC	$1.00
Sept. 23	Endependance Theatre, Endependance, VA	Unknown
Sept. 24	Grand Ole Opry, Nashville, TN	Unknown
Sept. 26	Recording Studio, Rock Hill, SC	$10.00
Sept. 27	" "	$10.00
Sept. 28	Vicco Theatre, Vicco, KY	$3.00
Sept. 29	Blue Diamond Theatre, Blue Diamond, KY	$2.00
Sept. 30	Keithley Theatre, Jonesville, VA	$1.00
Monthly Total		$66.00[66]

The band played at a fiddle contest in Bluefield, West Virginia, on Sunday, September 4, but neither Arthur Smith nor Howard competed in the fiddling portion of the contest. Howard didn't feel he had to "prove himself" in that way, that his music would speak for him. This was a personal decision he would follow for the rest of his life.[67]

On Thursday, September 8, the band was in Virginia for a performance at the Appalachia Theatre in Appalachia. Some sixty-five years later Joe Forrester still recalled playing at this theater. "It was tough times," he said, "and we were playing for tough people." He might remember it for another reason, as well, as this was the place where Mary Margaret made her last appearance with the Tennessee Valley Boys. She had become good friends with the band members and kept in touch by mail with both Joe Forrester and Billy Byrd.[68]

The Tennessee Valley Boys at this time included Joe Forrester on bass, Billy Byrd on guitar, Virgil "Speedy" Adkins on banjo, Howard on fiddle, and Herald Goodman who emceed and sang…and, of course, their big star, Fiddlin' Arthur Smith.

On September 26 and 27, 1938, the band went into a studio in Rockville, South Carolina, with Arthur Smith, to cut some sides on the Bluebird label. On September 26, they recorded "Tell Me" (BB B-8033, MW M-7684); "The Old Mountain Man" (BB B-8065, MW M-7680, RZAu G23937); "Is Your Name Written There?" (BB B8065, MW M-7682); "Tennessee Swing" (BB B7868, MW M-7683); "The Great Shining Light" (BB B-7999, MW M-7681); "That'll Do Now, That'll Do" (BB B8033, MW M-7684); "New Lamplighting Time in the Valley" (BB B-7999, MW M7681, Twin FT 8714); "The Lamplighter's Dream" (BB B-7935, MW M-7682, RZAu G23720); "Dad's Little Boy" (BB B-7935, MW M-7680, RZAu G23720); and "Banjo Rag" (BB B-7868, MW M-7683, RZAu G23937).

Arthur Smith was not a swing fiddle player, so Howdy Forrester stepped up and played hot fiddle licks on "Tennessee Swing" and other swing tunes they recorded. "Tennessee Swing" was re-released in 2003 on a CD entitled *Farewell Blues—Hot String Bands, 1936–1941*, Krazy Kat CD #30.

On September 27, the Tennessee Valley Boys recorded ten more songs: "Girl of My Dreams" (MW M-7689); "In the Pines" (BB B-7982, MW M-7685); "I've Had a Big Time Today" (BB B-7982, MW M-7685); "When the Roses Grow Around the Cabin Door" (BB B-8009, MW M-7687); "Give Me Old Time Music" (BB B-7982, MW M-7689); "The Farmer's Daughter" (BB B-7893, MW M-7685); "Gypsy's Warning" (BB B-7893, MW M-7686); "Why Should I Wonder?" (BB B-7943, MW M-7687, RZAu G23719); "I'm Lonesome I Guess" (BB B-8009, MW M-7688); and "Hesitating Blues" (BB B-8101, MW M-7688).

Howard plays on "Girl of My Dreams" and "In the Pines"; the latter song was re-released in 2002 on a County Records CD titled *Arthur Smith and His Dixieliners*, CO-CD-3526.[69]

This 1938 recording session was very important to Howard's career in country music and to his own self-esteem. He was only a lad of sixteen, but Arthur Smith, one of the biggest stars of the Opry, had actually recorded with Howard and the band. On "In the Pines," Howard plays twin fiddles with Arthur Smith, and then when Arthur sings, Howard plays "fill" in the background. On this recording, that "sweet Howdy Forrester tone" and his good musicianship are already apparent. These are two of the traits that would later make him famous, and Arthur Smith obviously could see this.

Throughout his life, Howard always looked up to Arthur Smith and said Arthur "taught him a lot." Arthur had his troubles with the Opry later on, but Howard always stuck up for him and was quick to defend his honor when people tried to steal his tunes or licks and pass them off as their own.[70]

As perceptive as Howard was, he undoubtedly realized that on this day, at this recording session, Arthur had given him a golden opportunity. Now it was up to Howard to make something of it. In addition to opportunity, he and Joe each received twenty dollars for the two days of work, a handsome reward for "making music with their friends."

October found the Forrester boys still on the road:

DATE	LOCATION	EARNINGS
Oct. 1	Grand Ole Opry, Nashville, TN	Unknown
Oct. 3	Strand Theatre, Vanceburg, KY	$3.00
Oct. 4	Park Theatre, Huntington, WVA	$3.00
Oct. 5	" "	$2.00
Oct. 6	New Westland Theatre, Portsmouth, OH	
Oct. 7	" "	
Oct. 8	Grand Ole Opry, Nashville, TN	
Oct. 12	Gem Theatre, Kannapolis, NC	
Oct. 13	Brookneil Theatre, Brookneil, VA	
Oct. 14	Grand Theatre, Leaksville, NC	
Oct. 15	Grand Ole Opry	
Oct. 17	Rural Retreat Theatre, Rural Retreat, VA	
Oct. 18	Hillsville Theatre, Hillsville, VA	
Oct. 19	Floyd Theatre, Floyd, VA	
Oct. 20	Stuart Theatre, Stuart, VA	
Oct. 21	Old Farm Hour, WCHS, Charleston, WV	$4.00
Oct. 22	Grand Ole Opry, Nashville, TN	
Oct. 24	Belfry H.S., Belfry, KY	$3.00
Oct. 25	Palace Theatre, Hamlin, WV	$3.00
Oct. 26	Logan H.S., Logan, WV	$3.00
Oct. 27	Magnolia H.S., Matewan, WV	$2.00
Oct. 28	Burch H.S., Delbarton, WV	$3.00
Oct. 29	Grand Ole Opry, Nashville, TN	
Oct. 31	Wharton Theatre, Wharton, WV	$3.00
Oct. 31	Van Theatre, Van, WV	$3.00
Monthly Total		$32.00

Joe Forrester's journal indicates that during the weeks when the chart above shows no pay entries, the band's lodging and expenses were paid.[71] Apparently, they received nothing extra above that.

On Monday, October 17, while the Tennessee Valley Boys were performing in Rural Retreat, VA, Herald Goodman added yet another fiddle to the mix, a young man from Georgia named Robert Rutland. Rutland performed under the name "Georgia Slim."[72]

Howard had heard about Slim, and when Goodman asked the band for ideas to improve their show, Howard recommended getting an additional fiddler and suggested Slim. Slim was playing in a fiddle contest at a nearby coal miners' town, and Herald and Howard went to hear him. A fiddler in a contest puts everything he's got into his tunes, and after hearing Slim play "Fire on the Mountain," Howard turned to Herald Goodman and said, "Hire him right now!" Herald, too, was sold on Slim and offered him a job.[73]

Slim was six years older than Howard, but they took to each other immediately. Both tall, slender, and good looking, their styles of playing and the ways in which they "heard the music" were similar, and they were very much soul mates. The two of them and Arthur Smith did some triple fiddling together, but the trio never recorded anything, so there is no way to know what they sounded like.

It is quite a tribute to the musicianship of the group that they could keep playing gigs in quick succession while integrating new people into—or removing them from—the group. Arthur Smith was still the featured performer, but Howard and Georgia Slim played "twin fiddles," another of Goodman's names he made up.

The band was still on the road in November, now with Georgia Slim in tow.

DATE	LOCATION	EARNINGS
Nov. 1	Clothier Theatre, Clothier, WV	$2.00
Nov. 2	Omar H.S., Omar, WV	$3.00
Nov. 3	H.S., Chapmansville, WV	$3.00
Nov. 4	H.S., Guyan Valley, WV	$3.00
Nov. 5	Grand Ole Opry, Nashville, TN	

Nov. 7	Mountain Theatre, Clintwood, VA	$3.00
Nov. 8	" "	$3.00
Nov. 9	Keen Mtn. Theatre, Keen Mtn., VA	
Nov. 10	Haysi Theatre, Haysi, VA	
Nov. 12	Grand Ole Opry, Nashville, TN	
Nov. 14	Narrows H.S., Narrows, VA	
Nov. 15	Pinbrook H.S., Pinbrook, VA	
Nov. 16	Jefferson H.S. Aud., Pulaski, VA	
Nov. 17	H.S., Christiansburg, VA	
Nov. 18	Galax H.S., Galax, VA	
Nov. 19	Grand Ole Opry	
Nov. 21	Bland H. S., Bland, VA	
Nov. 22	North Fork H.S., North Fork, WV	
Nov. 23	Leager H.S., Leager, WV	$1.00
Nov. 24	Gilbert H.S., Gilbert, WV	
Nov. 25	Theatre, Berwin, WV	
	Theatre, New Hall, WV	
	Theatre, Bishop, WV	
Nov. 26	Gus Foster's Radio Jam, City Hall,	
	Danville, VA	
Nov. 28	Majestic Theatre, Majestic, KY	
Nov. 29	Freeburn Theatre, Freeburn, KY	
Nov. 30	Dehue Theatre, Dehue, VA	
	Dance, Moonlight Nigh Club, Logan, WV	

On November 6, while they were back home in Nashville, Joe Forrester bought himself a new bass fiddle for $107.00 and promptly "broke it in" during their usual Saturday night appearance on the Opry.[74]

All of this traveling was beginning to wear on the band, especially having to run back into Nashville every weekend, which limited their touring area.

On Thursday, December 1, the band played a matinee at the high school in Coalwood, West Virginia, and in the evening performed at the War Theatre in War. On Friday they played at the high school in Richlands, Virginia and on Saturday returned home for the Opry.

Upon their return to Nashville, Joe Forrester discovered that the U.S. Post Office, where he had applied for a job earlier, had some "real work" for him and when the band left town on Monday, he did not go with them. The work lasted only a week (Christmas rush), although he would later work for the Post Office as his career job, and he rejoined the band on Saturday, December 10 for the Opry broadcast. This would be the Tennessee Valley Boys' last time to play together on the show.[75]

Sunday, December 11, they traveled to West Virginia to perform on the Radio Jamboree in Logan. On Monday and Tuesday, they played in the high schools in Pound and Nora, respectively. December 15 found them at the Harman Theatre in Maxie, Virginia, playing a matinee and then doing an evening show at the theatre in Big Rock.[76] The flyer announcing the shows said: "WSM Presents Herald Goodman and the Tennessee Valley Boys: Big Howdy, Georgia Slim, Forrester Brothers, Billy Byrd, Virgil Atkins, Cousin Herald, and Lespedeza." Lespedeza was the name Goodman had given to Joe Forrester, who became the comic of the show—at Arthur Smith's suggestion, appearing as a total hayseed who couldn't keep his britches on. His billing called him "Lespedeza, greener than the grass for which he's named."[77]

Joe wore a wig and big, baggy britches, held up with the requisite suspenders, which didn't quite seem to do the job. He would dance around his bass fiddle and at the end of a song, down would fall his pants! (His mother had dyed his underwear red, so it would really show up when the britches fell and he wouldn't look like he was naked.) To this day, Joe laughs with a twinkle in his eye when he reminisces about the fun he had using his bass as a prop for his antics.[78]

On Friday, December 16, the Tennessee Valley Boys played at Wayne High School in Wayne, West Virginia, to end their last week on the road out of WSM.[79]

They were home in time for Christmas holidays, but by then Herald Goodman had realized there was not enough work in and around Nashville to keep them gainfully employed. Being a regular on the Opry meant being available for the show every Saturday night, and that didn't pay enough to keep a man alive. (Joe Forrester notes several times in his ledger book that he was paid $1.00 for each of his Opry appearances.)[80] This meant the band had to have other engagements to play, but they were limited to quasi-local events, anything close enough to Nashville that would allow them to return for the Saturday night Opry broadcast. They had totally tapped out the local market, and Goodman felt the need to move on to greener pastures elsewhere.[81]

CHAPTER 3

On the Saddle Mountain Roundup

At the end of 1938, the Tennessee Valley Boys left Nashville and the Opry for an east Texas barnstorming tour: Howdy and Joe Forrester, Herald Goodman, Arthur Smith, Slim Rutland, Curt Poulton (originally with Goodman in the Vagabonds) playing guitar and doing some singing, and Gus Foster, a promoter and booking agent. They worked at a small radio station in Kilgore, Texas, and played in schools and theatres. They also played with Shelton's Sunshine Boys in Shreveport, Louisiana.[82]

The Forrester brothers had taken a room at the "Tulsa Hotel—Each Room with a Bath" in Kilgore and, while there, wrote the following letter home (postmarked February 22, 1939), to tell their mother about the new job they were getting:

Dear Mama and Clyde:

Goodman and Gus just got back from Tulsa. They are going to produce a big Monday night show and we are going in with the whole gang except Arthur.

We have a guarantee of $20 apiece every week. That's the happiest thing we've heard of yet. You should see this gang.

Clyde get ready we are going to bring a quart?? in. We will see you Mar. 3 or 4.

Love,
Joe and Howard[83]

Howard was so excited to be paid $20 a week that, when he received his first check, he admitted, "I went to a fine restaurant in Tulsa and bought me a T-bone steak."[84] About this time, Arthur Smith grew restless, as was his wont, and he left the Tennessee Valley Boys to head for West Virginia and a stint playing with the Bailes Brothers.[85]

In many ways, Howard was sorry to see Arthur leave the group. He had learned a lot from Arthur: many new tunes, some technique, how to play fill behind a soloist or a singer, and how to be a real showman on stage. On the other hand, Arthur's departure meant Howard got to play more solos and develop his own style. Arthur remained a lifelong friend of Howard and frequently stopped by Howard's home to talk and play music on his way through Nashville.[86]

By April 1, 1939, the band was working at the new job in Tulsa, Oklahoma, at a 25,000 watt radio station, KVOO, where Bob Wills had started out back in 1934. Herald Goodman began auditioning other acts, and before long he had put together a "barn dance," which Goodman, in his inimitable way, quickly named the Saddle Mountain Roundup. Admission to their show cost a maximum of forty cents per person.

The line-up featured the Tennessee Valley Boys, who now consisted of guitar player Curt Poulton, Joe Forrester playing bass and providing comic relief, Howard and Georgia Slim playing twin fiddles, and self-proclaimed "Cousin" Herald Goodman serving as emcee. Second in the line-up were the Three Young Maids from Sand Springs, Oklahoma. Other acts included the newly-hired Wilene Goldie Sue "Billie" Russell, christened as the "Orphan Girl" by Herald Goodman (and soon to become Mrs. Howdy Forrester); Rowdy Wright and his Jolly Cowboys; Steely Brothers, a hillbilly band; Cowboy Jim; Buster Brown, an Indian who yodeled; a twelve-year-old fiddler named Johnny Leach and his Girlfriend; the Sooner Sweethearts, an Oklahoma girls' trio; and Junior Webster, a singer with a wonderful voice.[87]

In addition to performing as a group, the Tennessee Valley Boys also served as the house band, accompanying many of the other acts, which cut down on the overall number of players who had to be hired and paid.

The band had an arrangement with KVOO, which gave them a commission to play the barn dance and do some radio programs. They had an up-front guarantee of a certain amount of money. Howard was now getting the $20 a week he had written about to his mother.[88] He was doing pretty well for a lad of only seventeen years.

The barn dance actually started on April 1, and the opening show was a smashing success. According to the KVOO Business Manager, Claymon Foster, "More than 4,000 people witnessed this opening, and we turned away approximately another thousand."[89] They put on a two-hour show, commencing at 9:00 p.m. The second hour of the show, from 10:00–11:00 p.m., was actually broadcast live over KVOO. The show played for eleven weeks at Convention Hall in Tulsa and then Goodman took the show on the road, playing every Saturday night in various towns in Arkansas, Oklahoma, and Kansas.

Their great success was all the more amazing since, at this time, Bob Wills was still running a dance hall there in Tulsa. Howard and Joe went to listen to Bob's show, after which Howard decided they really had to improve to be competitive—smoother bowing, playing in the higher positions—the practicing began in earnest.[90]

The Orphan Girl, Billie Russell, had sung and played guitar when she auditioned for the Roundup. However, she also played the piano and the violin and at some point in her career had picked up the accordion. Although her musical training was primarily classical, her grandfather, George Robbins, was a fiddler. From an early age Billie had been exposed to fiddle and guitar music. As a result, she could play in a fiddling style and during her college years had become a real fan of Bob Wills and the Playboys. Sometimes on the show, she and Howard and Georgia Slim would all play fiddles together.

Billie could also read and write music. She never really taught Howard to read music, but, according to Joe Forrester, Billie probably did write out (notate) some of his compositions for him so that he had lead sheets to submit for copyright purposes. (She would later perform the same service for Bill Monroe, when she played with the Bluegrass Boys.)[91]

In mid-May Howard and Joe received a postcard from their mother, dated May 10, which told how much she missed them:

Wed.
Dear Joe and Howard:

How are you this pretty morning? I'm spending the week on Pretty Creek [her family home]. This week, Mama has not been feeling well and I'm staying this week to help her a little. She is feeling better. I hope you all have wrote me two or three letters, I won't get them tho till Sat. as that is when I'm going home. Hope you are both well. Mama said tell you all she would write next week if she felt like it. I'll write a letter next week. don't forget to write.

Love,
Mama[92]

By June 17, Billie Russell, the Little Orphan Girl, was a regular on the show with her own spot, backed up by the Tennessee Valley Boys. She also played fiddle on the early a.m. radio show on KVOO and played with the group at local theaters and high schools.

By October of 1939, the Tennessee Valley Boys were touring again and were splitting their proceeds five ways between Goodman, Georgia Slim, Joe, Howard, and Red Penn, after they had paid the Orphan Girl, mileage, advertising, and fifteen percent artist service.

Joe's ledger for the month of October has the following entries:

DATE	LOCATION	PROFITS
Oct. 23, 1939	Haskell H.S. Auditorium	$7.30
Oct. 24	Preston H.S. Auditorium	$3.00
Oct. 25	Nuyacka H.S. Auditorium	$7.72
Oct. 26	Inola H.S. Auditorium	$7.50
Oct. 30	Macomb H.S.	$3.00
Oct. 31	Big Beaver Night Club	$5.00
Monthly Total		$33.52[93]

The band was trying to build up their audience appeal and recognition, so they had a bunch of promotional pictures taken and began selling them at their performances. Joe Forrester notes that they sold $1.70 worth of pictures at one of their shows.[94]

On Monday, October 30, they had several unfortunate experiences: a wreck that cost them $10 in repairs and an incident at the school where someone took them for about $15–20, resulting in paychecks of only $3.00 each for the day. A note in Joe Forrester's ledger (now a maroon-colored book) says: "Got took for about $15 or $20 at school—watch next time."

November's schedule found them quite busy:

DATE	LOCATION	PROFITS
Nov. 1	Talaquah H.S.	$3.19
Nov. 2	Gans H.S.	$2.83
Nov. 6	Unknown	$3.66
Nov. 7	Chief Theatre, Eufala, OK	$4.85
Nov. 8	Kellyville H.S. Auditorium	$10.73
Nov. 9	Childers H.S.	$5.84
Nov. 13	Grove Theatre, Grove, OK	$9.09
Nov. 14	Gore H.S.	$8.00
Nov. 15	Community Bldg., Siloam Springs, AR	$.77
Nov. 16	Nusho Theatre, Bixby, OK	$8.62
Nov. 20	School, Disney, OK	$6.80
Nov. 21	H.S. Auditorium, Talala, OK	$7.39
Nov. 22	Oak Hill Indian School, Jay, OK	$3.50
Nov. 23	H.S. Auditorium, Westville, OK	$7.00
Nov. 24	Cozy Theatre, Wagner, OK	$7.97
Nov. 27	H.S. Auditorium, Talihina	$.30
Nov. 28	H.S. Auditorium, Gavette, AR	$1.80
Nov. 29	H.S. Auditorium, Warner, OK	$2.75
Monthly Profit		$95.09[95]

Each of the brothers made $95.09 for the month from their shows, a better take than before. They also sold $53.50 worth of pictures. In this pre-television era, part of developing "star quality" was to provide people with great visual images and a reminder of the band and the show they had put on. Selling promotional photos was a big part of building their image and giving them a more professional look.

On November 2, the split changed from a five-way to a four-way, with Goodman no longer included. By November 6, they had paid Goodman off for all the pictures, so they could now have any picture sale money to keep as either profit or for new pictures when they needed them. After paying Goodman, they still had $9.50 left over and started a community bank account.

December found them as busy as ever:

DATE	LOCATION	PROFITS
Dec. 4	H.S., Schulter, OK	$3.68
Dec. 5	Wild Horse School	$5.67
Dec. 6	H.S., Lincoln, AR	$2.09
Dec. 7	H.S., Mannsford, OK	$9.22
Dec. 8	H.S., Hartshorne, OK	$3.68
Dec. 11	H.S., Claremore, OK	$.57
Dec. 13	H.S., Kansan, OK	$4.59
Dec. 14	H.S., Hulburt, OK	$5.50
Dec. 18	H.S. Auditorium, McCurtin, OK	$0
Dec. 19	H.S. Auditorium, Wolf, OK	$2.51
Monthly Profit		$37.51

They made only $37.51 each in December, but they sold $32.00 worth of pictures.[96] And they were picking up valuable performing experience; the quality and variety of their playing and singing had really improved. But they were in a situation similar to what they had with WSM and the Grand Ole Opry. They couldn't travel very far from Tulsa, as they had to be back to do their radio show—

every morning! It was nice to have the radio backing: a small salary guaranteed and air time to play music and plug their other shows— but the leash they were on (getting back to Tulsa on time) was rather short.

Any extra time they had was spent practicing, as Howard and Slim worked out their elaborate twin fiddle duets and got their bows synchronized on all the tunes.[97] This synchronization of bow-ing has become one of the mainstays of twin fiddling in today's old-time fiddle contests.

By the time 1940 started, Billie Russell was listed as one of the Tennessee Valley Boys, along with Howard, Joe, Georgia Slim, Red Penn, Goodman, and Junior Webster. And Billie and Howard had taken a real interest in each other, which was not surprising since they were both good-looking young people from poor backgrounds, highly-gifted musicians far away from home, and each pursuing a career in the tough music business.

Howard was a slim 5′11″ tall with wavy brown hair, soft hazel eyes, and a big smile, which revealed a row of perfect teeth.[98] Billie, on the other hand, was short. Uncle Dave Macon, a long-time friend, used to refer to her as "itty bitty Billie." She was small with a full head of long, dark, wavy hair, snappy green eyes, thick eye-brows, and high cheekbones. Her great-great-grandmother was a full-blooded Cherokee Indian, which made Billie one-sixteenth Indian and gave her a slightly exotic look.[99]

Howard's son Bob thinks that Howard and Billie were prob-ably dating "on the sly," as Herald Goodman had a strict prohibition on members of the show dating each other. However, Goodman didn't do anything about it when he caught them together at the movies. Perhaps he knew what a good fiddler Howard had be-come and didn't want to lose him from the band, or perhaps, as son Bob has suggested, "Goodman could tell they were pretty seri-ous about each other." In any event, Goodman allowed the courtship to continue, asking Howard at one point whether his intentions were honorable. When Howard assured him they were, that seemed to satisfy him.[100]

Between radio shows, rehearsals, individual practice time, work-ing out "twin fiddling" routines, and traveling to performances, it is amazing that Howard and Billie could actually find time to date—on the sly or otherwise! All the boys in the band, however, were nice, handsome young men, and when brother Joe Forrester was asked, "I'll bet you all had lots of young women chasing you?" he replied with a twinkle in his eye, "Well, yes…but once Howard saw Billie, that was it for him." As for Joe himself, he used to blush bright red whenever a girl even looked at him, which led to Herald Goodman calling him "Bashful Joe."[101]

The new year found them back on the road again:

DATE	LOCATION	PROFITS
Jan. 5, '40	Stockade Theatre, Ft. Gibson, OK	$0
Jan. 10	H.S. Auditorium, Shamrock, OK	$0
Jan. 11	H.S. Auditorium, Oilton, OK	$3.15
Jan. 16	H.S. Auditorium, Hacket, AR	$3.89
Jan. 17	H.S. Auditorium, Bryant, OK	$2.31
Jan. 18	Nusho Theatre, Cleveland, OK	$0
Jan. 19	H.S. Auditorium, Shidler, OK	$0
Jan. 23	H.S. Auditorium, Mason, OK	$3
Jan. 25	H.S. Auditorium, Collinsville, OK	$0
Monthly Profits		$12.35

Winter weather had set in, and not only was it sometimes difficult for them to get to their scheduled performances, but it was hard to generate much of a crowd, so their January earnings from shows were not much. Their January 10 show in Shamrock, Oklahoma, was canceled because the roads were bad and the gas was off at the school where they were to perform. Unfortunately, their expenses didn't get canceled out by the snowstorm. Keeping body and soul together was always a day to day struggle. They used most of the money the shows generated to pay off their bills for paper, advertising, and pictures.[102]

Sometimes, if the weather was bad, Joe Forrester would have to put his bass fiddle inside the car to protect it, rather than carry it on top as he usually did. The neck of the bass would be in the front of the car and the body would rest on the middle of the back seat. If Billie and Howard were sitting in the back seat, Joe said, "I'd be driving down the road, and it wouldn't be too long, I'd see that bass fiddle move over and one of them'd be scooting under the bass to get to the other side. We'd all laugh loud and long."[103]

It was apparent that their gigs were getting fewer and farther between, and they were not making the money they once had. Goodman was beginning to feel that they had pretty much tapped out this area, and as always, he was looking for greener pastures.

While they were working out of Tulsa, Howard, Joe, and Herald Goodman wrote a song together, which they titled "On the Saddle Mountain Roundup." Goodman later copyrighted the song in 1941. The words are significant:

> *Dust storms and heat,*
> *There's nothing to eat,*
> *I'm back on the trail once more.*
> *I'm going west, there I'll find rest,*
> *When my last ride is o'er.*
> *I hear the cattle lowin'*
> *By the waterhole tonight*
> *On the saddle mountain trail.*
> *They seem to know I'm going*
> *To my old pals tonight*   ·
> *On the saddle mountain trail.*
>
> *Through the dust and heat I'll ride*
> *Out through the great divide,*
> *I'll find a greener pasture*
> *When I reach the other side*
> *On the saddle mountain trail.*[104]

Notwithstanding that the name of their show was the Saddle Mountain Roundup, Howard and Joe were not really "cowboy" entertainers; they didn't sing or play that type of music. And they certainly were not cattle or horse people. Although this song could have been just a spoof written for the show, the words on the surface do not reflect who the boys were or what they did. And therefore, it may well be a metaphor for them leaving home and heading out on the trail in search of "greener musical pastures" out west.[105]

Sunday, February 4 found them playing at the Pettit Theatre in Homing, where they each made only $2.83 and only sold ninety cents' worth of pictures. On this day, Georgia Slim, who could probably see the writing on the wall, left the group to return to his mother's place in Georgia.[106]

In a 1969 interview with Earl Spielman, Slim opined, "I don't think [Herald Goodman] was interested in establishing a show and letting it go on and on and on. He'd peak it, get what there was to be made, pull out, go someplace else and promote another one, for example." For whatever reason, Goodman was starting to play theaters, not big barn dance-types of places, and, as Joe Forrester said, "trimming the show down."[107]

On Thursday, February 8, they played the Bufflo [sic] Theatre in Pawnee, Oklahoma, for a $3.50 take each and $3.90 in picture sales, and on Friday, their performance was at the high school in Gypsy, where they did much better, netting $6.58 each and selling $5.40 in pictures. But gigs were becoming harder to get.

They only played two shows the following week, in Strang and Webber Falls, Oklahoma, but the week after that, they played four days, February 20–23, at the high schools in Coyle, Chelsea, Checotah, and Boynton, Oklahoma.

The week of February 26, they played three shows: at the grammar school in Tiger District, at the high school in Oolagala, and at the Nusho Theatre in Cleveland, Oklahoma, and only netted $8.83 apiece, with an additional $4.90 in picture sales.[108]

On Monday, March 4, the band played at the high school in Tecumseh, Oklahoma. After the show, they settled their advance with Herald Goodman, and the Saddle Mountain Roundup was officially dissolved, after only one year. Goodman allowed the Forrester brothers to keep the name Tennessee Valley Boys.[109]

CHAPTER 4

The Dallas Polka

Howard, Joe, Red Penn, and his brother Chuck (who had played with Clay McMichen) went down to Wichita Falls in Texas, looking for work. Georgia Slim, who had returned from his visit to his mother, did not go with them, although he soon left for Dallas along with the promoter Gus Foster.

Billie also did not go with the boys. Although she and Howard were quite serious about each other, they knew they could not get married without having the security of a job or jobs, so Billie remained in Tulsa. The boys were unsure of what they would find in Texas, and Joe says, "It was safer and better for her to stay." It also meant one less room to rent, as the boys could bunk together, but Billie, being an unmarried woman, would have needed a separate room. Howard's son Bob thought that his mother and dad probably had an "agreement between them [that] if things worked out he was going to send for her."[110]

On the way to Wichita Falls, the boys made a short stop in Oklahoma City, where they tried without success to land a job with radio station WKY. Upon their arrival in Wichita Falls, Howard immediately penned a letter (postmarked March 7, 1940) to Billie, whom he often called "Bill":

Dearest Bill:

We got here last night about dark and spent the nite in a hotel and took an audition this morning at 9:15 [at Radio Station KWFT] and we will put our first program on in the morning at 6:45. Pretty fast, eh?

45

Boy, that ride from Oklahoma City down here was the lonesomiest [sic] thing I ever did in my life.... They seemed well pleased with the act at WKY but I think it was just another schrewy [sic] radio station. We have really got a spot starting Monday [March 11].

We play from 6:00 until 7:00 but they read the news all thru the spot and play organ music, too, so our part will amount to about 30 minutes.

You remember I promised I wouldn't say things were good when they weren't, so here's the set up and we hope it's good. We get to announce our dates and do most of the m.c. ourselves and hope to do all of it later on, but, honey, I did it on the audition and made them like it. Ha. (The Big Howdy.) If we get straightened out here and sold commercially, we will do fine because they were really glad to have us here and said they needed our act...

Well, here it is—I would rather be in Tulsa right now than any other place I know of and would I like to see you—but don't tell anyone I'm homesick or say anything about our setup. We rented an apartment today and we live with a nice couple who have two girls. One is about 12 and the other five and in the door staring me right in the face. She really is cute. You'll like her when you come down...

Love,
Howard[111]

On radio station KWFT they had a grocery store sponsor, and they played a fifteen-minute show in the store five days a week in the early morning. They made $40/month for the band from this commission. In addition, they could play whatever other performances they could get.

On Saturday night, March 16, working out of radio station KWFT, the Tennessee Valley Boys played at the Kerr Theatre in Davis, Oklahoma, and on Wednesday, March 20, at the Thompson Theatre in Healdton. They were "back in the saddle again," and, while they still weren't making a lot of money, at least they were in new territory and developing a new audience who seemed receptive to their music.

Sunday, March 24 found them at the Majestic Theatre in Temple, Oklahoma, and on Friday, the 29th, they played at the high school auditorium in Sunset, Texas.[112]

Howard missed Billie a lot, and on March 28, 1940, he wrote her from Wichita Falls:

Dearest Bill: [his affectionate name for her]

How are you? You little devil—…so you accused me of sleeping Sunday and being drunk? I'll have you know we left here at 11 o'clock Sunday morning and worked a theater all day. So there. Ha. Yes, and another thing. A hillbillie is good for only a little while, are they? I think you mean that, too, and if you think that I even want to get out and forget that I am a married man you're crazy. Don't take this too seriously. It was written with a good attitude…and if you find something that sounds a little "nutty" please excuse it as our sleep is limited to about four or five hours per day. Wonder if the Roundup will go over as big in Muskogee this Saturday nite as it did before. I hope so for Goodman's sake.

Don't kid me about wanting a job. You're in seventh heaven up at that radio station and don't deny it. It gets in your blood, don't it? Ah—come on now and tell the truth. You're still there, aren't you? Tell them we all send our regards.

We played our first dance Tuesday nite and have two more this week and they are all on a flat note* so that makes it good. They dance from 9 until 1:00.

Boy, are they crazy about square dances down here.

They can dance all night and never get tired…

I am *The* Big Howdy from the lone star state of Texas.

Ha. How about coming down and see me this summer? You'd better…

Love,
Howard[113]

*a flat note meant the band played for a pre-arranged fee, rather than receiving a percentage of the gate.

From this letter, it seems that Billie was still playing on the radio in Tulsa, quite likely with Herald Goodman and what remained of the Saddle Mountain Roundup. Whether Howard ever heard her or not is unknown, but with the schedule he was keeping, it is not likely.

It is clear that Howard and Billie were serious about each other. They obviously were not yet married, yet Howard seems to have considered himself as such and not free to go out, nor did he want to. This was fortunate for Billie, as the band members met plenty of unattached (and some attached) women on the road who would have been happy to take up with them, despite their somewhat impoverished circumstances.[114]

March 31, 1940, was Howard's eighteenth birthday, and he celebrated it with his band members, but without the love of his life, Billie Russell. He had actually played some band dates in taverns well before his eighteenth birthday, which meant he was playing in bars more than three years before he could legally drink in them!

Their itinerary for April was a grueling one:

DATE	LOCATION	PROFIT
April 2	Park Theatre, Iowa Park, TX	$0
April 3	Strand Theatre, Chilicothe, TX	$0
April 4	" "	$0
April 6	Wichita Club—Square Dance	$0
April 8	Joy Theatre, Ringling, OK	$0
April 9	Ritz Theatre, Lawton, OK	$0
April 10	Quail H.S., Quail, TX	$0
April 11	Gem Theatre, Ryan, OK	$0
April 12	" "	$0
April 16	H.S. Auditorium, Granite, OK	$0
April 17	Palace Theatre, Graham, TX	$0
April 18	Rock Tavern, Lawton, OK	$0
April 19	H.S. Auditorium, Erick, OK	$0
April 22	H.S. Auditorium, Acme, TX	$0

April 23	Grand Theatre, Walters, OK	$0
April 24	Cona Theatre, Nocona, TX	$0
April 25	Rock Tavern, Lawton, OK	$0
April 30	H.S.Auditorium, Dodson, TX	$0

The band members were being paid a small stipend by the radio station. They did not take any cuts out of the money they made playing shows and dances in April, as they needed to pay rent, make car payments, and generally get established in their new location. It appears from Joe Forrester's ledger and other records, however, that they actually grossed more money playing for dances than when they played shows.[115]

On April 2 Howard sent Billie a postcard from Wichita Falls, which read in part: "I sure enjoyed your bawling out. That was just what I needed to pep me up. But that singing was uncalled for, you little—"

This would seem to indicate that he had, in fact, heard her on the radio. According to Howard's son Bob, the "bawling out" is probably a reference to Billie's singing, as Howard loved to tease Billie. He signed the postcard as he always did, "Love, Howard."[116]

In May, they started the month with yet another engagement at the Rock Tavern:

DATE	LOCATION	PROFIT
May 2	Rock Tavern, Lawton, OK	$0.00
May 3	Wichita Valley Farms—Dance	$0.00
May 4	Rule Theatre, Rule, TX	$0.00
May 5	Square Dance, Rule, TX	$0.00
May 8	H.S. Auditorium, Post Oak, TX	$0.00
May 9	Rock Tavern, Lawton, OK	$0.00
May 10	H.S. Auditorium, Warren, OK	$0.00
May 11	Old Tin Barn, Olny, TX	$0.00
May 14	H.S. Auditorium, Humphreys, OK	$2.63
May 15	Roxy Theatre, Munday, TX	$3.12

May 16	Rock Tavern, Lawton, OK	$4.12
May 17	Texas Theatre, Seymour, TX	$0.00
May 18	Cona Theatre, Nocona, TX	$3.53
May 20	Ritz Theatre, Graford, TX	$0.00
May 23	Rock Tavern, Lawton, OK	$2.79
May 24	Club House, Wichita Valley Farms	$5.37
May 25	Old Tin Barn, Olny, TX	$6.60
May 30	Rock Tavern, Lawton, OK	$1.10
Monthly Profit		$29.26

As Joe's ledger shows, the Forrester boys were working hard, playing a lot of shows and some dances. It also shows how frugal they were, as Joe indicates on many days (marked as $0.00 for profit) that they each did not take a cut of the money they made, but rather paid rent, bought groceries, and paid for their advertising and other performance expenses. Joe also notes they spent $.40 for postage, probably for all the letters Howard was sending to Billie![117]

In his letter of May 18, he told Billie, "I'm studying about you...I'm coming up about the 31st...Joe may come with me, but we will set something anyway. I'll be studying about you until then."[118] Bob thought the "set something" might refer to their making final plans to get married.[119] And on May 23, Howard wrote from Decatur, Texas, to say "Boy, it sure is good to be in a big town once more.... We made some progress today."[120] This is probably a reference to their job situation improving.

On May 31, Howard sent Miss Wilene Russell a telegram from Wichita Falls: "Come prepared to stay. Bring fiddle. Howard Forrester, KWFT."[121]

Sometime during the next month, Billie arrived in Wichita Falls, and on June 29, 1940, in a ceremony before a Justice of the Peace, she and Howard were married, in Walters, Oklahoma, just across the state line from Wichita Falls. The marriage was witnessed by Billie's mother, Virginia Lee Kelley, and Red and Chuck Penn from the band. Howard's brother, Joe, was not at the ceremony, as he had just come off the road and was exhausted. For license purposes, Howard listed his age as twenty-one (he was actually only eighteen), and Billie listed her age as nineteen (she was actually seventeen).[122]

Howard's family was not very happy about him getting married at such a young age. And his Aunt Nell was not shy in telling him about it. She wrote him a very disparaging letter about him "marrying that little Indian girl." One of Howard's many strengths was loyalty to the people he cared about, and he was very loyal to Billie. He kept Aunt Nell's letter for many years and, even after all that time, it still rankled him a lot.[123]

The Little Orphan Girl was now back in business with the Tennessee Valley Boys, performing with them over KWFT as a regular part of their show. In addition to solos and some fiddling with the others, Billie also sang in a trio with Howard and Joe. Billie sang lead, Howard sang baritone, and Joe took the low tenor.[124]

After a time, Herald Goodman asked the Tennessee Valley Boys—with Orphan Girl in tow—to join him at WFAA in Dallas, which they did. Unfortunately, this arrangement didn't really work out as one of the members of the show whom Goodman had brought with him from the Saddle Mountain Roundup—a guitarist named Harry Adams—apparently had a drinking problem.

By now the Penn Brothers had left the group and gone home, and in early fall, the Forrester Brothers and Billie went to Kansas City, Missouri, to audition for a radio station there. Joe Forrester reported that the station liked them much better in person than on their demo, but they failed to get a spot on the radio as there was no sponsor available.[125]

Their next stop was at radio station WDZ in Tuscola, Illinois, where their old performing buddy, Curt Poulton, had found them a job. WDZ broadcast live talent all day long, with commercials, sponsors, and salaried musicians. They worked out of WDZ until early 1941, doing their usual routines with Big Howdy, Lespedeza, Little Orphan Girl, and Forrester Brothers duets. Their program aired at noon, which didn't leave them much time to play other performances at venues in the area. Howard said that after a while they left Illinois because of the weather, but Joe maintains it was because they "couldn't do much but play programs all day long."[126]

KWFT in Wichita Falls missed them, though, and asked them to come back, complete with salaries and sponsors. By April, 1941, they were appearing on "several programs a day."[127] It was a better life, but it didn't last long.

On May 26, Uncle Sam sent Joe Forrester his draft notice. He had several months before he had to report, so he took Howard and Billie to Dallas, where Georgia Slim Rutland and Gus Foster were doing a show called the Texas Roundup.[128] Also on the show were the Holden Brothers and the Buskirk Brothers. Howard called Paul Buskirk "one of the greatest mandolin players in the country." Howard played some Appalachian Mountain songs with the Buskirks, as they had been in West Virginia before coming to Texas.[129] After dropping Howard and Billie off in Dallas, Joe left for Nashville to get his affairs in order before reporting for induction into the armed services.

Despite being back with his "soul mate" Slim, Howard did not stay long at this job. Gus Foster, the promoter, had taken up gambling and would not—or could not—pay the band, so Howard and Billie headed for KTSA in San Antonio, where they played for a short while on a daily show at 6:45 a.m. They called themselves the Happy Hepcat Hillbillies; their group included U.S. "Scooter" Tonahill, Roscoe from Roscoe, Ken Lasater, Slim Harbert (formerly of the Shelton Brothers), and Howard and Billie.[130]

On December 7, 1941, everyone's world was turned upside down, when the Japanese bombed Pearl Harbor. Howard told his wife, "Billie, let's pack everything and go home." Howard was sure he would be drafted before long, so home they went.[131]

CHAPTER 5

Grandmammy, Look at Uncle Sam

Upon reaching Nashville, Billie was surprised when Howard moved the two of them in with Howard's mother, Emmie, and Howard's oldest brother, Clyde, at Emmie's little house on Elvira Street. But they all got along well, and Billie and Emmie became very close friends.[132]

Howard went to the Navy to sign up, probably following in brother Clayton's footsteps, as Clayton had enjoyed his Navy experiences and travel. Howard's actual draft notice, however, did not arrive until August 8, 1942, and even after that, he did not actually receive orders to report for duty until the spring of 1943. His brother Clyde, who was working as a carpenter and cabinetmaker, also joined the Navy, enlisting in the Construction Battalion (SeaBees).[133]

In the meantime, Howard needed a job, of course. He told Buddy Spicher in a June, 1987 interview:

> I went up to WSM as soon as I got back, and I met Honey Wilds in the hall, and I met J. L. Frank, who was Pee Wee King's manager. He said, "Do you want a job, kid?" I said, "Yeah, I'm lookin' for one." He said "Pee Wee needs a fiddle player. Go back and see him."
>
> This was 1942, and they were starting a tent show and Bill Monroe was on the tent show, and that's how I met Bill. I worked

the biggest part of—well 'til the end of the season with Jamup and Honey. Art Wooten was playing fiddle for Bill. Bill decided to take the tent on for another couple or three months. Art didn't want to work any more for some reason, so Bill asked me to play fiddle for him, and I did. So that's how I came to go to work for Bill Monroe.[134]

Two or three days later, Roy Acuff, who was also on the tent show, came to Howard and said he'd sure like to have him play fiddle. Howard told him he had just promised Bill he'd play with him, and that he wasn't one to go back on his word. Howard left the door open, though, by saying, "If the opportunity ever exists again, I'd sure like to take advantage of it."[135] It would take nine more years, but eventually Howard would walk through that door.

Lee Davis "Honey" Wilds and Lee Roy "Lasses" White had started a blackface minstrel show on WSM back in 1932, calling themselves Lasses and Honey. By 1934 they were also performing regularly on the Opry, but by 1940 Wilds had a new partner, Bunny Biggs, and changed the group's name to Jamup and Honey. They were one of the first Opry acts to take a tent show on the road. These tent shows brought variety and entertainment to small-town America. Both Roy Acuff and Bill Monroe were part of this tent show, though after a time, each recognized the huge potential profits, and each man started his own tent show. The tent shows would roam all over the southeast part of the country, then have to hurry back to Nashville on Saturday for the Opry show. Following the broadcast, the tent show would immediately hit the road and head out to the next town, where they would put up their tent and get ready to perform.

Small wonder that Art Wooten got tired of this "life on the road" and left the tent show, which opened the door for Big Howdy Forrester. Howard started out with Jamup and Honey and had a separate solo act on their show, but ultimately ended up in Bill Monroe's tent show, becoming a regular when Art Wooten left.[136]

From postcards Bob Forrester has, it appears that Howard was playing with Bill Monroe as early as February, 1942, and that he was both in the tent show and on the Grand Ole Opry.[137] Monroe's "band" for the 1942 tent show included: "Cousin" Wilbur Wesbrooks on bass, Clyde Moody on guitar, Dave "Stringbean" Akeman on banjo, Bill Monroe on mandolin and vocals, and Howard on fiddle.[138] Pictures of the band do not include Billie Forrester, who probably stayed with Jamup and Honey for a while longer. Clyde Forrester remembers that both Howard and Billie were on the road each week and back for the Opry show on Saturday night. Since they and Clyde all were living in Emmie's house at the time, Clyde was certainly privy to their comings and goings.[139] In any event, Howard played with Monroe from early 1942 until February 1943.[140]

Old-time fiddling was undergoing a transition to meet the demands of the newer type of music where the vocalist's role was on an equal par with the instrumentalist's. Working with Monroe, Howard developed new techniques for playing song melodies. He began to play the melody similarly to the way it was sung, but at the end of each phrase, where a singer would normally breathe, Forrester would add an improvised scale portion or an arpeggio, which would lead to the next major melody note on the tonic of the new chord.

This was the beginning of what would become the "bluegrass sound." Other fiddlers who heard Forrester on the Opry broadcasts adopted his new techniques, and Forrester fast became a highly influential fiddler.[141]

The long-awaited draft notice arrived on August 8, but Howard's actual orders didn't come until early 1943.[142] Monroe knew it was only a matter of time, however, before his "hot fiddler" was mobilized, so he began looking for a replacement, trying out such notables as Carl Story and Robert Russell "Chubby" Wise.[143] After all, the show must go on! Ultimately, Chubby got the nod and played with Bill until 1945, when he got wanderlust and went to play with Curley Williams and the Georgia Peach Pickers.

Chubby was ineligible to be drafted into the military, as he walked with a noticeable limp from a serious childhood injury. Following Chubby's departure, fiddler Jim Shumate took over Howard's job with Monroe.[144]

Howard was quite taken with Chubby Wise—his bluesy style of playing; his wild improvisations; his sweet, people-pleasing personality—and the two fiddlers became lifelong friends.[145]

By 1943, Monroe was grossing over $200,000 a year from show dates, many of them his own tent show. According to W-2s on file with the Country Music Foundation Library, however, Howard made only $405 working with Monroe for the first two months of 1943 and another $160.50 from WSM for his performances on the Opry. Billie Forrester, however, made $1,429 from Bill Monroe, also according to W-2s on file, so she clearly was not only playing with him, but spent the better part of the year doing so.[146] It is unclear just what instrument she played with Monroe at this time, but Joe Forrester recalls that "she did not have an accordion during the time before Howard went into the service," so it probably was not accordion.[147]

Billie could sing, dance, play guitar, piano, and fiddle, and harmonize with others in duets and trios, and may, according to research by Murphy Henry, have been a separate act on the show. Murphy quotes Cousin Wilbur Wesbrooks (Monroe's bass player): "In 1942, Bill Monroe took out a show with Jam Up and Honey, Uncle Dave Macon, Robert Lunn, Sam and Kirk McGee, and Sally Ann [Monroe's name for Billie]."[148]

Since the others listed had separate acts, perhaps Billie did as well. With the Tennessee Valley Boys, she had done a solo act with the band backing her up; this may be what happened with Monroe's Bluegrass Boys. Monroe gave Billie the name of "Sally Ann," perhaps taken from the fiddle tune of that name. And he sometimes gave her billing as "The Kentucky Songbird," although clearly she was not from Kentucky![149]

In any event, Billie spent the war years playing with Monroe and the Bluegrass Boys, and when in town, living with Emmie Forrester in her house. The men in the band looked after Billie on the road and kept other men from bothering her. They treated her much like a sister, and Chubby Wise even paid regular visits to Emmie Forrester all during the war to make sure she was doing okay while all her boys were away.[150]

In addition to playing and singing with the band, Billie was entrusted with the band's finances—that is, she took tickets at the door and took care of the cash box that had all their receipts from the shows they put on. Monroe was sometimes slow to get the receipts to the bank, and often Billie would have several thousand dollars in cash for which she was responsible. Billie called the fish tackle box they used for the receipts "the money bucket" and said she would "sometimes hide it under the bed and hope for the best." Bill Monroe clearly trusted her with his last nickel![151]

Billie also performed another service for Monroe. With her classical piano and violin training, Billie could read and write (notate) music, and she wrote out lead sheets for Monroe so that he could submit his songs, such as "Kentucky Waltz," for copyright. Not only was she a consummate performer, but she was invaluable to Monroe in many other ways, and Monroe knew it. Still, in his penurious way, Monroe never paid her anything extra for all her additional duties.[152]

As Howard was getting ready to leave for boot camp, Monroe, always the gentleman, promised him that his job would be waiting for him when he returned from the service.[153]

On February 26, 1943, Howdy Forrester reported for duty in the U.S. Navy.[154] Brother Joe had already gone into the Army on May 26, 1941. He had been sent overseas with the 22nd Regiment of the 4th Division and spent time in England and France. He was at Utah Beach for the D-Day invasion of Normandy and fought with the 4th Division in four campaigns. He was overseas for twenty-one months, and, although his original call up had been for a period of one year, he ultimately spent four years in the service. He came home a technical sergeant. A musician at heart, his trusty guitar, probably a 1935 Martin D-18, had gone along with him on the ship to Europe, and he never missed a chord![155]

Howard was first sent to boot camp at Naval Training Station, Bainbridge, Maryland, and then to Chelsea, Massachusetts, (outside Boston) where he attended a six-week course at the Naval Hospital Corps School, studying pharmacy. He was then transferred to U.S. Naval Hospital, Pearl Harbor, Territory of Hawaii, where he reported for duty with his fiddle under his arm. He would be there for the next twenty-five months, working his way up the ranks to pharmacist's mate third class.[156]

His first twelve months at Pearl Harbor were served in what Howard called "the nut ward," dealing with psychologically-damaged sailors and soldiers. Following that, he was transferred to work in the hospital's laundry, where he reported that he was "terribly bored." He made repeated efforts to get out of the laundry by applying for shipboard duty on any ship headed for the war zone. Unfortunately, as his chief told him, "Forrester, you are too good at what you do here. No one is going to approve your transfer request."

Finally, Howard resigned himself to the fact that he would probably finish out the war at Pearl Harbor and, thus, he would probably come home alive. "I guess I'm just asking to get killed," he said. "I'll just settle down and accept this." And he began making plans for his life after the war, as always with the music playing in his head.[157]

Howard was getting regular letters from Billie, mostly about her travels and adventures on the road with the Bluegrass Boys. They were logging thousand of miles, playing at any theatre, civic auditorium, armory, ballpark, fairground, skating rink, courthouse, school, or other venue that would have them. The schedule was a killer, and Howard was quick to recognize that, after his own "barnstorming" days with Herald Goodman. One of these letters to Billie said: "Baby, I think of you a lot making the long jumps and the nerve racking grind that goes with so many weeks of the same thing over and over. You have had a pretty long stretch on this job without any vacation. You had better conserve some of your energy."[158]

Later, however, he took another tack with her, as he realized that his own plans for a band would also require hard work: "If you think that schedule is hard, you should see the worksheet on my band that I hope will be working in a few years."

A month later, he wrote this:

> How would you like to be stationed with me back there with a small jam outfit in a night club? If the time off could be arranged for me to play every nite, we could really have a setup. This is a

plan that has come to me in my day dreams, but it might be that it could be arranged…[159]]

Unfortunately for subsequent generations of fiddle fans, Howard never did start his own band after the war. The Fates intervened. But, meanwhile, dream though he would, Howard had his Navy obligations to fulfill.

Howard's buddy, trumpeter Harvey Blair (who had played with Henry Bussey), was also stationed at Pearl Harbor, and he and Howard organized a band (more like an orchestra) together and played at the officers' and chiefs' clubs on the base. The band had full brasses and saxophones; Howard played bass and sometimes fiddle. By his own admission, he wasn't too great on the bass!

Since Howard could not read music, he had to memorize all his parts, which meant lots of extra practice for him. The Navy base at Pearl Harbor was operating at capacity because of the war, and there wasn't any suitable place for Howard to rehearse his music. He began practicing in the "head" (restroom) where, with all the moisture from the showers, the music really rang out. In short order, he became known as the "Shithouse Fiddler."[160]

Late-night practices and gigs left Howard somewhat sleep-deprived, and often he would fail to show up for morning muster. Someone else would sing out "Here" for him when his name was called, but invariably the chief would say, "We know where he is; let him sleep." Because Howard was such a good worker, he was never punished for this.[161]

The four Forrester brothers kept in touch with each other all through the war. Clayton, who was mechanically inclined, repaired planes during the war. A letter dated January 23, 1944, from Clayton to Howard's wife Billie indicates that Corporal Clayton Forrester was stationed with a bomber squadron in England. He wrote:

Hello sis, I got your letter just awhile ago sure glad to hear from you.… I haven't heard from Howard lately except for a "V" Mail Xmas card with some south sea island babe on it, ha. I suppose he is fine though…

Love,
Clayton[162]

Older brother Clyde actually got to visit Howard during the war. Clyde, who was in the Navy Construction Battalion (SeaBees), went to the Eastern Pacific on the *USS Pennsylvania*. One of the port calls on the way out was at Pearl Harbor. Clyde knew from Howard's letters that he was stationed at Hospital 128, so he asked his chief for permission to go across the island and visit Howard at the hospital. The chief told Clyde he could not grant him permission to leave the ship, but that if it were *his* brother who were in Hawaii, he would definitely go to see him. Clyde took that as tacit approval and immediately left for Hospital 128 and a visit with Howard.

The brothers had lots to catch up on and, before they realized it, it was quite late and past curfew, which made it impossible for Clyde to return to his ship. Some of Howard's buddies at the hospital, however, arranged for an ambulance to transport Clyde back to the ship, with the proviso that if the ambulance were stopped at a checkpoint, Clyde must lie down and pretend to be a seriously-injured sailor. The ruse worked, and Clyde was returned to his ship without incident. Clyde's ship then lifted anchor and sailed for Saipan and Okinawa, with him safely on board.[163]

Howard served out the rest of the war in Hawaii, clearly having drawn the "easiest" wartime duty of any of the four Forrester boys. His letters to Billie and his mother indicate that he was playing for dances and really "in the groove," although he was anxious to get home "to some real practice and then find a job."[164]

Meanwhile, Billie Forrester was still playing with the Bluegrass Boys. In February 1945, she cut eight sides with Bill Monroe on Columbia Records: "Come Back to Me in My Dreams," "Footprints in the Snow," "Kentucky Waltz," "Rocky Road," "Nobody Loves Me," "True Life Blues," "Bluegrass Special," and "Goodbye Old Pal." The band included Billie Forrester, Bill Monroe, Clyde Wesbrooks, Tex Willis on guitar, Dave "Stringbean" Akeman on banjo, Howard Watts (Cedric Rainwater) on bass, and possibly Curley Bradshaw on second guitar.[165]

As the war ended, Howard telegraphed his mother from San Francisco on November 13, 1945, saying: "Back in the states at last. Should be home within twelve days. Love, Howard."[166]

By November 19, Howard was back in Centerville, Tennessee, and he telegraphed Billie, who was in Tulsa at the time, visiting her mother: "Billie, be at Chisca Hotel Wednesday [Nov 21]. Have room reserved. Will be there in afternoon or night. Love, Howard."[167]

Clearly, he wanted to spend some time alone with Billie, before they had to return to the family home on Elvira Street. With Emmie, Billie, and all four sons home, the Forrester house was going to be a very busy place!

The Chisca Hotel in Memphis is where Howard was discharged from the Navy on November 21, 1945.[168] He declared that he probably was "not very military," but he had enjoyed serving his country.[169] The Navy awarded him the Asiatic-Pacific Campaign Medal for service in that theatre during the war.[170]

For some time, Howard had been saying he would "be home by Christmas." Now he had made good on that pledge. Emmie Forrester was thrilled to have her boys back home, and Christmas 1945 was a happy time at the Forrester house. All four Forrester boys considered themselves extremely blessed to have come home from the war intact.[171]

In December 1945, Howard returned to work, playing with Bill Monroe and the Bluegrass Boys. Joe Forrester said that "Bill sent word to Howdy that his job was open for him when he got out of the service."[172] (Of course, federal draft regulations also required that returning veterans were entitled to have their old jobs back.)

His wife, Billie, was still playing with the band, and now it became even more of a family affair, as Howard told Bill Monroe, "Well, I got a brother that needs a job." And Bill said, "Well, bring him on." Thus, Joe Forrester also became a Bluegrass Boy, playing bass with the group. The band now included Monroe, three Forresters, Lester Flatt on guitar, and the newly hired Earl Scruggs on banjo.

Life on the road with Monroe was hard. Each of the band members received $50 a week for their services, but out of this had to come all of their expenses, such as lodging and meals. And they were on the road most of the time. Frequently, they would leave Nashville at midnight on Saturday after the Opry and drive all night to be at a Sunday gig the next day. They would often play three or four shows a day and then on Friday night, after doing a show, they would drive all night to be back in Nashville for the 8:00 p.m. Opry show. Sometimes, they logged three thousand miles in a week![173] Howard's son Bob said: "You mention road trips with Bill in those days, Mama would just kind of roll her eyes."[174]

There were no speed limits on the roads in Tennessee in those days. According to Joe Forrester, "We drove as fast as we wanted or could handle."[175] The roads were not wonderful, either, and flat tires were a common occurrence. Band members took turns driving Monroe's stretched-out Chevy, and it is a wonder they did not drive into the ditch more often, considering how little sleep they got and how hard they worked. When asked how they put up with all this, Joe Forrester made a wry face, then laughed, and said: "Well, we were a lot younger then. When you're young, you've got them big dreams."[176]

Howard, Billie, and Joe all stayed with Bill Monroe through the end of March of 1946, when they left after one week into the tent season. Joe Forrester says they left because the traveling was killing them,[177] but Howard told Doug Green in an oral interview sponsored by the Country Music Foundation that it was because he wanted to play other kinds of music.[178] He respected Bill Monroe a lot, but he was least enthusiastic about playing bluegrass. Bill Monroe wanted it done his way, always, and his way was fast. He would say, "Howdy, can't you play it a little faster?"

CHAPTER 6

Rutland's Reel

The Fates intervened in their lives again that spring, as Billie real-ized that she was pregnant. Notwithstanding that, when Howard received a call from Art Davis, who had a band in Tulsa called the Rhythm Riders, the Forresters packed their bags and headed out on the road to Tulsa.[179] This actually was a great thing for Billie, as her maternal grandmother, Sudie, lived in Tulsa. Billie had helped Sudie buy a little house in Tulsa during the war, so they moved in with her.[180]

The Rhythm Riders performed each weekday at 4:45 p.m. on KTUL Radio, on a show sponsored by OK Rubber Welders, a tire recapping outfit. Davis offered them a guarantee of $50 a week for the radio show performances, plus an additional $10 a night when they played for a dance. They could make $80 to $90 per week and, best of all, they weren't traveling!

They were playing western swing music, with Howard and Art Davis playing fiddles, Jay Davis on rhythm guitar, Joe Forrester on bass, and a pregnant Billie playing accordion.[181] The KTUL news-letter referred to the "Forrester boys" as a "steal from the Old Barn Dance of WSM."[182]

Howard loved to play western swing music, but other than a great break at the end of "Old Grey Bonnet" (*Leather Britches* LP, Stoneway STY-150) and some unpublished jam session tapes, he never recorded any western swing music. Bob Forrester thinks this was probably because too many others, most notably Bob Wills, had already recorded all the great swing tunes. Howard felt his own "voice" was the elegant fiddle sound, so that is what he recorded.[183]

Later in life Howard and Billie looked back on this job as one of their favorites. The job, however, did not last long, because in May of 1946, Howard's friend, "Georgia Slim" Rutland, notified them that he had reorganized the Texas Roundup on KRLD, and the three Forresters packed up and headed for Dallas, taking Sudie with them.[184]

Robert Rutland had served in the U.S. Air Corps as a Bombardier and Gunnery Officer for forty-six months and had just been released in April 1946.[185] He was anxious to get back to his music making and what better way than with his old soul mate, Big Howdy Forrester!

Rutland had a connection to the radio station KRLD in Dallas to get back on the air, and he pitched Howard and Joe on coming down to be partners with him. They picked up a singer—Dewey Groom—and a steel guitar player, Dub Hendrix, to join their group.

Howard and Joe went in on a percentage deal with Rutland; Slim got the biggest percentage, and Howard and Joe shared the rest. Howard's comment was "We did very well." Dewey and Dub each got fifty dollars a week, but Billie was not part of the group. They had to keep themselves really small, because there wasn't enough money to pay other musicians. KRLD didn't pay them an actual salary. And, of course, Billie was pregnant, which made it difficult for her to perform, even if she had really wanted to.[186]

The show on KRLD was lots of fun for them to do. They were on the air weekdays from 6:45–7:00 a.m. and from 12:45–1:00 p.m., times when the farmers and workers were having meal breaks and could listen to them. Their show opened and closed with the tune "When It's Roundup Time in Texas" and featured lots of western swing music and old-time fiddle tunes, played by Howard, Slim, or a combination of the two.

Dewey Groom, whom Slim called "the boy with the curly hair," played guitar and sang in a style reminiscent of Gene Autrey. Many of his songs on the air were patriotic tunes, in keeping with the mood of the country immediately following the war. He sang tunes like "Did You See My Daddy Over There?" and "Stars and Stripes on Iwo Jima." Both Dewey and "Cornbread" Dub Hendrix (on steel) had also been in the war, and you can hear the war's influences in the way the band treated the patriotic songs.[187]

Howard and Joe Forrester sang a number of vocal duets, with Howard fiddling in between verses. Howard actually had a much higher voice than Joe, not what would be expected since Howard was quite a bit taller. Much of their music sounded like the music of Bob Wills' Playboys, although at times both Howard's and Slim's fiddling was so jazzy that it sounded like they had been listening to and practicing licks from Stuff Smith and Joe Venuti!

Georgia Slim also sang some solos, and they all had a great time ad libbing and trying to top each other's lines. And, of course, Joe was back in his role as "Lespedeza," making wisecracks and generally being a backwoods hillbilly. Slim would read letters over the air from their listeners, and the band would perform music as requested in those letters.[188]

Bob Wills heard them perform on KRLD, and Howard got word that Wills wanted to hire him and Slim for his own band, but they already had commitments and chose to keep them.[189]

Some of their listeners tried to foment a rivalry between Slim and Howard as to which man was the better fiddler. Howard and Slim would play along with that and try to outdo each other with their "hot fiddling." Howard finally told Slim he would not try to play "Fire on the Mountain" (which Slim played at breathtaking speed) if Slim would promise not to play "Old Joe Clark," one of Howard's hottest hoedowns.

There really was no rivalry between them, though, and they remained the best of friends. They often did very elaborate "twin fiddling" together, and they had matching suits made, and both grew goatees and mustaches to match. This "pretend rivalry business" would manifest itself in a very bizarre fashion years later.[190]

At one point they had a contest to grow their goatees into beards. Pictures of them from this period show them looking like a couple of hippies…or old mountain men. When they got ready to end the contest, they staged the "shaving" as part of their show, complete with two lady barbers to do the deed. The barber who shaved Howard finished first, so he was the champ and got his picture, along with that of the barber, in the local paper! He recalls, "I'll tell you what—that day we turned people away at the theater, which was a good promotion."[191]

While they were on air, they were allowed to pitch their gigs elsewhere, which Slim did with alacrity. They played all over Texas, Oklahoma, and New Mexico, for anyone who would pay them— theatres, picnics, fairs, parties, dances, taverns, and even political rallies. They actually played for one of Lyndon Johnson's rallies in Tyler, Texas, during his 1948 senate race. (Johnson was a protégé of the great Sam Rayburn, former Speaker of the House; Joe Forrester's first wife was related to Rayburn.[192])

Slim talked a lot about his mother on the radio, and it was clear that both he and Howard missed their mothers.[193] The two men arranged for their mothers to come visit them that summer in Texas; Slim's mother boarded the train in Tipton, Georgia, and rode it to Nashville, where she was joined by Emmie Forrester for the rest of the trip. The two mothers also became good friends.[194] It is unclear how they got along with Billie's grandmother, Sudie, who was 1/4 Indian and quite outspoken.[195]

Unlike Howard, Slim enjoyed playing in the fiddle contests held around Dallas. He was the local favorite and almost always won. At one contest the famous fiddler Eck Robertson came to play. Slim began to sweat as Eck strode onto the stage and announced: "Ladies and gentlemen, I'm not only the greatest fiddler in Texas; I am the greatest fiddler in the world."

Howard said that when Eck finished playing "Sally Goodin," "Damn, if I didn't believe him!" Eck *almost* beat Slim that day.[196]

In August, 1946, the Forresters received a letter from their old friend, "Uncle" Dave Macon, which said in part: "Tell poor Little Bitty Billie I am fully in hopes God will be with her in her confinement and if you are both blessed with a baby boy name him Dixie Davie Forrester."[197]

Billie didn't suffer unduly with her pregnancy and, of course, she had Sudie there to help her. They all lived together in a little house on Edgefield in Dallas.[198]

In December, Howard received a letter from Honey Wilds (of Jamup and Honey), answering an earlier letter from Howard inquiring about summer employment:

Dear Mop-head—

Alright, alright, I know I should have written sooner...but anyhooow—Here it tis—Yes, we are going to need an outfit for this summer—we have talked about you as a fiddler—we would like to have you—the rest of the outfit will have to be as good as you—So let me hear from you—And will tell you more about it—

Honey
Wilds[199]

Apparently, with Billie pregnant and fairly steady work for the band in and around Dallas, Howard chose to remain there and did not respond to Wilds' offer.

Zeke Clements, the cowboy singer and songwriter, also contacted Howard about moving to California. Bob Wills, Spade Cooley, and others had already gone west, and their bands were playing to overflow crowds. Zeke loved the sound of the fiddle and thought that Howard could do well in California. But despite the lure of money, fame, and the fast-growing movie industry, Howard thought California was much too far away from his family in Nashville and declined to go.[200]

The new year opened with a bang as, on January 4, Billie delivered a baby boy. Fortunately for him, the Forresters did *not* take Uncle Dave Macon's suggestion for their son's name, but instead named him Robert Allen Forrester—Robert for Great-uncle Bob and Allen for Howard's father. Some of Howard's friends in the music business wanted to call the new baby "Little Howdy," but Howard, who did not even like his *own* nickname of Big Howdy, refused to let that happen. Robert Allen Forrester became "Bobby" and later "Bob" and grew up under the tutelage of both his parents and his "grandmother" Sudie, whom Billie called "Mama."[201]

In 1947 the band began appearing on Hal Horton's "Cornbread Matinee," which aired live from 12:00–12:30 daily on radio from the Arcadia Theatre. And they performed evening gigs as Hal Horton and his Texas Roundup at such places as Tiger Field and the Corsicana Chamber of Commerce. Admission to their show was 50 cents for adults and 25 cents for children.[202]

The band also continued with other gigs, playing in May at a big dance at the Crystal Springs Ball Room (one of Bob Wills' old haunts), where the flyer gave Howard top billing: "Howdy Forrester and the Texas Roundup."[203] In June they played as entertainment and for a square dance at the Fiddle Band Contest and Fiddler's Frolic at Fair Park in Crockett, Texas. There were twenty bands to compete and an anticipated crowd of ten thousand.[204] They also played at the Bonham Fair and the Texas State Fair.

A publicity brochure for the band from this time period, entitled Georgia Slim and the Texas Roundup, lists Howdy Forrester as Program Director, which provided him with good on-the-job training to later become Roy Acuff's booking agent.[205]

Howard's and Slim's mothers both came to visit them again, Emmie, no doubt, lured by the birth of her grandson.[206]

In mid-1947, Howard, Joe, and Slim leased a club in Dallas to play dances two nights a week. They named the club "Bob's Barn" after Slim (Robert Rutland). They added members to the show: Billie Forrester on accordion, singer Ludie Harris, "the Blond Bombshell," who also played guitar and/or bass, and Felipe Harris on drums. Harris and Billie sang duets; Howard (tenor), Joe (lead), and Slim (baritone) sang trios; Howard and Slim played fiddle tunes and did twin fiddling together. Felipe Harris, the drummer, was Mexican, and many bands would not hire him because of it, but Howard and Slim had no such prejudices and knew a good deal when they saw one.

After a while it became clear that the area would only support one dance night per week. They changed their schedule and played Bob's Barn solely on Saturday night, where, according to Joe Forrester, they drew really good crowds.[207]

During this year, Georgia Slim and Howard did a recording session of twelve commercial sides on Mercury 78 rpm singles. On them Howard plays two solo fiddle tunes: "Grey Eagle" and "Tennessee Wagoner." The sides were re-released as *Twin Fiddling—Country*

Style: Georgia Slim Rutland, Big Howdy Forrester, on Kanawha LP 601, and re-released again on CD in 2006 as *Twin Fiddling, Texas Style: Georgia Slim and Howdy Forrester*, Tri-Agle-Far Records CDTR 710. The sides are impossible to find, but the recent CD release clearly shows Howard's and Slim's playing styles, both together and separately.

In October, Hank Thompson invited Howard and Slim over to WFAA Studios in Dallas, where Thompson was just starting an eigh-teen-year recording alliance with Capitol Records. The song that sent him down that road to stardom was the one he recorded that day with Forrester and Rutland backing him up: "Humpty Dumpty Heart" (CAP 40065), re-released in 1999 on a Proper Records CD set entitled *doughboys, playboys, and cowboys—the golden years of Western swing*, Proper Box 6. The twin fiddlers kick off the melody, then play an entire verse in jazzy harmony, take another small break, and finally finish the song—a tribute to how much Thompson liked their fiddling. They also recorded three more songs with Hank that day: "Today" (CAP 40065), "Don't Flirt with Me" (CAP 40085), and "Rock in the Ocean" (CAP 40085), with twin-fiddled breaks and back up. Their intonation is flawless, and their bow strokes are perfectly matched. All four of these songs were re-released in 1996 as a Bear Family boxed set of CD's, *Hank Thompson and His Brazos Valley Boys*, BCD15904LK.

In addition to arranging tunes, Howard also was composing original fiddle tunes, one of which was "Rutland's Reel," which he wrote as a tribute to his friend Georgia Slim. The opening melody of "Rutland's Reel" was taken from an old book of tunes that Slim had gotten from his grandfather, but the rest of the tune is pure Howdy Forrester invention.[208] In 1962 Howard would record this tune on his LP album *Fancy Fiddlin'—Country Style*, MGM E-4035, later re-released on CUB 8008.

In late 1947, Billie also got a chance to record, making thirteen movie "shorts," featuring her playing accordion and singing for Hollywood Hillbillie Jamboree.[209] Although it did put her name and face before the public, according to the contract she signed with Tommy Scott, she was only paid $1.00 for her work! Joe Forrester insists, however, that she actually was paid $50 per short.[210]

In 1948, Howard, Joe, and Slim continued to manage Bob's Barn, where they booked dances and shows and, of course, themselves to play. By the end, they were only playing there one night per week and booking others for the open spots: Mexican dances on Saturday night, black dances on Monday, and so forth. They were still appearing on the radio from Monday through Saturday, 5:45–6:15 a.m. at 1080 on the dial.[211] And they were still playing dances elsewhere. A flyer from that time period shows "Howdy Forrester and the Texas Roundup at the Legion Hut in Eagletown, OK, $1.00 per person."[212]

In between all the music making, Howard was able to find time to finish his high school education through a correspondence program. Somehow he knew he needed to do this, perhaps because Billie was better educated than he was or perhaps because he knew that fiddling alone would probably not pay his way through life. This additional education would stand him in good stead when he later worked in the office for Roy Acuff.[213]

The band enjoyed a high profile in Dallas, and Howard met a lot of the "ranking fiddle greats" from Texas, such as Major Franklin, Red Steeley, Vernon Solomon, and Benny Thomasson.[214] Howard was actually driving around the countryside with Slim one day when Slim told Howard he had to stop and see a buddy of his about something. When Howard said that was fine with him, Slim stopped at a house way out in the country. It turned out to be Benny Thomasson's house, and they all spent the afternoon playing tunes and swapping stories with each other! And that was how Howard met Thomasson.[215] They became good friends and often jammed together.

According to an interview Thomasson had with Stacy Phillips: "He [Georgia Slim Rutland] came to my house many times, him and Howdy Forrester. Them boys were both fine fiddlers. I taught them a lot of stuff, 'Say Old Man Can You Play the Fiddle,'[216] somewhere in the 1940s. They were at my house every other night or two."

In January, 1950, Howard and Slim were at Hank Thompson's house when he decided to record a tune called "Beautiful Texas." Using a portable recorder with Lee Gillette at the controls, they recorded right there in Hank's living room, with Howard and Slim playing twin fiddles, Lefty Nason on steel guitar, and Rip Giersdorf on bass. For some reason, Capitol never released this song, but recently it came to light on the Bear Family CD set *Hank Thompson and His Brazos Valley Boys*, BCD15904LK.[217]

Despite the successes, things were winding down for the band in Dallas, and it became more and more difficult to get enough paying gigs to keep themselves afloat. According to Howard, Slim didn't want to put a lot of money into the club, and neither Howard nor Joe felt they were advancing their careers in Dallas. So in mid-year, Joe and Howard turned over their share in the club to Georgia Slim, bade him farewell, and returned to Nashville. Slim continued to operate the club until 1951 or 1952, at which juncture he returned home to his native Georgia, where he ran a music store.[218]

CHAPTER 7

Brilliancy

Back in Nashville, Howard and Joe found employment at the U.S. Post Office, which, of course, gave hiring preference to returning veterans. Brothers Clayton and Clyde also went to work for the Post Office and, for a short time, it was a Forrester family affair. Clyde worked on the sorting table, where the mail sacks were dumped after they came in on the trucks. The dust raised by the dumping did not agree with Clyde, and after a short time, he left the Post Office and returned to what he loved best, carpentry and cabinet making, which became his lifelong career.[219]

Howard had an "outside" job with the Post Office, driving a truck and picking up mail from the collection boxes. Although it was steady work and a steady paycheck, Howard found it hard to focus on his job. While he was driving around town, notes would be running through his head, and he would find himself composing or arranging fiddle tunes. Numerous times he nearly had serious accidents as a result of this inattention to his driving. Fortunately, he realized that he was a menace to himself and to the community doing this kind of work and bade the Post Office goodbye. Clayton and Joe, however, had long careers as letter carriers there, and both finally retired from the Postal Service. Joe's career as a traveling musician had ended, although he would always maintain his tremendous skill as a rhythm guitarist and would play for family parties and gatherings as often as possible.[220]

Since Sudie had come to Nashville with the Forresters, Billie was able to attend Draughon's Business College, where she took an advanced secretarial course while Sudie took care of son Bob for her.[221]

As for young Bob Forrester, Howard enrolled him in Catholic school, as soon as he was old enough to attend. Although Howard professed to be an agnostic most of his life, he was an astute observer of people. While the Forresters were in Texas in the 1940s, they played many gigs at churches. The Protestant churches would sometimes fail to pay the band, short their pay, or at best, pay them late. But Howard noticed that the Catholic churches always paid them the agreed-upon amount, paid them on time, and usually fed them and took better care of them. While Howard was in the Navy at Pearl Harbor, he also noticed that the Catholic chaplains were always the first to respond in an emergency, always there to comfort the sailors and soldiers, even at great personal risk to themselves, and even if the service members were not Catholic! Many of the Protestant chaplains spent the bulk of their time at the officers' club instead. All of this made a profound impression on Howard, and he vowed that if he got out of the war alive and if he ever had children, they would go to Catholic schools. He kept his promise, and Bob went to Catholic school, where he received what Howard called "a first-rate education."[222]

Shortly after returning to Nashville, Howard entered his first— and only—fiddle contest ever, playing at the old ballpark there. He won the contest handily, but always said of contests: "I have nothing to prove in a contest. I know I can play, and I don't have to prove it to anyone else. Besides, if I win, people will say, 'I knew it was rigged so that one of the Big Boys would win,' and if I lose, people will say: 'I always knew that Howdy Forrester wasn't that good,' so either way, I lose."[223] He was a fiddler without ego; he never tried to show anyone up or to prove that he was better than others. In fact, when his dear friend Perry Harris and Opry Manager Bud Wendell started the Grand Master Fiddler Championship in Nashville, Howard worked them as a judge, but never competed in them, although undoubtedly he could have won with ease.[224]

After Howard left the Post Office, he needed a job and needed it badly. He had two mouths to feed besides his own now, and, of course, his own mother and Sudie to look after as well. For a while he worked helping his brother Clyde on various construction jobs in Nashville.[225]

Meanwhile, in April of 1950, Billie graduated from business college and was hired by the Social Security Administration. Over time she worked her way up to be a mid-level manager in charge of a twenty to thirty person phone unit, and she stayed with the federal government until she retired in 1980, thirty years later.[226]

Also in April, Howard, Joe, and Billie, and friends Lawrence Timon and C. L. "Lester" Harris played in a band competition sponsored by the local paper, *The Nashville Banner*. Their band, called Lawrence Timon's Riverwood Riding Academy Band, won first place.[227] Billie also played accordion at the Old Hippodrome "All Free Square Dance Contest," one of her last truly public performances.[228] After that her playing was limited to family gatherings and parties.

At some point she probably realized that, notwithstanding her great musical talents, she was never going to have a stable, secure life in the music business. Like Howard's brother, Joe, she wanted more from life than endless traveling, playing, and singing the same tunes over and over, and always wondering where the next meal— or the next gig—was coming from. And she also had a son to raise. Life on the road was no place for a young child.

Near mid-year, Lloyd "Cowboy" Copas, one of the reigning stars of the Opry, called and asked Howard to play backup fiddle for him on the Opry, as Dale Potter had just been drafted.[229] Copas was a tenor, whose voice was well-suited for "lilting and melodious love songs" which led to announcer Grant Turner naming him "Waltz King of the Grand Ole Opry."[230] Howard's beautiful slid double stops, excellent sense of timing, and smooth bowing were a perfect match for somebody like Copas. Howard played for Copas for about a year and really enjoyed it. In addition to his voice, Copas was, in Howard's opinion, "one of the finest rhythm guitar men in the world. I loved to play a fiddle tune and have Copas back me up, and he was always good about that."[231] Just playing the Opry was not enough income to keep Howard afloat, however, and he kept looking for other employment.

In July, Howard and Joe played for a square dance and barbeque in Only, out in Hickman County where Uncle Bob lived. The flyer said the dance was "given by C. A. Townsend, with music by Howdy and Joe Forrester, sets called by Johnny Elliott—All Candidates Invited," so undoubtedly there was some electioneering involved.[232] In any event, the Forrester brothers really enjoyed re-connecting with family and friends back home.

Howard continued to work on construction jobs with Clyde, and in 1951, while they were pouring concrete at Emmie's house, Brother Oswald (Pete Kirby) from Roy Acuff's band, the Smoky Mountain Boys, called Howard and told him, "Roy Acuff wants to hire you." Howard started working with Roy and the Smoky Mountain Boys on the Grand Ole Opry in October. "This is the last fiddle job I'll ever have," Howard said to Clyde. Whether he meant that if this job didn't last, he would give up fiddling as a career and get a "real" job, or whether he was just prescient about what a good—and lengthy—job Roy was offering him, no one really knows. As it turned out, though, it *was* his last fiddling job, one that lasted nearly to the day he died.[233]

In the late 1940s and up until 1951, Roy Acuff had a succession of top-notch fiddlers: Tommy Magness, Arthur Smith, Floyd Ethridge, Hal Smith, Tommy Jackson, and Benny Martin.[234] But once he hired Howard, that was it; the fiddle slot in the band was set, for many years to come. Howard was a stalwart in the band.

Acuff's band, at that time, consisted of Robert Lunn ("Talking Blues Man"), who was a good dancer and comedian; Joe Zinkan on guitar and bass, Lonnie Wilson on guitar, Brother Oswald playing Dobro, Jimmy Riddle on harmonica and piano, Acuff, and Forrester. Roy also had the three LeCroy Sisters and one other girl to open the show with square dancing. Howard was the only real fiddler in the band, although on very rare occasions, Roy would play something on the fiddle. They had a "show" with comedy, something moving all the time, not just a fiddle band standing on stage playing music. Roy was the consummate showman, and Howard felt that "entertainment" was the key to Roy's—and their—success. The band was Roy Acuff and the Smoky Mountain

Boys—*not* six big-name players—but Roy could fill an auditorium with twelve thousand people![235]

Howard and his Uncle Bob made a home recording of their own fiddling during this time, a recording that clearly shows the influence Uncle Bob had on Howard's playing. Howard often attributed much of his style to the influences of Uncle Bob, Georgia Slim Rutland, and Fiddlin' Arthur Smith.[236]

On October 24, 1951, Howard went into the studio with Lester Flatt and Earl Scruggs and did some hot fiddling on the following eight tunes, all recorded for Columbia: "'Tis Sweet to be Remembered" and "Earl's Breakdown" (20886), "Get in Line Brother" and "Brother I'm Getting Ready to Go" (20915), "Over the Hills to the Poorhouse" and "My Darling's Last Goodbye" (21002), "I'm Gonna Settle Down" and "I'm Lonesome and Blue" (21043). These were originally issues on 10″ 78 and 7″ 45 rpm singles in 1951–2. Howard and Everett Lilly played twin fiddles on "I'm Lonesome and Blue" and "My Darling's Last Good Bye," the first bluegrass twin fiddles for which there are definite attributions.

"Earl's Breakdown" was the first of the sides to be released and was the big hit from this session. Neil V. Rosenberg, who compiled a Flatt & Scruggs discography for the *Journal of Country Music*, opined "Lots of bluegrass fiddlers have honed their chops on Howdy's break for that tune, which is a great one."[237] "Earl's Breakdown" was re-issued by Columbia on a "Hall of Fame" single and on EPs in the later 1950s. It appeared on Flatt & Scruggs' first LP in 1957, which was one of the first bluegrass albums ever published, and was re-issued on four more Columbia and Harmony albums between 1960 and 1973.

Four of the other songs appear on *King of Bluegrass, Great Original Recordings, Vol. 1*, Harmony HL7340, in 1965. All eight songs were re-issued between 1977–9 on albums by County as *The Golden Years*, CCS101, on Rounder as *The Golden Era*, 5505, on Rounder *Don't Get Above Your Raisin*, 5508, and on Time/Life as *Country & Western Classics: Flatt & Scruggs*, TLCW04, in 1982. In 1991, the Bear Family issued a boxed set of CDs, *Flatt & Scruggs: 1948–1959*, BCD15472.[238]

With all these re-issuances it is clear that people in the music business thought these cuts were great music and well worth preserving. Howard was in good company, recording with Flatt & Scruggs; other fiddlers they used on various tunes included Benny Martin, Paul Warren, Everett Lilly, and Howard's good friend, Chubby Wise.[239]

Meanwhile, Howard was enjoying playing on the Opry; he got to play a variety of music, and Roy let him play it "his way." Their segment usually opened with a square dance and Howard fiddling away on some hot breakdown. Then, when band members would sing, Howard would lay in behind them with "fill," coming in on breaks, occasionally with some neat little improvisation. Roy would always have him play some solo piece, and sometimes Howard actually took a turn at singing. And, of course, with his good musical instincts, Howard would play little fiddle licks here and there to help keep the show humorous and moving along. He was always moving as he played, swaying to the music, dancing as he played, and always his eyes were twinkling and his mouth was smiling. He clearly loved what he did.[240] And the audience clearly loved his playing, as he received quite a bit of fan mail.

This was interesting, in and of itself, as Howard on stage did not look like other old-time fiddlers. In her book, *Roy Acuff, the Smoky Mountain Boy,* Elizabeth Schlappi described Howard like this:

> Howdy does not appear to be an old time country fiddler: he doesn't have chin whiskers running down to the fiddle, he doesn't hold it on his chest, and he doesn't slouch when he plays. Howdy tucks his fiddle under his clean-shaven chin and stands straight, with feet placed in the manner of a concert violinist. Furthermore, he insists on using a tuning fork. But looks are deceiving. When the music pours out it is powerfully evident that Howdy Forrester is, indeed, one of the finest of all the traditional country fiddlers, and certainly the finest fiddler Roy ever had. In fact, Howdy is the finest fiddler he has ever known.[241]

Howard's cousin Floyd Pruett (Uncle Bob's grandson) still lived out in Hickman County, and he listened to Howard on the Opry every Saturday night. If Howard played the tune "Liberty" on the show, it was his way of signaling Floyd that he was coming out to Hickman County to visit on Sunday. Floyd would round up family members, get a bottle of "moonshine," and they would have a good old-fashioned jam.[242]

The Smoky Mountain Boys teased Howard at first, as they realized he didn't know the ropes yet. One night on the Opry, Howard turned to Bob Lunn and said, "What's next?"

Bob told him, "As soon as Roy stops talking, you start playing 'Silent Night.'" But this time Howard saw the gleam in Lunn's eye and didn't bite.[243]

Sometimes, being new, Howard stumbled into his own mistakes. One night Roy was getting ready to close the show, which usually meant doing a gospel number. Roy chose "I Saw the Light" and signaled Jimmie Riddle to kick it off. Howard missed the signal and began singing before any of the others, his clear, high-pitched voice filling the auditorium and echoing off the rafters. The band started laughing so hard that they couldn't play, and Roy had to close the show.[244]

Such was the job of being a rookie. Howard learned to pay real close attention at all times, as Roy's show was basically unscripted. A musician had to be really good and always alert to play with Roy. One night he would call a tune in A; next time he sang that tune, it might be in G—or even C!

In addition to the Opry, Roy took the band to play various engagements around the country and, in fact, all over the world. At first they flew everywhere in a DC-3, but the landing strips were often too far from the playing venues, so Roy got them a bus to ride in. Finally, they ended up just using three automobiles and taking turns driving.[245]

Shortly after Howard joined the Smoky Mountain Boys, Roy took them to Canada to play some shows. Howard was very serious about his work with Roy, and he did not always understand the drinking and bantering and high jinks of the other band members. It began to bother him to the point that he had decided to tell Roy after they returned from Canada that he was quitting the band. But once again Fate intervened.

Upon arrival at their hotel in Canada, the Smoky Mountain Boys got in line to check in. Suddenly, another tourist tried to muscle his way in front of Roy Acuff at the head of the line. Roy fixed the man with a stare and said, "I'm checking my band into this hotel first and then you and I will go outside and settle this." (For a small man, Roy was very forceful.) After checking in, Roy pulled the man outside and pummeled him good. After witnessing this, Howard said to himself "That's the Boss right there," and he decided not to quit the band after all![246]

The band played at the Astor Roof Hotel in New York City in 1952. Billie got to accompany Howard on this trip and actually "came out of musical retirement" long enough to square dance with Brother Oswald during the show.[247]

In 1953 the Smoky Mountain Boys traveled to the Far East to put on shows as part of a USO tour, something Roy really liked to do. He was very patriotic and, in fact, once said that he would rather play for the troops than do almost any other kind of show. This tour took them to Japan, Okinawa, Korea, and Wake Island, where the soldiers and sailors were really appreciative of Roy's show.[248] Howard received a Certificate of Esteem from the Department of Defense for his "patriotic service in providing entertainment to members of the Armed Forces."[249]

The music business was changing fast, and Howard tried to learn it all—listening to Stephane Grapelli, Joe Venuti, and his idol, Fritz Kreisler. Some of the big band leaders, like Paul Whiteman and Ted Fio Rito, had started using strings in their bands. Howard listened to them, as well, but had no desire to play that way.[250]

The Smoky Mountain Boys were spending about 250 days a year on the road and, in the 1950s, played in every state in the Union. During a trip to Pennsylvania Roy Acuff pioneered the concept of playing in parks on week nights, which drew large crowds and helped fill up the time between the big weekend shows. When not on the road, the Smoky Mountain Boys worked at Acuff's Dunbar Cave in Clarksville doing maintenance and other chores.[251]

In 1953, as a reward for all his hard work, Roy gave Howard two weeks off, and Howard the family man took Billie and eight-year-old Bob on a car trip to Florida. They drove all the way to the tip of the state, down one side and up the other, pausing frequently for dips in the ocean.[252] It seems amazing that after 250 days on the road, Howard would even want to move from his comfortable recliner, much less go on an arduous road trip with an eight-year-old child! But Howard loved his family and loved to travel and see new things.

In 1954, Roy and the Smoky Mountain Boys went to WSM's large Studio C in the National Life & Accident Insurance Company building to do some serious recording. One of the many sponsors of the Opry shows was the Royal Crown (RC) Cola Company, and over a period of seven to ten days, the band recorded fifty-two fifteen-minute radio shows for RC Cola. The group never repeated a song on any of the shows, actually recording some 160 tunes, many of which were never commercially recorded and released. Each show segment opens and closes with a plug for RC Cola, and the segments contain vocals, Howard's fiddle tunes, other instrumental tunes, and lots of good hillbilly entertainment.[253]

The shows were pressed on 16" acetate disks, one show on each side, and were sent out to various radio stations around the country to play. After the broadcasts (one each week), the disks were to be returned to the Royal Crown Company. Most of the stations who received the disks were in the South and southeastern parts of the U.S. One of the stations, of course, was WSM in Nashville, home of the Opry.

No one knows just how many records were mailed, nor how many were actually played on the air. And Royal Crown has no records to indicate these shows actually existed! However, some forty-five years later, four sets of disks turned up in private collections in California, Michigan, Mississippi, and Virginia.

In 2001 RME Music, Inc., actually released *Roy Acuff and His Smoky Mountain Boys, Vols. 1–5* (no CD numbers) of the RC Cola shows on CD. Where the rest are, or if they will ever be released, no one seems to know. The jacket liner from Volume 5 quotes WSM's Grand Ole Opry announcer, Eddie Stubbs:

This collection offers the listener the ability to get an understanding of what Roy Acuff's sound and style during this period were all about. The band has never sounded better.... The name Howdy Forrester has been legendary in the realm of fiddle playing based largely on his live performances with Roy Acuff. Howdy is showcased on all the RC Cola Shows with his unique style on hornpipes, breakdowns, or anything he chose to play, easily displaying what helped to make him a legend.[254]

In 2006 a new compilation of Roy Acuff shows was released over the Internet for download or purchase on CD: *The Roy Acuff Show Collection: the Great 48*. They are, as the name implies, forty-eight show segments, some of which contain tunes and songs identical to the RME compact discs. However, there are a large number of tunes played by Howdy Forrester that are *not* in the RME segments, including "Tennessee Waggoner," "Brilliancy," "Rickett's Hornpipe," "Trot Along," "Eighth of January," "Little Betty Brown," "Turkey in the Straw," "Sally Goodin," "Leather Britches," "Soldier's Joy," "Arkansas Traveler," "Fire on the Mountain," "Cincinnati Hornpipe," "Wake Up Susie," "Rakes of Kildare," "Flop Eared Mule," "Grey Eagle," "Mississippi Sawyer," "Dusty Miller," "Sugar in the Gourd," "Billy in the Lowground," and "Stoney Point."[255] A number of these tunes are not on *any* of Forrester's own commercial recordings, either. I immediately ordered a CD, which arrived in a plain brown wrapper, without any markings on the CD. Fortunately, I had printed out the website listing of all the segments on the CD, so I knew what I was listening to. I went back to the website to see if I could find a CD number or other identifying information for the Discography in this book. The website is gone, and my Internet search turned up nothing.

In 1954, Howard's son Bob turned seven and was baptized into the Catholic Church, along with Howard's wife, Billie. Howard thought religion and all that talk about heaven was "just too good to be true," and while he wanted to believe it, he just couldn't. So, although he admired the Catholic Church, he did not join the church at this time.[256]

Near the end of 1954, the band went on another USO tour, this time to Alaska over the Christmas holidays, and once again, Billie "unretired" long enough to go on the tour with Howard, where she actually played and sang some. The band left Nashville on November 28 and stopped in the Northwest to entertain troops there. They arrived in Anchorage on December 4 and, after engagements there, traveled to Nome for a show on December 19. By December 21, they were in Fairbanks, and the weather had gotten so cold that on December 26, even the dog sled races were canceled, as it was -46 degrees! Howard quipped, "If it's too cold for the dogs up here, it's too cold for me!"[257]

The country music newsletter *Pickin' and Singin' News* of January 15, 1955, printed a letter from a fan at Eielson Air Force Base (twenty-six miles south of Fairbanks, Alaska), which said in part:

> I had the pleasure of assisting with a local broadcast of the Roy Acuff USO show, along with Joe Perry who is Engineer-Program Director-Announcer of our AFRS station.... Roy along with Oswald, Pap, Odie, Jimmie, Jerry Johnson, Howdy and Sally Forrester really went all out to make a real good show that was interesting from start to finish.
>
> Yours truly will have to admit that I saw it three times—first at Ladd AFB on the 20th...the second on the 22nd...and again on the 24th...it sounded something like the Grand Ole Opry in respect to the ovation they received.... Thanks sincerely to Roy and the gang's effort and time away from their loved ones during the holiday season and we want you to tell Roy we won't forget it...
> > Sincerely,
> > Cousin Doug
> > [T/Sgt Douglas R. Stuckey][258]

While they were in Alaska, both Howard and Billie were initiated into the Royal Order of Polar Bears Club at Barter Island, the farthest north night club in the world.[259] Howard also was sworn into the Order of the Arctic Realm for having crossed the Arctic Circle.[260] On December 30, they returned to Anchorage and on January 6, arrived back in Nashville.

Howard really fit well in Roy's band. Howard valued family and friends above almost everything else in life, and Roy's band functioned much like a family. In an unpublished interview of Howdy Forrester by writer Danny Twork, Twork said, "The name Howdy Forrester and the name Roy Acuff go together like branch water and bourbon. They're just natural."[261]

There wasn't much turnover of personnel in Roy's band, and band members spent much of their "off duty" time together, pursuing various activities. In between Opry segments or performances on the road, band members would usually return to Roy's dressing room for a jam session. And often, in their free time, band members would go to Roy's amusement park at Dunbar Cave and help Roy make improvements or just hang out and fish or play music or talk.

In the mid-1950s, band member Shot Jackson actually supervised the band in the building of two house boats, which the "boys" used extensively for parties and other events. One boat stayed on the lake at Dunbar Cave and the other was tied up at Roy's house on Old Hickory Lake.[262]

In addition to fostering a family atmosphere in the band, Roy actually was one of the few band leaders who paid his band a living wage, whether or not they were out on the road, and he paid them their wages on time, as well. He understood that "his boys" had lives and responsibilities apart from the band and needed a steady income to live on. This is probably one of the primary reasons his band members were so loyal to him. Roy also gave them little "perks," such as taking the wives with them on a trip to Florida or on a deep sea fishing expedition.[263]

Roy used to tell his band, "Fellas, if at some time I can have your homes paid for, you can kindly beg or steal something to eat, but no one can kick you out of the house if you own it. I don't think that your taxes will get so far behind that you can't maybe pay them. The one thing that I want you to have is a shelter over you and your family's head."[264]

Howard took these words of wisdom to heart, and with his steady income from Roy's band and Billie's job at the Social Security Administration, they were able to acquire fourteen acres of land in Nashville. In 1952 brother Clyde built them a house on the acreage, where they and Sudie raised Bob and hosted lots of family parties and many evenings of fiddling with friends. Much later in life, when it was time to downsize a bit, Howard was able to sell his modest home for $370,000 to the developer who was building the Rivergate Shopping Center![265]

Roy was a very innovative boss to work for. In the early 1950s, television was in its infancy, but Roy sensed the potential that was there. He worked hard to get the Smoky Mountain Boys onto television. They made a number of appearances on the Kate Smith show, which broadened their appeal to audiences all across the country.

Roy also got all kinds of engagements for his band to play, including one in Liberty, Texas, in 1956, where they actually played in hillbilly attire for the Liberty Bicentennial Observance.[266] But for most gigs, including the Opry, he let the band members dress as they chose. For most of them, including Howard, this meant country casual attire—slacks and a shirt (often plaid) and sometimes a string tie. Roy usually wore a suit, the only band member to do so.

The Smoky Mountain Boys also played on military bases around the United States. In the mid-1950s they played on an Air Force base in North Carolina, where one of the young dental officers became quite enamored of Howard's playing and befriended him. The dentist, Dr. Perry Harris, became a lifelong friend of Howard's, and they often took trips together. Harris could pick a little banjo, but mostly he just loved fiddle tunes, especially the way Howard played them.

Harris later went back to school, becoming first an MD with a specialty in otolaryngology and later a plastic surgeon. After his stint in the service, he relocated to Nashville and became one of Howard's best friends.[267]

In January, 1955, Roy and the Smoky Mountain Boys began a two-year partnership with Kitty Wells and her band and Johnny (Wright) and Jack (Anglin).[268] They played on the same Opry segments, and they toured the United States and Canada together, billing themselves as the King and Queen of Country Music. They set attendance records wherever they went. In November, 1955, the combined show played the Palace on Broadway in New York, the first country music troupe ever to do so.[269] In February, 1956, they played in the main auditorium at Ohio State University and filled every seat, despite the new popularity of rock 'n' roll, which was sweeping college campuses.[270]

Kitty was under contract to Decca Records, and she and Roy made some recordings together during this period. Howard and Kitty's fiddler, Ray Crisp, play twin fiddle harmony behind Roy and Kitty on "Good Bye, Mr. Brown" and "Mother Hold Me Tight" (Decca 29935), later released in a Bear Family boxed set *Kitty Wells— The Golden Years: 1949–1957*, BFX15239.[271]

In 1957, the Smoky Mountain Boys played a concert of music written solely by Fred Rose of Acuff-Rose Music Publishing. This was a tribute concert played at the park and co-sponsored by the *Nashville Tennessean* and the City Park Board of Commissioners. Musicians were provided by AFM Local 1257 and included: Howdy Forrester, Roy Acuff, Lonnie Wilson, Shot Jackson, Jerry Johnson, Brother Oswald (Pete Kirby), and Jimmie Riddle. The concert was made possible by a grant from the Music Performance Trust Fund of the recording industry and drew a huge crowd, proof of the lasting appeal of Rose's music.[272]

During this year, long-time Smoky Mountain Boy Robert "Talking Blues Man" Lunn went to Starday Records to record an album entitled *The Original Talking Blues Man—Robert Lunn*, SLP-228. He took with him Smoky Mountain Boys Brother Oswald (Pete Kirby) to play dobro, banjo, and "jug," Jimmie Riddle to play harmonica and washboard, and fiddler Howdy Forrester. They added Junior Huskey on string bass and Gene Martin on guitar. They gathered around the microphone in the recording studio and put on an old-fashioned jug band show—picking, singing, telling jokes, and talking the blues. Various band members also played solos, including Howard, who played "Fiddlin' Trombone," a tune he later recorded as "Trombone Rag" on his solo album *Howdy's Fiddle and Howdy Too!*, Stoneway STY-127.

Also in 1957, Howard was invited back to the recording studio, this time by the Stanley Brothers and the Clinch Mountain Boys, where they recorded four cuts for Mercury, featuring Howard and Benny Martin fiddling some hot bluegrass tunes: "Daybreak in Dixie," Mercury LP-20884, "If That's the Way You Feel," Merc-Starday 71258, "A Life of Sorrow," not released at this time, and "I'd Rather be Forgotten," Merc-Starday 71258. These cuts were later re-released in 2003 on a 2-CD set titled *The Stanley Brothers and the Clinch Mountain Boys—The Complete Mercury Recordings*, B0000534-02.[273]

In September 1958, Howard cut his first solo album, *Fancy Fiddlin'—Country Style*, but according to son Bob, the album was not released until 1960, first as MGM E-4035 and then as CUB 8008. Roy Acuff had asked Howard to make an album, but up until then, all the published fiddle albums had been square dance albums, with the tunes arranged strictly for dancing and the calls imbedded over the music. Howard said the only way he would make an album was if he were allowed to play his tunes his way, which meant they were not set up for square dancing and there were no calls on the recording. Roy told him, "I'll guarantee you, if you want to do an album, I'll get you one and you do it just exactly how you want to."[274] And so the album was made.

Many of the twelve tunes on this album were Howard's original compositions or arrangements: "Rutland's Reel" (written as a tribute to his good friend "Georgia Slim" Rutland), "Fiddler's Waltz," "Leather Britches," "Dog in the Rye Straw," "Brilliancy" (a pastiche of old hornpipes), "Strictly Forrester," "High Level Hornpipe," "Say Old Man," "Cruel Willie," "Clarinet Polka," and "Sally Goodin" and "Grey Eagle Hornpipe," two of his signature hoedown arrangements.[275] The band backing Howard included: Buddy Harmon on drums, Ray Edenton on guitar, Pig Robbins on piano, Bob Moore on bass, and Jimmie Riddle on harmonica.[276]

In 1959, Howard was back in the studio, this time with Roy Acuff and the Smoky Mountain Boys, where they recorded an album titled *Once More It's Roy Acuff*, Hickory LPM-H101, featuring many of Roy's recent Hit Parade songs.

Then Roy took the band on a private (not USO-sponsored) trip to Hawaii and Australia. The trip lasted over two months (2/21–4/25), but did not turn out exactly as planned. The first stop was in Hawaii, where the band spent about ten days performing, mostly for military audiences. On March 3 they arrived in Sydney, Australia, where they had been booked on a percentage basis to do a series of shows. Roy usually worked on a straight payment contract and, although attendance at the Sydney shows was decent, it was not good enough to make expenses. The show was a good old country music show, and Roy even used some local Australian performers to fill in, but the Australians did not understand or take to that kind of music. After a very poor showing at a concert in Adelaide, Roy canceled the rest of the band's appearances.

In an attempt to recoup some of the money the band had lost, Roy decided to make a series of black-and-white TV films called *Roy Acuff Open House*. There are thirty-nine recordings of thirty minutes each, on which Roy sang a number of songs he had rarely sung before or since, tunes like "When You Wore a Tulip" and "Four Leaf Clover."[277] Unfortunately, he did not know who held the copyrights to these tunes and ended up paying big royalties when he returned home and discovered that they were not only *not* in the public domain, but also not owned by Acuff-Rose!

The series of films was later duplicated and sent to television stations around the country. Roy Acuff and his band, including Howdy Forrester, became well known all over the country, not just in Nashville. Roy later gave the copies of the films to the Armed Forces Radio Network, and they were played repeatedly for servicemen overseas.[278]

Australia boasts many kinds of strong liquor and various beers from around the globe, and Howard and Jimmie Riddle were busy trying as many of them as they could. But once the taping started, they swore off alcohol until the taping finished—consummate performers all.[279]

In these films, Howard was clearly at the "top of his game." He was only thirty-seven years old, but his playing had matured significantly. He held his fiddle liked he owned it, and he had a stage presence that made the audience feel he was the greatest fiddler in the world. He had become not only the consummate fiddler, but a great showman as well. He had that kind of bravado—backed up by the finest fiddling—that made the audience love him. If he had seen himself play (without knowing himself), he would have said,

"Now he can really show," his highest compliment for another musician.[280]

By December, the band was well-recovered from its Australian junket, and Roy took them on another USO tour from December 13, 1959 until January 13, 1960.[281] Roy did not like to spend Christmases at home and frequently booked the band to be away during that time. That the trips were made on behalf of the armed forces may have helped make the band's absences more palatable to their families, although Billie did not like it one bit.[282] This tour went to the Caribbean: the British West Indies, Panama Canal Zone, Puerto Rico, and Cuba, where they were air-lifted in to Guantanamo Naval Base and performed for servicemen who had not been off the base for the eighteen months since Castro had come to power! Howard got to see Bermuda, the Turks Island, San Salvador, Eleuthera, and Antigua, and the Miraflores Locks at the Panama Canal.[283]

In January of 1960, Howard's first solo album, *Fancy Fiddlin'— Country Style*, (MGM E4035/CUB 8008) was finally released, and on March 28, Howard received a letter from Acuff-Rose Artists with high praise for the album: "Dear Howdy: Let us add our congratulations to the many you undoubtedly are receiving on your excellent new album. It should have been titled 'Howdy at His Absolute Best'...Best regards, Acuff-Rose Artists Corp. W. D. Kilpatrick"[284]

He also received critical acclaim from concert impresario Harry Draper in the *Nashville Banner* on March 10 in a column titled "Round the Clock": "One of the best violinists around is Howdy Forrester who plays the fiddle with Roy Acuff's Smoky Mountain Boys. *Forrester's technique is strictly legitimate.*—Harry Draper"[285]

Howard was very proud of this album, although he was quite realistic when he said: "I know there is only a small group of fiddlers who'll ever buy my records. It doesn't bother me. That's just the way it is."[286]

This MGM recording, however, became one of the most sought-after fiddle recordings of its time, and fiddlers of today still search old record stores and the Internet looking for copies, which are almost impossible to obtain!

In the fall of 1960, the Smoky Mountain Boys played a week-long run at the Showboat Casino in downtown Las Vegas and returned a year later for another run.[287] Even Tinsel Town loved Roy's homespun entertainment and Howard's fancy fiddle playing. This led to tremendous success on the club circuit, and the band played The Flame in Minneapolis, The Mint in Las Vegas, Rivoli Hall in Chicago, and The Headliner Room at Harrah's in Reno.[288]

The sophistication of Howard's fiddling, with its marriage of classical style and country tunes brought in people who might otherwise have turned up their noses at a country "hillbilly" band.

October 2–December 17 found the Smoky Mountain Boys gone on yet another USO Tour, this time to Germany, Italy, and France. The trip started somewhat ominously with engine trouble, which grounded them for two days in the Azores. Then they were off to Germany for the first set of performances for the troops.

On November 16, while the band was in Berlin for performances, Howard and harmonica player Jimmie Riddle slipped across the border into East Berlin for a visit to the Soviet sector. Howard reported that the difference between West and East was like the difference between daylight and dark![289]

While on this trip, Howard (the history buff) talked to a number of German soldiers who had served in World War II. He was amazed that not a single one would admit to having fought the Americans! To a man, they all insisted that they had only served on the Eastern (Russian) front.[290]

Howard and Jimmie also sneaked off to the Hohner factory, where Jimmie purchased twenty-five chromatic harmonicas—in all the different keys—for only $72.00!

After Germany, the band went into Italy and played in a number of cities. They got to do a little sightseeing, including the Leaning Tower of Pisa. They went back to Germany for the rest of November and then to France for performances before the trip home.[291] The Chief of USAREUR Special Services presented Howard with a Certificate of Esteem for "his outstanding showmanship and high caliber of entertainment."[292]

Howard loved these trips. He was always restless and eager to see and experience new things. He took trips to England, Scotland, Hawaii, Florida, and Kentucky. One of the highlights of his many overseas trips was to discover the music of the country he was visiting. He bought recordings nearly everywhere he went and, upon his return home, would listen to the new music and try out on his fiddle some of the things he had heard. Howard brought home music of every genre—classical, opera, jazz, big band, blues, gypsy music, African drumming, Latin American rhythms, Far Eastern music…. As a result, his son Bob also was exposed to music from all over the world, although the result was not necessarily what Howard might have wanted. Bob took up the drums and joined a rock 'n' roll band, playing for dances and parties in the Nashville area![293]

Bob had taken several years of violin lessons and that, coupled with listening to and watching his dad fiddle all his life, had led to Bob's becoming a fairly credible fiddler. According to Howard's brothers, Joe and Clyde, Bob could have been as good—or perhaps even better—at the fiddle than his dad was, since Howard never had the benefit of *any* formal music instruction. Unfortunately, fiddling was not the "be all and end all" for Bob that it was for his father, and he did not practice very much. Howard thought he had talent, though, and on occasion they would play together. Howard did not push Bob to become a fiddler, as he felt fiddling should be "all about having fun."[294]

In 1961, Howard returned to Dallas and played a show at the famous Longhorn Ballroom with his Texas Roundup buddy, Dewey Groom, who now owned the Ballroom.[295]

The Smoky Mountain Boys went to Spain and Morocco for their next USO tour from December 12, 1961 to January 10, 1962. Band members, including Howard, were shocked by the primitive conditions they encountered on this trip. They couldn't believe there were "people [still] living as they did in Biblical times." Howard's comment was, "We don't know how well off we are!"[296]

When they returned, they recorded another album on the Hickory label, *Roy Acuff—King of Country Music*, Hickory LPS-109 (later re-issued as HR-4504). One of the cuts on this album, "Wreck on the Highway," was re-released in 1995 by Razor & Tie on an album titled *When I Stop Dreaming: The Best of the Louvin Brothers,* RE 2068.

In 1962, Howard was gone for nearly two months as Roy took the band overseas for a USO tour that took them to Sicily, Italy, Crete, Turkey, Lebanon, Saudi Arabia, Ethiopia, Jordan, Cyprus, Greece, and Libya.[297]

In December of 1962, Bashful Brother Oswald (Pete Kirby) recorded an album *25 Years on the Grand Ole Opry*, with Junior (Roy Madison) Huskey, Cowboy Copas, Jimmie Riddle, and Howard. After the session, Oswald asked Howard to play a tune for a fiddle album, so Howard played a tune called "Trot Along," which would later be re-issued on the compact disc *30 Greatest Fiddler's Hits,* Deluxe DCD 7823. Bob Forrester had dropped by the studio on his way home from school; at the close of the tune, Oswald's voice can be heard on the sound track saying, "How do you like that, Bobby?" The same musicians, Oswald, Riddle, Huskey, and Copas backed Howard on this tune. (Copas was Howard's friend from his early days on the Opry.) This recording is significant because Cowboy Copas was killed a few months later in a plane crash while returning from a benefit show in Kansas City.[298]

The other Forrester tune on *30 Greatest Fiddler's Hits* was the song "Still on the Hill." This tune was originally recorded in 1963, on the Starday album *Country Music Cannonball*. Starday, located in Nashville at the time, did compilations of various performers.[299]

One evening the Smoky Mountain Boys played for a square dance up at WSM for John McDonald, the broadcaster for "Noon-time Neighbors," which aired at noon on Fridays. Then the band went over to Starday for one of the compilation sessions, this one produced by Tommy Hill. Gene Martin did a tune; then Jimmie Riddle played one, and then it was Howard's turn. The producer needed one more tune to fill up the album.

Howard, according to son Bob, took an old one-part tune called "The Sells Brothers Circus Rag," which he had learned from Uncle Dave Macon, and, virtually on the spot, added second and third parts to it, including his signature slid double stops, a high part, and a key change, and the group recorded it, under the title "Still on the Hill." Bob, who had accompanied his dad to the studio, actually sat in and played drums on the recording.

Because the tune was later re-released on compact disc, the Forresters have received more royalties from this tune than from any other tune Howard ever composed or recorded! Howard had never played the tune before, and Bob says he never heard him play it again after that recording session.

Howard was always doing that—creating parts to a song, playing it, and then forgetting it. He was able to make a part for a song that fit the original song like a glove.

"The Sells Brothers Circus Rag" was the signal tune used by the circus to notify the light man when the elephants defecated in the ring. The light man would then switch the spot light to another ring, and the clowns would run out into that ring to distract the audience, while the roustabouts cleaned up the elephant's mess.

Howard, who had a great sense of humor, thought it was hysterically funny that this tune, of all his work, brought him the most royalties. He called this tune his "greatest hit," and, forty-one years later, son Bob is still receiving royalties on it![300]

Howard loved a good joke and had a great laugh that was highly infectious. He couldn't tell jokes very well himself, but his friends used to tell him lots of jokes and stories just to hear that fabled laugh. One of them told him that if he wasn't making a living playing the fiddle, he could easily get a job making laugh tracks for movies and commercials![301]

Several years later Starday would publish another compilation album (a 2-record set) entitled *Grand Ole Opry Spectacular* (SLP 242), containing forty performances by various Opry stars. Side two of the first record opens with Howdy Forrester playing a hoedown, just like he always opened Roy's Opry segments. The album jacket lists the tune as "Chasin' the Squirrel," but the tune is actually "Trot Along," for which Howard receives thunderous applause.[302]

During this year, Roy also took the band to the studio again, where they recorded *Stars of the Grand Ole Opry*, Hickory LPM-113, a compilation of some of their favorite songs.

In June of 1963, Howard returned to the recording studio without the Smoky Mountain Boys and recorded another album of his own, titled *Big Howdy—Fiddlin' Country Style* on the United Artists label, UAL 3295, containing the following tunes: "Grandmammy Look at Uncle Sam," "Town and Country Fiddler," "Memory Waltz," "Howdy in Hickman County," "Apple Blossom Polka," "Pretty Polly Ann," "Doc Harris Hornpipe," "The Weeping Heart," "Wild Fiddler's Rag," "Cathy with the Raven Black Eyes" (named for Bob Forrester's then girlfriend), "The Last Waltz," and "Cluckin' Hen."[303] Actual lead sheets for these tunes are included in the appendix of this book.

Howard composed every one of these tunes, and they are some of his best work. It took him about a month to write all of them.[304] Howard had this to say about the experience: "When I went to the studio to record, the back up guys thought it would just be breakdown fiddling [three chords on an old guitar], but when I began to play, they realized that it was a lot harder and they sat up and really started playing."[305]

Tommy Jackson produced this album and arranged for it to get recorded. The band included Bob Moore on bass, Buddy Harmon on drums, Hargis (Pig) Robbins on piano, Ray Edenton on rhythm guitar, and Jimmie Riddle on harmonica. Even Bob Forrester had a role in this recording. Since Pig Robbins was blind, he could not see when Howard would signal the others that the song was about to end, so it was Bob's job to tap Pig on the shoulder so he would quit playing on time.[306]

While they were recording this album, one of the band members opined, "We need a really great tune like 'Faded Love' [Bob Wills' huge hit] on this album." No one could think of a tune to match "Faded Love," but since all the other tunes on the album were Howard's original compositions, he said he would try to think of something. He went right home and wrote the tune "Weeping Heart," which is definitely of the "Faded Love" genre. They recorded it the very next day.[307]

One of the tunes on this album, "Cluckin' Hen," calls for the fiddle to be cross-tuned and is based in part on an old Hickman County tune, which Howard learned from his Uncle Bob.[308] Howard liked the nice resonance cross-tuning provided to various tunes and he used to travel with a second fiddle, which he kept cross-tuned.

Roy Acuff also liked the sound of a cross-tuned fiddle. Once, when the Smoky Mountain Boys were up in Canada performing, the band was clapped back for an encore. Roy asked Howard to get his cross-tuned fiddle and play "Bonaparte's Retreat" for the crowd. Roy was a sharp showman, and he sold the crowd on Howard playing the encore for them.

Howard complied with the request, but when he got out on stage and looked out into the crowd, he suddenly realized he was in Quebec (*French* Canada) and that people there might not appreciate him playing "Bonaparte's Retreat." He said, "I looked into the abyss, and I thought the people there might kill me, but Roy had sold them on me, so I played it anyway." The Canadians loved Howard's playing so much they ignored the title of the tune and clapped him back for yet *another* encore.[309]

Howard loved Canada and Canadians, and he often said that if it weren't for his family all being in Nashville, he would go to Canada, as he thought he could do quite well there. The Canadians really liked his playing. Howard became fast friends with Rudy Meeks, the Canadian National Fiddling Champion, and they took a number of trips together. Meeks later won first place at the Grand Master Fiddler Championship in Nashville.[310]

Tommy Jackson produced another album, this time for MCA, titled *Square Dances Without Calls*, DL7-8950 (and later MCA-162). Tommy does most of the fiddling on it, but Howard plays the lead on "Clarinet Polka," "Jesse Polka," and "Snowflake Reel," although he is not credited on the album cover. Grady Martin plays on this album as well, also uncredited. Grady had been drinking quite heavily, but he played his break anyway, and it was perfect on the first take.[311]

Oddly enough, on this album the "Clarinet Polka" is performed in the key of G. Usually when that is done, the tune is called "Grandfather's Polka." It is surprising that Howard, who was fastidious about his tunes, allowed it to be called "Clarinet Polka," especially since he later recorded the "Clarinet Polka" on a solo album—in its original key of B-flat!

In 1963, the Nashville Symphony was having a tough time making its budget, so it appealed to the country music people to help put on a fundraiser at Ryman Auditorium; Roy Acuff, who loved classical music, answered the call. The Smoky Mountain Boys did their part of the show, and then Roy had Howard play "Say Old Man," which was one of his signature hoedowns. Both the audience and the symphony musicians were duly impressed.

After the show, the symphony's violinists took Howard back stage and asked him to teach them to play "The Orange Blossom Special," one of the flashiest of fiddle tunes. Howard reported that they had great difficulty picking it up—all the shuffle bowing and fast licks—and, of course, no music for them to read. They had to learn it the "fiddlin' way"—by ear.[312]

The symphony had a guest conductor that day, a British chap named Harry Newstone, who could play the harmonica. He and Jimmie Riddle decided to play a duet together, but neither of them knew the other's tunes. Howard and Jimmie Riddle had a flashy version of "Clarinet Polka" that they often played together. Howard played his part for Newstone, who whipped out a paper and pencil and wrote out the notes as Howard played them. Then Newstone and Riddle went on stage and performed the tune together on their two harmonicas![313]

Roy Acuff published two more albums that year, the first containing material from two of the overseas tours he and the Smoky Mountain Boys went on to entertain the troops, titled *The World Is His Stage—Roy Acuff and the Smoky Mountain Boys*, Hickory LPM-114.

Howdy fiddles behind Roy on most of the tunes, plays a wild western swing-style break on the "New Fort Worth Rag," accompanies singer June Webb with some very innovative fiddling on "Oh, Lonesome Me," and dazzles the crowd of servicemen with his own highly-regarded version of "Sally Goodin." He also plays a double-stopped break, emulating the singing of Melba and Jane, on "Have I Told You Lately That I Love You."[314]

The second album, *American Folk Songs*, Hickory LPS-115, contains well-known folk songs like "Red River Valley," "Great Titanic," and the perennial bluegrass favorite "Put My Little Shoes Away."

With the advent of rock 'n' roll, nearly all the bands had become "electrified" and, after a long hold out, Roy had finally succumbed as well. But he never liked the sound, and on June 12, 1963, when he recorded *American Folk Songs*, he pulled the plug on the electricity. The album contains twelve tunes, eleven of which he had never recorded before. They are all really old country songs, which he arranged himself. Howard was thrilled with the recording and "felt this session was even better than the old 'golden Acuff sound' of the 1940s."[315]

It is clearly apparent why Roy kept Howdy Forrester in his band all those years: the elegant style, fluid playing, and inventiveness alone made him an important part of the Smoky Mountain Boys. But above all, Howdy's fine fiddling makes Roy sound better as Howdy leads him back in after breaks and adds just the right touches—in the right style—to every tune. Howdy always said he was lucky to work for Roy Acuff, and that is certainly true. But Roy was very lucky to have Howdy Forrester in his band.

In 1964, Roy took the Smoky Mountain Boys on two tours—the first one a private tour to Japan (5/30–6/17/64) and the second one a USO-sponsored tour to Germany over the Christmas holidays (12/21/64—1/3/65). The Japan tour was very memorable for several reasons. First, the band was in Tokyo when the big earthquake of 1964 occurred. Roy was in a cab and didn't even feel the quake, but Howard and Jimmie Riddle were eating in the dining room and watched the chandelier in the middle of the ceiling end up on the wall, along with their dinner!

The Japanese loved their show, which was performed with the aid of an interpreter and an illustrated program in Japanese. However, Roy was still not sure they understood what the band was saying and singing or what American country music really was all about.

Howard had this to report: "The Japanese people are fond of country music. The crowds were good at the start and got bigger as we went along. They sing along with us. I doubt if any of them knew what the words mean, but they sang them just the same and appeared to be having much fun."[316]

The second memorable event of this tour was that the audience included a young man named Shoji Tobuchi, who was mesmerized by the playing of Big Howdy Forrester. Shoji had been taking Suzuki violin lessons since he was seven, but he had planned that he would eventually follow his father into the corporate world. His plans derailed when Roy Acuff and the Smoky Mountain Boys came to play on his campus.

Shoji was captivated by the music, especially by Howdy Forrester's rendition of "Listen to the Mockingbird." He decided to become an entertainer and, while his father was away on a business trip, his mother sent him to the United States to seek his fortune. He called Roy Acuff, who arranged for him to be a guest on the Opry, where Shoji fiddled his way to two standing ovations.[317] The rest, as they say, is history.

Shoji eventually settled in Branson, opening his own dinner theatre and becoming a famous fiddler himself. Howard was paid to come to Branson on Shoji's birthday by Shoji's uncles, who treated Howard to dinner and front row seats for the show. As a surprise birthday gift to Tobuchi, Howard played for him. Tobuchi felt he owed his career to Forrester's influence on him, and he still talks about Howdy on many of his shows.[318]

CHAPTER 8

The Last Waltz

By 1964, Howard was tired of all the traveling and then playing the Opry every Saturday night. People used to come up to him and tell him how lucky he was to get to play on the Opry all those years. He would roll his eyes and say to his wife and son, "People say they would give anything to have my job on the Opry. Well, I would give anything just to get *off* the Opry."[319] But, of course, he never did.

Roy Acuff had no hobbies; the Smoky Mountain Boys were his life, and so he kept them busy, playing all over the country and even the world.

They also made three recordings this year; the first was *The Great Roy Acuff*, Capitol DT-2103 (re-issued in 1970 as Hilltop JS-6090 with four songs omitted.) On this album, Howard presents many different takes on fiddling. On the tune "Sweep Around Your Own Back Door," he plays a bluesy fiddle break (à la Chubby Wise). On "Swamp Lily" he plays a fast moving line of counter melody behind both Roy's singing and the piano break. He exhibits great rhythm and timing to fit all those notes in around Roy's slow singing—in the key of B-flat, no less! On "Little Moses" he plays a fast moving break and fill in an "airy" style, which matches the words Roy sings: "There's going to be a meeting in the air."

The second album was *Hand Clapping Gospel Songs*, Hickory LPS-117, later re-issued as *I Saw the Light*, Hickory LPS-158. It contains many of Roy's favorite religious songs like "Turn Your Radio On" and "That Glory Bound Train."

The third album, *Country Music Hall of Fame*, Hickory LPS-119, contains a lot of Acuff's favorite train songs and gospel numbers.

With all this frenetic activity going on, even Roy could see that Howard was wearing out. One day he approached Howard about trying his hand at something else and offered him the chance to "come inside Acuff-Rose and learn the talent booking business." Howard worked for Jim McConnell, learning the business, and in 1965, Roy made him the manager of the Acuff-Rose Artists' Corporation (ARAC), Personal Appearance Division.[320] He was responsible for booking such artists as Roy Acuff, Bill Carlisle, Mickey Newbury, Roy Orbison, Eddy Raven, Tex Ritter, Bill Monroe (his old boss), George Hamilton IV, Stu Phillips, plus numerous artists in the pop field and some English acts. By 1968, Acuff-Rose had twenty-three acts for which Forrester did the booking.[321] He mostly booked shows, but he also booked some clubs as well.[322]

Howard had an assistant at Acuff-Rose, Jean Thomas, who handled administrative duties for him. Jean had some musical training and could read and write music. She remembers that, in addition to performing secretarial duties, she may have written out some of the lead sheets for Howard's original compositions, so that he could get them copyrighted.

Jean worked for Howard for the twenty years he did booking and found him to be "laid back, not very outgoing, but an outstanding judge of character and very knowledgeable about country music." She thought he was very genuine and really liked working for him. "I don't know what I can say about him that's good enough," was her overall comment.[323] As for Howard, he prized Jean and her many talents, telling people she was one of the big reasons for his success in the booking business.[324]

In June, Howard took time off from his booking duties to make the USO tour to the Dominican Republic with the Smoky Mountain Boys. The country was in the midst of a revolution, and some of the fiercest fighting took place while the band was there. Roy, ever true to the adage that the show must go on, refused to cancel or delay the shows, and the band played to very appreciative audiences.[325] This would be one of the last road trips Howard would make with the band, although he would continue to play the Opry with them and to do other local performances as time allowed.

Roy Acuff loved classical music, and he always bought season tickets to the Nashville Symphony. Since his wife Mildred favored Big Band music, Roy would often ask Howard to go to the symphony concerts with him. Howard loved these excursions and got to hear many of the famous violin soloists who came to play with the symphony. As he listened to the music and watched the performers, he made mental notes of things to try when he got home.

One afternoon Roy took Howard to see the Russian violinist Nathan Milstein play. Their presence together in the third row actually caused more of a buzz among the audience than Milstein's playing did![326]

At Christmas time Roy took the band on yet another USO tour, this time to South Vietnam, Okinawa, Japan, Korea, and the Philippines. Howard did not go with them. Roy used various fiddlers to fill in for Howdy, including Jimmy Lunsford, Jackie Phelps, and Benny Martin, who made most of the overseas trips with Roy. Someone once asked Howard if he had ever gone on the Vietnam tours with Roy, and he replied with his characteristic good humor, "Oh, no. They shoot agents over there!"[327]

Despite Howard's retirement from the road trips, his popularity did not ebb. In September, an admirer said of him: "Howdy Forrester is the fiddlin' ambassador of hoedown to Mozart."[328]

And, of course, Roy Acuff continued to make record albums, two of them in 1965. *Wabash Cannonball: An American Legend*, Hickory LPS-125, is a collection of American train songs. It features some fierce and wild fiddling by Howard on "Night Train to Memphis" and "Sunshine Special," a nice kickoff on "Fireball Mail," and beautiful double stops (in the key of F!) and a nice counter melody on "Midnight Train."

The second album is *Sacred Songs*, Metro MS-508, a large selection of the gospel songs and hymns that helped define the Acuff sound.

In 1965 Howdy's son Bob turned eighteen and graduated from high school. He was still playing in his rock 'n' roll band, but

Howard insisted that he enroll in college. Based on his own long years on the road, Howard told Bob:

> Music is a hard way to make a living. If it happens for you, that's fine, but I wouldn't count on it. In the meantime, you are going to college, and if you don't, we'll just strangle you now and be done with it! Education will open doors for you. I am lucky Roy Acuff thinks I am a good fiddler. There is no merit system in the music business. You can be real good and starve to death.[329]

Needless to say, Bob signed up for college, although at age eighteen he thought his dad knew nothing. Bob earned a BA in history from Vanderbilt University and later a Master's degree in mathematics from Peabody (now part of Vanderbilt), which he parlayed into a college professor's job, teaching mathematics at Volunteer State Community College. Howard, who only had an eighth-grade education, was extremely proud of Bob, and by age twenty-four Bob had decided that his dad was a genius!

One Saturday night after playing the Opry, Howard stopped in to hear Bob's rock 'n' roll band play. After listening to the band for a while, Howard was asked to play a fiddle tune, which he did. The band then began playing "Whole Lot of Shakin' Goin' On" and, when one of the band members nodded at Howard to play a break, Howard went off into a perfect rock 'n' roll flight of fantasy, leaving the band, including Bob, speechless. "Forget Jimi Hendrix," Bob said, "Daddy's the real deal. He really ate that song up."[330]

In December of 1965, Billie's grandmother Sudie died of heart failure at the age of more than eighty. She had lived with Billie and Howard all those years and had virtually raised Bob, as Billie worked full time and Howard was on the road a lot.[331]

In 1966, Roy and the Smoky Mountain Boys went back to the studio and cut an album of gospel tunes and hymns titled *Simply Roy Acuff*, Hilltop JS-6028. Roy loved the old gospel songs and as Ron Grevatt of *Music Business Magazine* put it, "Religious and inspirational song material have always occupied a key part of the Acuff repertoire."[332] Howard's Sunday school-teaching uncle must have been very proud of him.

They also made a second album that year: *Roy Acuff Sings Hank Williams*, Hickory LPS-134. Part of the fiddling on this album is done by Tommy Jackson and the rest by Howard.[333]

One of the extra jobs Howard had performed for Roy Acuff was that of road manager while the band was gone from Nashville. Howard was meticulous about making all the arrangements for travel, hotels, and local transportation and for seeing that players and instruments were at the assigned locations in time for the various performances. He was also the liaison with the escort officers. Roy would miss Howard's personal touch in this area, and the road trips never ran quite so smoothly once Howard went to work in the office.

By the late summer of 1967, Howard announced that he would no longer play professionally, but music in general—and fiddling in particular—were in his blood, and within three months he was back at it, much to Roy's delight.[334] He even went "back to his roots" and played for a square dance out in Hickman County that year.[335]

And Roy took him back to the studio with the Smoky Mountain Boys to record *Famous Opry Favorites*, Hickory LPS-139. Most of the songs are pretty laid back on this album, but Howard plays a lot of pretty double stops with that perfect intonation for which he was famous. And he does cut loose with nice fiddle breaks on the Bill Monroe tune "Uncle Pen" and "I'm Movin' On," and plays a nice moving line behind Roy on "Filipino Baby."[336]

Bob Forrester turned twenty-one in 1968. While on a trip to Florida with his dad, they went into a bar for a celebratory drink, a sort of rite of passage. It was one of the very few times Bob remembers his dad ever going to a bar to drink.[337]

In 1968 Roy and the Boys also recorded an album titled *Roy Acuff: A Living Legend*, Hickory LPS-145. Again, most of the songs are slow and mellow, but Howard plays beautiful double stop breaks on "Rising Sun" and "No One Will Ever Know," and nice double stops behind Roy's singing in "Mommy Please Stay Home with Me," "Easy Rockin' Chair," "Waltz of the Wind," and "Last Letter." Most of the songs on this album are in the key of F, not a very friendly key for fiddlers and definitely one that makes for tougher double stops.

In 1969, Howard had two serious losses in his life. His wonderful mother, Emmie Forrester, had a heart attack and, after several days in the hospital, passed away. His mother had played such an important role in his life, and, even when he was an adult, she was one of his strongest supporters and biggest fans. Parties and gatherings at the Forresters would no longer be the same without Emmie there.[338]

While he was still mourning this loss, his old soul mate from KRLD, "Georgia Slim" Rutland, passed away from a massive heart attack. Howard and Joe Forrester, Roy Acuff, Lester Flatt, and Arthur Smith were the honorary pallbearers. Slim was only fifty-three years old, and Howard took his death very hard.[339] Howard was only forty-seven, but the idea of his own mortality began to weigh on him.[340]

He didn't have much time to grieve, however, as Roy kept him busy making records. Howdy, Roy, and the Smoky Mountain Boys recorded an album called *Treasury of Country Hits*, Hickory LPS-147. Roy owned Hickory Records, so he could record just about any time he had something to say.

In 1970, Howard fiddled on two more albums, as Roy and the Smoky Mountain Boys recorded *Roy Acuff's Greatest Hits*, Columbia CS-1034, and *Time*, Hickory LPS-156.

Since Howard was not traveling all over with the Smoky Mountain Boys, he had more time (finally) to spend with family and friends. These were the heydays for session fiddlers, and many of the top names were in Nashville making recordings. Howard's house was always open to any of his friends who were "passing through," and he spent many long hours playing and swapping tunes with such notables as Johnny Gimble, Benny Martin, Vernon Solomon, Benny Thomasson, Major Franklin, Tommy Jackson, and his really close friends Chubby Wise and Arthur Smith. Howard was a "night person," and once he started playing music with friends, the hours flew by. Often they would play until the wee hours and sometimes all night.

Once, when the Smoky Mountain Boys were playing in Florida, Roy let them take their families along for some rest and relaxation. Early one morning Billie and Bob could not locate Howard. After an exhaustive search, they found him and Jimmie Riddle, the harmonica player, sitting on the beach, the waves lapping their toes, playing tunes and watching the sun come up. They had been playing all night and had worked up dozens of tunes—many of them Mexican—to play on the Opry! (They tried never to play the same tune twice.)[341]

Howard loved these gatherings with his friends, and he also loved to barbecue for them. He would put a slab of meat or some ribs on the barbecue, pour glasses of 100-proof bourbon and branch water (his favorite drink), and the music would just flow out of his fiddle. He was a spicy food gourmet, and he would season up the meat with hot sauce and jalapeno peppers until it was sizzling. Eat and sweat, drink and fiddle—Howard was in his element. His family said he loved hot food so much that sometimes he actually would put hot sauce on a slice of pie and have that for dessert![342]

His friends loved these soirees as well, and they were all enamored of his fiddle playing. Johnny Gimble would always ask Howard to play "Grey Eagle Hornpipe," and Johnny would always stop playing and just sit there and listen in awe. The middle part of "Grey Eagle" had come from Howard's Uncle Bob, but the tune itself was not very accessible. Johnny's comment when asked about Howard was: "Howdy Forrester is the best breakdown fiddler I was ever around!"[343]

He and Howard got together to play anytime Johnny was in town. They would play at the Forresters' home or Howard would pack up Johnny and Barbara Gimble, his own wife Billie, brothers Joe and Clyde, and son Bob, and head down to Hickman County for a big fiddle jam.

One of these jams took place on Thanksgiving, 1971, at Howard's home in the Sherwood Parish Apartments. (He had already sold his house on Gallatin Road.) They played dozens of tunes, including: "Hang Your Head in Shame" with Howard on lead, Johnny on five-string fiddle, Joe Forrester on guitar, Dick Gimble (Johnny's son) on bass, and Bob Forrester on drums; "Over the Waves"; "Home in San Antone" with Howard playing the break; "Big Taters in Sandy Land" with Johnny on electric mandolin and Howard on fiddle; "Twinkle Little Star"; "Little Coquette," with

Billie Forrester on piano and Howard taking a swing-style break, and "Gardenia Waltz," a tune Johnny wrote and Howard called "one of the prettiest waltzes I ever heard." Fortunately, they taped the entire jam session.[344]

Another of these jams took place on November 6, 1972, in Bucksnort, where Howard's cousin Floyd Pruett lived. They played hours of music—hot hoedowns and rags, other fiddle tunes, western swing-style pieces, and some very jazzy tunes, where Johnny was at his best. Johnny and Howard traded off on breaks, took turns playing lead, and did some nice twin fiddling. They recorded the entire afternoon of fiddling, drinking, and merriment. At the outset of the tape, one of them says "It's November 6, 1972." Another says, "No, it's November 5." Howard's retort was: "Let's have another drink, and then we'll decide!"[345]

Howard was always at his most relaxed down at Floyd's in Hickman County, where he would drink a little corn liquor and play a lot of tunes.[346]

One night they were on their way to Floyd's house for a jam. Grady Stringer, a Dickson County fiddler of some note, followed them there, which didn't make Howard very happy. He was already angry at Stringer because he had tried to take credit for some of Arthur Smith's tunes or licks. So when Stringer asked Howard if he played "Billy in the Lowground," Howard glared at him, stuck his fiddle under his chin, and just took off on "Billy." Bob Forrester says his dad played that tune for five minutes or more, putting everything possible into it, as only he could do. When he finally stopped playing, there was dead silence in the room. Grady packed up his own fiddle and left without a word, and they didn't see him again.[347]

Another time Johnny and his band were in town, and they and Howard had a great time jamming backstage at the Opry in Roy Acuff's dressing room. They recorded this session as well, although none of these tapes has ever been published, despite the great music contained on them.[348]

The jams in Roy's dressing room were legendary. The Ryman Auditorium backstage area was seriously limited, with only two or three small dressing rooms to accommodate dozens of performers changing costumes, warming up, and storing personal effects and instrument cases while they were on stage. So Roy rented space in a building a few doors down the alley from Ryman, where he created a huge dressing room for himself, complete with a garage for his Mercedes!

Along with the Smoky Mountain Boys, the biggest stars and hottest fiddlers and pickers would come to Roy's dressing room between acts to jam, talk, and drink. There was always a bottle of George Dickel and extra glasses on the bar, and people partook freely.

One old fiddler from Carolina always tried to get Howard to drink more than was prudent, in the hopes that he could get Roy to let him fiddle Howard's tunes on the Opry. But as Les Leverett, the fabled WSM photographer (and frequent visitor to Roy's dressing room), said: "Howdy Forrester was a real professional. He never drank so much that we couldn't understand what he was playing."[349]

In those days, Irving Waugh was the President of WSM, Inc., which hosted the Opry. Irving was a tough businessman, and the Opry stars both respected and feared him. One night between shows, Howard and one of the Stony Mountain Cloggers went out to the alley behind the Ryman, where Howard had parked his car. They were planning to get a little nip of whiskey from the flask Howard always kept in his trunk. It was late, and downtown Nashville was dark and fairly quiet. Howard had just taken the lid off his flask when his friend peered over Howard's shoulder into the darkness and said, "Oh…hello, Irving." Howard jumped at least a foot off the ground before he realized it was a joke![350]

In 1971, Roy Acuff felt it was time to record yet another album of the gospel tunes his native Tennesseans loved so much, so he, Howard, and the other Smoky Mountain Boys made another album on the Hickory label, *I Saw the Light*, Hickory-LPS-158. This album contains twelve of Roy's favorite songs, and he added the Jordanaires for additional vocal punch. Many of the tunes are up tempo, and Howard plays a continuous, fast-moving style of fill behind the singers.[351]

In March of 1971, Howard went to the RCA Victor studios to record with Lester Flatt and Mac Wiseman for an album called *Lester 'n' Mac*, LSP-4547. They used the ultra-modern facility called "Big Victor" or Studio A and over the course of three days recorded twelve tunes using Flatt's regular band of Haskell McCormick, Vic Jordan, Jake Tullock, Howard Johnson, Roland White, Buck Graves, and fiddler Paul Warren. They added Hargus (Pig) Robbins on piano, Jerry Carrigan on drums, and Big Howdy Forrester to do twin fiddling with Paul Warren.

In August of 1971, Howard, Johnny Gimble, and another fiddler named Sammy Dodge played for a recording called *Calhoun Twins: Jet Set in the Caribbean*, STOP Records LP10001. Members of the band were: Shot Jackson on dobro, Lloyd Green on steel guitar, Willie Rainsford on piano, Dale Sellers and Bobby Hardin on rhythm guitar, Kenny Case on lead guitar, and Bob Forrester on drums.[352] Jackson actually produced this album and later went on to manage the Calhoun Twins. None of the three fiddlers is credited on the album liner.

Howard also liked playing with Benny Martin, as both of them were very aggressive players, with different styles but the same approach.[353] Some of their "twin fiddling" was immortalized on *The Stanley Brothers and the Clinch Mountain Boys—The Complete Mercury Recordings*, re-released on CD in 2003.[354]

With all these fiddlers coming in and out of Nashville, it was only natural that someone would want to create a fiddle contest in which to showcase their talents. Those "someones" were Howard's good friend, Dr. Perry Harris, and the Manager of Opryland, E.W. "Bud" Wendell. They got some support from the Country Music Association and in 1972 launched the first annual Grand Master Fiddler Championship, held at Opryland in conjunction with the International Fan Fair.

Twenty-five of the top fiddlers in the world were invited to compete. Anyone else who wanted to play in the contest had to play in elimination rounds. Only the top five fiddlers from the elimination rounds were allowed to compete in the finals with the invitees. The grand prize winner that first year was Texas fiddle great Vernon

Solomon. Howdy Forrester was one of the judges, once again having refused to participate in a contest.[355]

This fiddle contest would become an annual event, and the Forrester family was always an integral part of it, as brothers Clyde and Joe and son Bob participated as judges for many of the contest years. Howard sometimes judged or played tunes at the opening of the contest to give the judges a "gold standard" by which to measure the contestants.[356]

Howard always preferred fiddle "festivals" over fiddle contests, and in the early 1970s, he played at Bill Monroe's Fourth and Fifth Annual Bluegrass Festivals in Bean Blossom, Indiana, and Lester Flatt's Festival in North Carolina. Kenny Baker and his fiddler friend, Ron Eldridge, were also at Bean Blossom, and Kenny brought Howard to their trailer for a jam session, along with Tex Logan, Doc Harris, Charlie Collins, Oswald, and Mac Wiseman.

Bill Monroe had nine or ten fiddle players at Bean Blossom that year, all on stage at one time: Paul Warren, Curly Ray Cline, Gordon Terry, Buck Ryan, Howard, and others, and Monroe recorded them all together on the MCA label: *Live at Bean Blossom*, MCA 2-8002.[357] Just before the fiddlers went on stage, Tex Logan did a rather lengthy interview with Howard, which was published in the September 1973 issue of the *Muleskinner News*.

Howard also went to the annual Renfro Valley Fiddlers' Convention, where the first year he presented the Grand Champion Trophy in the fiddle contest portion.[358]

One year, Howard, Chubby Wise, and Lester Flatt all went to the Renfro Valley Festival together. Chubby liked to gamble, and there was a big poker game set up for that night. Lester took Chubby aside and warned him not to go to the poker game. "These guys are pros," he warned, "and they'll clip you." Chubby, being Chubby, went to the game anyway.

The next day Chubby's watch was gone. Lester noticed Chubby playing pool, walked up to him, and asked, "Hey, Chubby, what time is it?" Chubby just froze. The poker pros had cleaned him out![359]

Another year at Renfro Valley, Howard, Roy, and the Smoky Mountain Boys were there to do a show. There was a fiddle contest scheduled for the next day, and dozens of top fiddlers were there to compete. Roy Acuff turned Howard loose on the show to fiddle for twenty minutes and "show those boys what they need to do tomorrow." Howard really brought the house down, and finally Roy ended up letting Howard finish the show.

The next day, Howard, Chubby Wise, and Willie Williams judged the contest, and then for the festival finale, Howard, Chubby, and Tater Tate played triple fiddles, and each did a few solos.

After one of the performances at the festival, Howard was jamming with Kenny Baker, Ron Eldridge, and a host of other fiddlers and pickers. As usual at these jams, the alcohol was flowing freely. One of the tunes someone played moved Howard to start dancing. He forgot his fiddle case was behind him—and open—and he tripped over it and fell. His fiddle went flying. Howard wasn't hurt, and they all had a good laugh until Howard picked up his fiddle to play and realized that both the bridge and the sound post had fallen. Howard had to borrow a fiddle from Ron Eldridge to play for the show that night.

After the show, Howard borrowed a post setter from one of the fiddlers, re-set his own post and bridge, and played his own fiddle on the show the next day![360] As meticulous as Howard was about his instrument, though, he probably stopped at the luthier's on his way home to get the post re-set properly!

Howard really enjoyed attending these festivals and went to many of them. He always felt that instead of fiddle contests, there should be more fiddle festivals. He was a believer in cooperation, not competition, and felt that festivals were a better way to showcase the fiddle. "There's not one greatest fiddler," he posited. "Winning only means that you were good that particular day."

He also felt that the contests were artificial. Often they were rigged so the home-town favorite would win. "Even Jascha Heifetz is not going to beat Frazier Moss down in Smithville," Howard opined.[361]

In 1972, Roy and the Smoky Mountain Boys released yet another album on the Hickory label, *Why Is*, Hickory LPS-162. Most of the songs on this album were tunes they had recorded on other albums. One fiddler friend called this a "sampler album."

Howard had a favorite fiddle he always played, which he called "The Mustang," because it was clear that the top had, at some time, been replaced. The wood and workmanship on the top did not exactly match the rest of the fiddle. Howard had traded a bow to Benny Martin to acquire the fiddle.

The fiddle was of German origin, made in 1842. Son Bob thought it might be a Roth. Pedigree aside, "The Mustang" had a huge, powerful sound, and with Thomastik perlon core strings Howard could fill a hall with a really robust sound. He loved that fiddle and played it on the first two albums he recorded.[362]

Howard had a luthier in Dallas, Tom Coburn, whom he had met while he was there in 1949, who did all the repairs on his fiddle. After Howard returned to Nashville, he continued to take his fiddle to Tom in Texas when it needed work. Howard's brother, Clyde, who was a cabinetmaker, even built a wooden bow case for Howard so he could send his bows to Tom for rehairing. For many years Tom took good care of Howard's fiddle.

Sometime after the second album (United Artists) had been recorded, Howard began to have trouble with his fiddle, and he took it to Tom for a tune-up, but when he got it back, it wouldn't play properly. Howard always felt, with fairly good reason, that Coburn had sabotaged his fiddle—it was really dead.

In 1946, while in Dallas, Howard and Slim Rutland had recorded some tunes for the Mercury label. One of the tunes Howard had recorded was "Tennessee Wagoner," a flashy hoedown played as only Howard could play it.

Tom Coburn was one of those fans who had tried to foment a fiddling rivalry between Howard and Slim when both men were playing with the Texas Roundup on KRLD. Somehow, Tom had gotten the idea that Slim was the one who had recorded "Tennessee Wagoner," and he bragged to a lot of people that this proved that Slim was the better fiddler. (The record jacket didn't actually indicate who was playing which tunes.)

Years later, after the 1973 publication of the interview by Tex Logan, everyone knew the truth about "Tennessee Wagoner" and that Howard was the one playing it on the recording. Coburn was really embarrassed by this, and Howard always felt that, to get even, Coburn had sabotaged his fiddle.[363]

Howard's good friend, H.G. Roberts, had a friend, Argyle Graves, who knew a really good violin maker/repairer in Southern Illinois, named Earl Batts. Howard wrote Batts a letter, told him what had happened, and asked if he could restore his fiddle. Batts, who was a skilled repairer of classical violins, was not sure he wanted to work on some old fiddle, even if the owner did claim to play on the Grand Ole Opry. But instead of refusing Howard outright, he said, "Come see me, and I'll listen to you play. Then I'll decide what I can do."

Howard went to Illinois and played for Batts for over thirty minutes—one fancy fiddle tune after another. Batts was shocked at Howard's tremendous skill level and said, "I think I can work on your fiddle," and he fixed it right up.

"I set that bridge on there just like I set it for Heifetz," Batts told Howard. Howard was thrilled with that, and his prized fiddle played perfectly. He and Batts became fast friends, and Batts did all his subsequent repairs.[364]

Howard later bought a fiddle from H.G.'s father-in law for $1,000. Bob Forrester thought it was a really sweet fiddle, so Howard gave it to him and Bob still plays it today. Howard, of course, continued to play the Mustang.[365]

Howard was very protective of his fiddle; on tour, he would carry it on the plane with him, never letting it out of his sight. Once, a trip took the Smoky Mountain Boys and him through the crowded Atlanta Airport, and people kept jostling him. Howard looked at Charlie Collins and Onie Wheeler and said in a loud voice: "If people don't stop pushing me, I'm going to start singing!"

"Go ahead," Wheeler told him. "People will certainly leave you alone then!"[366]

In the summer of 1973, Roy Acuff purchased a fine Pietro Guarneri violin from Salvatore Piccardini, a retired concert violinist in Ripley, New York. The violin was Italian, made in the 1700s, during the golden years of Italian violin making. Roy never played this violin on stage, as Roy often did tricks with his fiddle and bow and probably did not want to risk the expensive instrument in that way. Instead, he gave the Guarneri to his favorite fiddler, Big Howdy Forrester, to play. From then on, Howard played the Guarneri on the Grand Ole Opry, because Roy had given it to him, and he had the greatest respect for Roy.

Roy would always introduce Howard as "my fiddler, Howdy Forrester—he plays a Stradivarius, you know." It was an inside joke; Roy knew the audience would recognize the name Stradivarius and know the fiddle was really expensive. Guarneris are equally expensive, but Roy figured the audience would not recognize that fact, and so, ever the showman, he always called it a Strad.[367] Although the Guarneri was a fine fiddle, Howard still preferred his Mustang and used that for recording and other performances.

Roy also purchased several good quality bows to go with the Guarneri—a Bausch silver-mounted bow made in Saxony about 1900 and a Lupot copy made in Germany of about the same vintage. Howard used them on the Opry and, upon his retirement, returned them to Roy, who passed them and the Guarneri on to his next fiddler, Dan Kelly. In 2002, Kelly sold the two bows to a museum to be put on display.[368]

In May of 1973, President Richard Nixon invited the Smoky Mountain Boys to the White House to play at a dinner honoring the prisoners of war who had returned from Vietnam. The President dispatched Air Force One to Nashville to transport them to Washington. John Wayne, who was in Nashville buying cattle at the time, went with them. Other invitees on the plane included: Bob Hope, Sammy Davis, Jr., Ricardo Montalban, and Jimmy Stewart, who had all boarded the plane in California. Wayne was hung over and looked terrible, but he turned on his charm and shook hands with everyone.

Despite the fact that Howard was no longer traveling everywhere with Roy, he, of course, went on the trip to Washington. Ever the family man, Howard tried to call son Bob from Air Force One, with Wayne and Hope at his side. But, alas, Bob Forrester was out coaching a baseball game and missed the call! Jimmy Stewart took Howard to the cockpit and proceeded to explain everything on the "747" to him.

Bob Hope, of course, was the Master of Ceremonies for the show. Howard and the Smoky Mountain Boys received a standing ovation for their performance and an encore request from Hope himself.

At the close of the show, all the performers lined up on the stage, and Richard Nixon shook hands with each one. Howard hated Nixon, but the show was being televised, and the audience was full of returned prisoners of war who had made great sacrifices for the country, so when his turn came, Howard shook the President's hand as well.

The return trip to Nashville was on Air Force Two, and this time Howard was able to reach son Bob on the in-flight phone.[369]

The White House performance was a bittersweet one for Howard, as he was a life-long Democrat (a Yellow Dog Democrat, Bob says) with no love for Richard Nixon. Howard had grown up during the Hoover years of the Great Depression and he—and indeed all the Forrester family—did not believe Republicans would ever do anything to help the "working man." Howard, ever humble, considered himself one of these working class men—just plain folks. In fact, the Forrester family pretty much considered "goddamnrepublican" to be all one word![370]

In July, Howard and his friend Perry Harris began teaching a course "Fiddlers on Fiddling" to the music majors at the University of Tennessee. The class met every Thursday for six weeks, and participants received a Certificate of Completion.

Each week Howard would bring in another one of his fiddler friends and have him or her demonstrate his or her style by playing some tunes. Then he would point out the differences among their playing styles. Some of the fiddlers who played for the class included: Johnny Gimble, Roy Acuff, Kenny Baker, the Cates Sisters, Vassar Clements, Ed Hyde, Doug Kershaw, and Mack Magaha.[371]

Howard had fun with the class. His students could all read music perfectly, and he could read almost none, but *he* could play by ear, improvise, make up tunes on the spot, and knew hundreds of tunes by heart. Someone asked him if he could read music, and his comeback was "Not enough to hurt my playing!"[372]

The classical violinists were most impressed with Howard's command of the fiddle. He, in turn, told them he was in awe of all the technique they knew, the fact that they knew exactly how double stops were to be tuned up and played, whereas he had learned to play double stops just by trial and error. It was a fun class for Howard, the high school dropout, to teach, and both he and the classically-trained musicians learned that, as the Buddhists say, "There are many roads that lead to heaven," i.e., many ways to become a violinist.[373]

In 1973, one of Howard's busier years, Lester Flatt and Mac Wiseman again asked Howard to record with them on the RCA Victor label for an album called *Over the Hills to the Poorhouse*, RCA APPLI-0309. There are ten tunes on the album: "Ain't Nobody Gonna Miss Me When I'm Gone," "The Girl I Love Don't Pay Me No Mind," "There's More Pretty Girls Than One," "Waiting for the Boys to Come Home," "When My Blue Moon Turns to Gold Again," "Over the Hills to the Poorhouse," "I'm a Stranger in This World," "'Tis Sweet to be Remembered," "Blue Ridge Cabin Home," and "I'll Go Stepping Too." Besides Lester and Mac, the band includes Ray Edenton, Haskell McCormick, Paul Warren, Charles Nixon, Marty Stuart, Bobby Osborne, Johnny Johnson, and Jimmy Riddle. Howard once again twin fiddles with Paul Warren.

Buoyed by his many successes this year, Howard went into the studio solo (this time Stoneway) and recorded an album of fiddle tunes entitled *Howdy's Fiddle and Howdy Too!* Tunes on this album (STY-127) include: "Topeka Polka," "Grey Eagle," "Black & White Rag," "Run Johnny Run," "Cruel Willie," "Durang's Hornpipe," "Sally Goodin," "Fiddler's Waltz," "Trombone Rag," "Bully of the Town," "Brown Skin Gal," and "Build a Little Boat." Many of these tunes feature Howard's innovative double stops: "Black & White Rag," "Bully of the Town," and "Brown Skin Gal," and, of course, "Fiddler's Waltz," which was his own composition. And he added an additional part to "Topeka Polka," a tune which he had learned in Texas. This new part featured a key change to E-flat, a difficult key for most fiddle players to handle. Howard loved to challenge himself in this way.

Howard's friend, Dr. Perry Harris, wrote the album notes and had this to say about Howard's fiddling:

> It is a great honor to be asked to make a few comments about this album and the man whose great talent we hear…some things will be obvious to anyone who hears this masterpiece.
>
> I truly admire [Howard] for the intricate and fantastic fiddle work that he does and demonstrates so well on this album. His expertise is unsurpassed.
>
> Howard's fiddling has the inspiration of his uncle Bob and the great talent from the Master. What else need be said? Just listen!!
>
> > Perry F. Harris, DDS, MD,
> > FACS"[374]

In 1974 Howard played at the Bluegrass Festival at Capon Bridge, West Virginia, where the audience was mostly college students. Howard was pleased to see that more young people were becoming interested in old-time music.[375] He also played at the first annual Kerrville Bluegrass Festival in Texas, where he appeared on stage with Chubby Wise, Byron Berline, and Paul Warren—a fantastic foursome of fiddling.

The festival "got off to a fairly inauspicious start," according to Rick Gardner, a photographer who was in the crowd:

> It rained so hard Friday evening the area was flooded and no one could get to the site. The show was moved to an auditorium in town and about 100 people showed up. In the middle of the show, a car skidded off the road, knocked down a power line, and we all sat in total darkness for an hour till they hooked it back up. Some of the performers, notably Mac Wiseman, didn't get there at all![376]

During this year, there was a videotaped Hall of Fame special shot at the House of Cash, featuring stars of the Grand Ole Opry like Hank Snow, Roy Acuff (with Howdy Forrester, of course), Ernest Tubbs, and Bill Monroe. The video was about an hour long and was to air on television, although Bob Forrester does not recall ever seeing it.

Howard played "Roll in Sweet Baby's Arms" for this taping, and afterwards Bill Monroe, not known as a man of many words, opined, "That Howdy Forrester is a powerful man on that fiddle."[377] This was extremely high praise coming from Monroe.

Howard also went back to Texas to the Stoneway studio to record again, this time producing an album called *Big Howdy* (STY-136), which contains the following songs: "Clarinet Polka," "Over the Waves" (a tune his wife Billie had taught him), "Dill Pickle Rag," "Indian Creek," "Trot Along My Honey," "Uncle Bob," "Say Old Man," "Beaumont Rag," "Liberty," "Apple Blossom Polka," "Ragtime Annie," and "Howdy Waltz."[378]

Some of these tunes are clearly old traditional ones Howard had learned over the years, but others are his own inventions, such as "Apple Blossom Polka" and "Howdy Waltz," which feature his signature double stop treatment. The tune "Uncle Bob" is based on an old Hickman County tune, which his Uncle Bob had taught him.[379]

And Howard recorded again with Roy and the Smoky Mountain Boys, an album called *Back in the Country*, Hickory H3F-4507.

Howard may have felt that with all these recordings and all his appearances on the Opry he was really creating a legacy that needed to be documented. Or perhaps, with so many of his friends and acquaintances passing away, he was feeling a little more mortal. In any event, Howard gave two very important interviews during 1974: the first to Doug Green of the Country Music Foundation, who recorded the interview as an oral history and placed it on file in the Country Music Foundation Library.[380] (Green became Ranger Doug in the band Riders in the Sky.)

The second interview was one Howard gave to his best friends, Perry Harris and H. G. (Howard) Roberts, who published it in the June 1, 1974 issue of the *Devil's Box*, the monthly publication of the Tennessee Valley Old Time Fiddlers' Association. The *Devil's Box* cover for that month actually included a picture of a very young Howard and Georgia Slim Rutland fiddling together.[381]

Taken together, these two interviews shed a lot of light on Howdy Forrester's life and music and just who he was as a human being. His hobbies included gourmet cooking (especially barbe-cue and polk salet—the country version of salad), traveling to new places, and taking early morning walks. And he was an avid reader, always reading the daily paper and books on the myriad of sub-jects that interested him (almost everything!). He was a real U.S. history buff, especially about the Civil War, and he made trips to the various battlefields to see what was there. This may have led to his composing the tune "Se-Cesh," based in part on an old Hickman County tune, which was later used in the Ken Burns' PBS Special "Music of the Civil War."

Somehow, Acuff-Rose Music was given credit for the song, but son Bob and records at BMI both confirm that Forrester was the composer.[382] A transcription of "Se-Cesh" was published in the Spring 2005 edition of *Fiddler Magazine*.[383]

Howard loved his wife and family, and they, in turn, found him fun to be with. Bob said, "If he hadn't been my father, I'd still have wanted to hang around with him. I know he should be in the Country Music Hall of Fame, but if there was a Hall of Fame for fathers, I'd nominate him for that, too."[384]

When not working, Howard was at home with his family, and he spent lots of time with son Bob. Even after a long road trip with Acuff when Howard would return really exhausted, he would rally himself and take Bob to the local theater for a movie. They would sit in the over-sized seat at the end of the row, and Bob would snuggle up to his dad. Other times, they and Billie would all go to the drive-in movie or have friends over and play music.[385]

Howard was basically a night person, and, despite his early morning walks, he was grumpy in the morning. He didn't want any early morning conversations. He was always the first employee into the office to work at Acuff-Rose, however, arriving at least an hour before the others. Usually he and Billie would grab cups of coffee on the way to work, and Howard would spend the time before the others came to work sipping coffee, reading the news-paper, and "easing into the day."

Howard was a plain man, not given to flashy clothes. His fa-vorite "at home" attire was a pair of slacks and a sleeveless undershirt. He did not wear jewelry—not even a wedding ring or a watch, and he didn't carry pictures in his wallet.[386] Yet, his fiddling was very elegant and sophisticated.

In 1974, Howard realized another of his dreams; he took a trip to Scotland to see the land of his ancestors. Since he couldn't be at home with his family and friends, he took them with him on the trip: wife Billie, Canadian fiddle champ Rudy Meeks and his wife Ila, H. G. and Dot Roberts, and Dr. Perry Harris.

As they fiddled and sang their way around Scotland, Howard kept hoping to find another Howard Forrester there who would also be a fiddle player. Although he didn't find anyone by his exact name, he did meet a few of his relatives and made many new fiddler friends, with whom he corresponded upon his return to Tennessee. Some of them actually visited him in Nashville and still correspond, nearly twenty years after Howard's death, with his son Bob.

In June of 1975 the Country Music Association and the Grand Ole Opry jointly sponsored the Family Reunion of Country Music in conjunction with the fourth annual Country Music Fan Fair. Howard was one of the featured players at the reunion, which included all sorts of "greats" from the country music scene.[387]

Howard was always pleased when he was asked to perform in these kinds of shows. He used to tell Bob somewhat wistfully: "I know I am not the world's *greatest* fiddler. But I hope that, when the list of the best fiddlers is compiled one day, my name will be somewhere on that list."[388]

It must have been difficult for him to really believe that he was the great fiddler people thought he was. Coming from a poor background, lacking *any* formal music instruction, and having learned all he knew by trial and error, finding himself at the center of the fiddling world must have caused him some real insecurities and perhaps some sleepless nights. Bob Forrester thinks this may be one of the reasons his Dad drank so much—to keep the nagging doubts about being an imposter at bay.[389] It may also explain why he was a life-long nail biter, which is evident in the many photos of him.

Being asked to perform for all the various shows probably helped validate to him that he really did rank up there with the best. A quote by Dave Garelick in the *Devil's Box* shows that other people considered Forrester to be a top-drawer fiddler: "Any fiddler who comes anywhere near the Howdy Forrester sound is definitely worth listening to."[390]

Howard was also Kenny Baker's favorite fiddler:

> Howdy was the greatest fiddler that ever walked across the stage. Really and truly, the way he done hoedowns—anything he played—it was done so masterfully. He knew exactly what he wanted to do and how he wanted it to sound. As far as I'm concerned, anytime Howdy laid a number down, you'd pretty well have to say it was done *right*.[391]

Howard was inducted into the Alabama Fiddlers' Hall of Fame and also the New York Fiddlers' Hall of Fame (the second such inductee, right after Bob Wills). It is clear that the *world* considered him to be one of the very best fiddlers. Howard found the Hall of Fame inductions somewhat amusing and declined to attend, sending brother Joe to collect the awards in his stead.[392]

Howard recorded two more fiddle albums for Stoneway in 1975: *Leather Britches* (STY-150) and a twin fiddle album titled *Fiddle Tradition* (STY-149), on which he plays with his friend Chubby Wise.

Leather Britches contains the following tunes: "Blackberry Blossom," "Old Grey Bonnet," "St. Anne's Reel," "Rye Bread," "The Howdy Polka," "Hollow Poplar," "Memphis Blues," "I Saw the Light," "Rose of Sharon," "Red Apple Rag," "Leather Britches," and "Eighth of January." Most of the tunes are old-time tunes rendered new by Forrester's arrangements of them.[393] The tunes "Rye Bread" and "The Howdy Polka" are Forrester's own compositions.

Backing him up on this album are Clyde Brewer on piano, Larry McCall on drums, Chubby Wise and Richard Puckett on guitar, E. J. Hopkins on mandolin, and Buck Henson on bass. During the recording session, Chubby Wise, an ace fiddler himself, kept his eyes on Howard's fingers as they moved quickly over his fiddle. "I'm trackin' ya', Howdy; I'm trackin' ya'", he said, as he matched his chords to the places where Howard's fingers fell.[394]

Some fiddlers, Johnny Gimble among them, did not feel these Stoneway albums were very good. Johnny told Howard he should have recorded them in Nashville, where he could have used A-line session players for backup. Howard replied that no studio in Nashville had *asked* him to record; Stoneway Records, in Texas, had asked him, and that is why he went there.

His friend Perry Harris even offered to pay to have Howard recorded in Nashville with top session players, but Howard's pride would not allow him to accept.[395]

Despite the perceived lack of top drawer back-up players, however, Howard's fiddle playing is dazzling on these albums. For instance, on the *Leather Britches* album, he totally departs from old-time fiddling style with "Memphis Blues," which he plays in New Orleans jazz style, and the last part of "Old Grey Bonnet," which features a highly improvised western swing-style break by Howard. These two flashy "departures from type," plus the two original compositions and the many other Forrester arrangements, make this album well worth owning and clearly show the breadth and depth of Howard's playing and composing.

The second album, *Fiddle Tradition*, features Howard and Chubby Wise playing twin fiddles together. Despite the fact that both men were consummate fiddlers, their styles were dramatically different—Howard's big but very sweet and old-timey with improvisations that stay within the music at hand, and Chubby's very bold and bluesy, with improvisations that are entirely outside the music. Actually, many of Chubby's improvisations are a series of "licks," which he drops over the chord changes to make what is virtually a new song. It is more of a guitar player's way of thinking about improvisation, and since Chubby played the guitar, it makes sense that he might improvise in that way. Still, it is great fun to hear the two fiddlers playing together. Much of the music on the album sounds like Chubby is telling jokes and Howard is laughing at them, as they try to outdo each other on their breaks.

Tunes on this album include: "Cindy," "Convict and the Rose," "Liberty," "In the Pines," "Whispering Hope," "The Waltz You Saved for Me," "A Kind of Love I Can't Forget," "Red River Valley," "I'm

So Lonesome I Could Cry," "Grandfather's Clock," "Bottle in the Hand," and "Over the Waves."[396]

Several sources, among them the *Encyclopedia of Country Music*, indicate that Howard and Chubby recorded a second twin fiddle album on the Stoneway label, titled *Sincerely Yours*. Bob Forrester told me he didn't believe that this was true, that he knew of *no* second twin fiddle album his dad had made with Chubby Wise. After a lengthy search, I located the album in question, and, clearly, there is no sign of Howdy Forrester on this album—not in the credits—and *definitely* not in the music. Every tune is vintage Chubby, with his usual signature licks; there is none of Howdy Forrester's elegant playing on this album and no twin fiddling with anyone else either.[397]

Howard loved Chubby and loved the fact that they played in such different styles. "Chubby's so fascinating," Howard said. "After you hear two bars, you know that's Chubby. Diversity is what makes fiddling great," he explained. "It shouldn't all sound alike." Howard really liked the way Chubby could play and often said, with the greatest respect, "Don't ever follow Chubby on stage after he's just played the 'Lee Highway Blues'" (one of Chubby's signature tunes, which always brought the house down with applause).[398]

Howard's bold, but sweet, happy style is probably a reflection of all the love and attention Emmie Forrester gave her boys, the tight-knit family that Howard grew up in. And Chubby's lonesome, bluesy playing probably mirrors Chubby's troubled life and his struggle for survival. His mother kicked him out of the house at age twelve, after he had just broken his leg and was on crutches.[399]

Howard also went to the studio with Roy and the Smoky Mountain Boys, where they recorded three albums: *Wabash Cannonball*, Hilltop JS 6162, *Smoky Mountain Memories*, Hickory H3G-4517, and *That's Country*, Hickory H3G-4521. The first album, *Wabash Cannonball*, includes one of Roy's signature tunes: "Great Speckled Bird." On *Smoky Mountain Memories*, Howard plays a great double stop break on "Just a Friend"; the double stops he chose and the shuffling rhythm give a slight Cajun sound to his break. In "Touch the Morning," Howard's fast fill is mostly played up in third position on the E string, most unusual but very effective. In "Thank God" he plays a harmony behind the vocals, again in the upper octave. One thing about Howard, he wasn't afraid to try new musical ideas, and because he knew all the notes way up the fingerboard on his fiddle, he could use those notes to get effects other fiddlers couldn't.

On *That's Country* Forrester plays a great double stop break and a nice harmony part behind Roy's singing on "We Live in Two Different Worlds." He plays a fast fill behind the melody in "Turn Your Radio On," a counter melody to Roy's vocal in "Shut Up in the Mine in Coal Creek," and a fast hoedown style break and back up in "Zeb Turner's Girl."[400]

In 1976, Howard recorded yet another album for Stoneway: *Howdy Forrester, Stylish Fiddling* (STY-168), containing these tunes: "Willow Springs," "The Blue Danube," "Golden Eagle Hornpipe," "Legend in My Time," "I Love You Because," "Ida Red," "Gypsy Lament," "Slippin' Around," "Springtime Polka," "Evening Shades," and "Don't Let Your Deal Go Down."

Two of the tunes on this album—"Springtime Polka" and "Gypsy Lament"—are Forrester's original compositions. "Gypsy Lament" is very *triste* and gypsy-like—filled with flashy, off-the-string bowing and rich double stops in D minor, F, and D, slid around à la Fritz Kreisler—a very inventive piece of writing. Some of the other tunes are popular songs of his day to which he adds many things. In the Don Gibson song "Legend in My Time," Howard opens the theme on an octave double stop (G and high G) in third position. His signature double stops in this tune include some fourths, which even good fiddlers find hard to tune up, and his fiddle seems to almost cry at times when he slides into notes.

"I Love You Because" features gorgeous double stops, beautiful tone, and an interesting counter-melody, which Howard plays against the piano melody line. "Blue Danube" is, of course, a classical waltz by Johann Strauss, Jr., but Howard takes it over and makes it his own through a strong rhythmic structure, lots of double stops, and a key change from D to B-flat.

The name *Stylish Fiddling* fits this album well, as the tunes are very different from the usual assortments of straight ahead hoedowns and contest style tunes found on most fiddling albums.

Howard's back-up band for this recording session included Clyde Brewer on piano, Buck Henson on bass, Jerry Ontiberoz on drums, Danny Ross on guitar, Paul Buskirk on guitar and dobro, and Ron Rebstock on mandolin and banjo.[401] The cover for this album was actually designed by Howard's nephew Steve Forrester, whose real job was making display cabinets for museums.[402]

Howard's friends continued to come by his house for barbecue and fiddling sessions. One of the most fun fiddlers to watch and listen to, according to son Bob, was Chubby Wise. Chubby would be fiddling along, improvising over the chord changes of a tune, when suddenly his brow would knit and he would get this really serious look on his face. "He's painted himself into a corner he can't get out of," Howard and Bob would say to themselves. But then…Chubby would drop some little lick into the tune and bingo! He would end up right on the proper note for the next chord! Bob says Chubby always seemed to be able to solve any improvisation problem he had created for himself, one of the few fiddlers who could do that with regularity.[403]

Another frequent guest was Paul Chrisman (Woody Paul), fiddler in the band Riders in the Sky. Woody Paul was a big Howdy Forrester fan, and Howard always took time to help him with his tunes and licks.[404]

Howard liked to jam with Kenny Baker as well. They had a contest going on between them; each time they met, they would play each other a new tune, something the other had never heard before. Fiddler Ron Eldridge has tapes of some of these "fiddlin' feats," and when Howard plays for Kenny, he really pulls out all the stops and unleashes a flight of fantasy filled with every bit of technique and ornamentation he can muster—double stops, key changes, higher positions—it's all there.

Once when Kenny had finished playing his latest masterpiece for Howard, Howard looked him in the eye and said, "Just when I think I know just what you're going to do, you hit the bastardest note I ever heard. It just baffles me!"[405] They were always on their toes when they played for each other, and, although they played in very different styles, each had the greatest respect for the other's playing.

Howard always had time for other fiddlers, even ones he didn't know. In the mid-1970s, a California fiddler named Roscoe White was on his way down south to judge a fiddle contest. He and his guitar-backup wife, Ossie, had heard one of Howard's recordings and fallen in love with his music. Their flight had a layover in Nashville and, on a whim, they called Howdy Forrester over at Acuff-Rose where they had heard he worked. After a brief phone conversation, Howard invited them to come see him and provided directions to his office.

Howard spent several hours swapping stories with them, told them a lot about his days barnstorming in Texas, and gave them a cassette of his playing. They were quite taken with him and sat up until the wee hours playing and re-playing the cassette![406] If you were a fiddler, you were a friend of Howard.

In June 1976, Roy Acuff took the Smoky Mountain Boys to Lester Flatt's 4th Annual Mt. Pilot Festival at Mt. Airy, North Carolina, where they played afternoon and evening shows. An advertisement for the show in *Bluegrass Unlimited* magazine of March, 1976, lists Howard as "the great Howdy Forrester."[407]

During this year, country singer Sonny James published a bicentennial salute to *200 Years of Country Music*, Columbia KC-34035. *Music City News* reported that one of the cuts on this album was "Blue Moon of Kentucky," with fiddling by Howdy Forrester, who was, of course, a former Bluegrass Boy. His friend, Kenny Baker, who was originally scheduled to play, had injured his hand—who better to replace him than the greatest fiddler of them all?[408]

In 1977, Bud Wendell and Doc Harris asked Howard's brother Joe to serve as a judge for the Grand Master Fiddler Championship, and Joe agreed to do it—proof positive that one does not have to *be* a fiddler to be able to identify good quality fiddling. Of course, after listening to—and backing up—Howard all those years, Joe said he would have to have been deaf not to know good fiddling when he heard it![409]

Howard was still playing the Opry with Roy Acuff and still doing small gigs on the side. And his music was being played on the radio.

In those days people really paid attention to individual tunes, who was playing them, and how well they were played. Howard received a fine praise letter from the Country Music Association for a tune he had composed:

Dear Howdy:
    Just a note to say that I heard your recording of "Gypsy La-ment" on the Martha White Show the other morning. It was excellent and revealed the versatility of your talent...

Sincerely,
COUNTRY MUSIC
ASSOCIATION, INC.
(Mrs.) Jo Walker[410]

In January of 1978, Howard appeared with Roy Acuff in a three-hour taped special on NBC, titled "Fifty Years of Country Music." Hosts for the show were Roy Clark, Glen Campbell, and Dolly Parton.[411]

Roy also released a compilation album called *Roy Acuff—Greatest Hits, Vol. 1*, Elektra 9E-302, featuring tunes previously recorded in 1962 and 1963 (RCA Victor), 1964 (Bradley Studios), and 1968, 1973, 1974, 1977, and 1978 (Acuff-Rose Studios). Howard plays on all the tunes and twin fiddles with Tommy Jackson on the 1964 and 1968 cuts and with Robert White on the 1974 cuts.

The following year, the Grand Ole Opry asked one of Washington, D.C.'s bright lights, Senator Robert Byrd of West Virginia, who was then Senate Majority Leader, to play on one of the Opry shows. Byrd, who was known to his friends as Fiddlin' Bob Byrd, was quite an accomplished fiddler and could often be heard fiddling away in his office in the Senate Office Building. For a time, his chief of staff was fiddler Joe Meadows (who was himself a Bluegrass Boy for a while), and Joe and Bob Byrd had some great times playing together for the hoi polloi of Washington.

Byrd accepted the invitation to Nashville, and after playing on the show, spent a considerable amount of time back stage playing twin fiddles with Big Howdy Forrester. His high regard for Forrester's playing is evident in the letter of March 16, 1979, which he sent Howard following this encounter, a letter brother Clyde Forrester has proudly hanging on the wall at his house:

> Dear Howdy:
>
> I am writing to express my appreciation to you for extending such warm hospitality to me during my recent visit to Nashville, and appearances on the Grand Ole Ory. Being able to appear and play my fiddle on the Grand Ole Opry was a great pleasure. Also, in addition to the performance, I shall always remember the special friendship that I was able to make on this wonderful trip.
>
> Again, Howdy, thank you for your kind thoughtfulness in making my visit to the Grand Ole Opry a most memorable experience.
>
> With personal regards, I am
>
> > Cordially yours,
> > Robert C. Byrd

A pen and ink notation at the bottom of the letter says: "I thoroughly enjoyed the twin fiddling with you, Howdy."[412]

A video recording was made of Howard and the senator fiddling together, and NBC's Today Show aired the video before commercial breaks for the next week.[413]

Later that year, Bob Forrester asked his dad to play for a mathematics professors' conference he was attending. When Roy Acuff heard about it, he decided to come, as well, and brought the entire Smoky Mountain Boys band with him. They put on a thirty-minute show and brought the house down. Afterward, Howard and Roy went to the hospitality suite and drank and told stories to the crowd. Bob said it was the most excitement the math professors had experienced in a very long time![414]

In March of 1980, Howard's wife Billie retired from the Social Security Administration, with thirty years of service and a decent pension. She was a hard worker and had been promoted repeatedly over the years, finally reaching the level of mid-management. Did she miss the glamorous (and rigorous) life she might have had as a musician on the road, a life she had traded away for the security of a steady income and nights spent at home in her own bed? Bob Forrester doesn't think so. He felt there was enough excitement for her just living with Howard and his many accomplishments and helping entertain the dozens of family members and musician friends who came to visit them regularly.

"Mama loved to play," Bob said, "because we'd play around the house, you know, and we'd play at family gatherings. It was a standard thing to play at family gatherings, and we had a *lot* of family gatherings.

"I don't ever remember mama talking about how little money there was at times. Not that she ever regretted it. I don't think for a minute she would have done it different. Her and daddy would talk about their experiences all the time up until daddy died. They'd sit up at night, and I'd go over, and they'd sit and talk. They had so much to talk about. They wouldn't trade anything for their experiences."[415]

In 1981, Roy Acuff and the Smoky Mountain Boys, Merle Haggard, and others were invited to perform at Carnegie Hall, a place which featured prominently in Howard's "impossible dreams" and to which he never thought he would go. But go he did. He was so proud of getting to play there that he pasted his back stage pass to Carnegie Hall on the side of his fiddle case! "I got to do a sound check and play at Carnegie Hall, Bob; that's pretty good for an old country boy."

The show was sponsored by the producers of Wild Turkey Whiskey, and Howard reported that the Wild Turkey was flowing back stage, front stage, and everywhere else that night![416]

In those days, nearly all of the country music stars drank; liquor was their drug of choice, and Howdy Forrester was no different in this regard, *except* that he never let liquor interfere with his playing. (A number of Opry stars, Arthur Smith among them, lost their place on the Opry because of their penchant for alcohol.)

One night the Smoky Mountain Boys were playing at the new Opry House. Between sets, Howard, his friend Doc Harris, and fiddler Kenny Baker went out to Howard's car (about thirty feet away) to get a little nip of whiskey. One nip led to several nips, and by the time they returned to the Opry House, they were pretty red-faced. Who should approach them as they entered the building but the taciturn Bill Monroe! Before he could reprimand them, however, Howard quipped, "Now, Bill, you know when I was with you I liked to have a drink every now and then." Monroe just burst out laughing.[417]

Also in 1981, Howard was made an honorary colonel in the Louisiana Militia and later in the Alabama and Kentucky Militias. The city of Madison, Alabama, also made him an honorary deputy sheriff. Howard thought all these "honors" were pretty funny, but it did show that people really liked and respected Howard and his music.[418]

Roy released another album this year, titled *Roy Acuff: Back in the Country*, Elektra E-1-60012, featuring all the Smoky Mountain Boys and a host of other musicians. On three of the songs, Howard is joined on fiddle by Billy Jack Saucier and on "Smoky Mountain Memories" by both Saucier and another fiddler, Robert White. The band on these four tunes includes other musicians, with Grady Martin on guitar, Hargis (Pig) Robbins on piano, and Roy Acuff, Jr., on back up vocals.

The other seven songs feature Howard, Roy, and the Smoky Mountain Boys. On "Jesus Will Outshine Them All," Howard plays a nice harmony line to Roy's vocal line, and opens "Wednesday Night Waltz" with an entire verse of double-stopped melody played up the neck of his fiddle into fourth position!

In March of 1982 NBC aired a two-hour special: "Roy Acuff— 50 Years the King of Country Music." Howard, Jimmie Riddle, and Brother Oswald all got to play on the program, which was basically a retrospective of Roy's musical life and impact on the country music business.[419]

The hard life of the music business was beginning to catch up with Howard, and in mid-1983 he was hospitalized briefly with chest pains, but the doctor told him his heart was okay. Howard took this as a wake-up call, though, and retired from Acuff-Rose, although he continued to play the Opry show on Saturday nights.[420]

In May both he and Billie joined Roy Acuff on the stage of the Ryman Auditorium to play for Brother Oswald's wedding to Euneta.[421]

Howard also returned to the recording studio during this year, making an album with his fiddler friend Kenny Baker, titled *Red Apple Rag*, County Records #784. There are thirteen tunes on the album. Howard plays four of them: "Sugar Tree Stomp," "Little Nancy Roland," "Fiddler's Dream," and "Little Brown Hand—Adieu False Heart," and Kenny plays seven of them. Together they play two tunes: "Paris Waltz" and "Snow Deer." Kenny Baker was a bluegrass fiddler, and his style is quite different from Howard's. Their back-up band included Charlie Collins of the Smoky Mountain Boys on guitar, Wynn Osborne on banjo, Bobby Osborne on mandolin, and Roy Huskey, Jr., on bass.[422] Bob Forrester is the uncredited drummer on this album.[423]

Kenny Baker really respected Howard's playing. One of Bob Forrester's college math students was taking fiddle lessons from Kenny, who told him, "If you want to learn to fiddle, son, listen to Howdy Forrester—he's the best goddamn all round fiddler you'll ever hear in your life!"[424]

Another fiddler who was really taken with Howard's playing was John Hartford, who spent a lifetime researching, collecting, transcribing, and playing old-time fiddle tunes. In the 1980s, perhaps realizing that Howard's days on earth were running out, John began making regular visits to Howard's home on Tod Pries Drive. Armed with a tape recorder, manuscript paper, and pencils, Hartford began recording and transcribing many of Howard's tunes—and Howard's tales. They spent hours and days working on this project, Howard fiddling and John scribbling away, then playing the tunes back to Howard to make sure he had captured them accurately.

Because of John's passion for old-time tunes, many of the transcriptions are of old Hickman County tunes, which Howard had learned from his Uncle Bob Cates. The *Devil's Box*, which was then the official publication of the Tennessee Valley Old Time Fiddlers' Association, published a number of these transcriptions, which included among others "Dugler with a Shoofly On," "Balance All,"

"Old Hollow Poplar," "Homemade Sugar and a Puncheon Floor," and "Hawk Got a Chicken." (A more complete list is included in the bibliography of this book.)

Howard knew hundreds of tunes, many of which were indigenous to Hickman County and not played elsewhere. Unfortunately, Howard's life was rapidly winding down, and Hartford was unable to memorialize the entire treasure trove of tunes in Howard's head.[425]

Roy Acuff was making a lot of money from all the performing and recording he and the Smoky Mountain Boys were doing, and it was simply part of his character that he liked to "share the wealth." In August of 1985, he gave Howard a ten thousand dollar bonus check, as a way of showing his appreciation. Howard was quite stunned and so pleased that he actually framed a copy of the check![426]

By 1986, Howard was forced to leave the Opry when he became seriously ill and was diagnosed with esophageal and stomach cancer. In November of that year, the doctors removed most of his stomach, and no one held out much hope for Howard to recover. But against all odds, Howard was up and playing again on the Opry by January of 1987—and playing faster than ever![427]

One Saturday night, son Bob was returning from Kentucky and turned on his car radio to catch the Opry broadcast. It sounded like Herman Crook's band was playing, and Bob thought fiddler Earl White was really "eatin' up 'Sally Goodin.'" The next morning Bob mentioned the great performance to his dad. "Hell, son, that was me!" his dad retorted.

Bob replied, "No wonder Earl sounded so good." Clearly, his dad was back in the saddle.[428]

A video made at a February 1987 family gathering (some of the Smoky Mountain Boys were also present, as Howard considered them family as well) shows Howard looking tired and gaunt and clearly having lost a lot of weight. Nonetheless, he got out his fiddle and began playing with a vengeance. One tune after another rolled off of his bow.

It was as if he knew his time was about up and he had so many tunes he still wanted to play, so he sped them up to try to get more of them played in the time he had left.

One interesting aspect of the video is that his vaunted intonation is somewhat lacking. When Howard became ill, he lost a *lot* of weight, which meant his fingers became thinner as well. He had to make different adjustments between his fingers to be able to play in tune, and it took him a while to get used to this. On the video, however, he plays for a long time, taking requests from family and friends and playing lots of really fast breakdowns, as well.[429]

Howard was not a smoker, not even as a young man, so why he got esophageal cancer is anyone's guess. He did love to drink whiskey, however, and he drank a lot of it in his day. He even kept a little flask in his car, and at the close of a long recording session, he would say, "Let's do this and get off, fellas, and then we'll go to the car and get a little drink."[430]

Howard did almost all of his drinking at home, however, and he didn't frequent taverns. Even when he drank a lot, he just got happy and mellow and went to sleep. Ever the professional, Howard never allowed his drinking to get out of hand or to interfere with his fiddle playing, his job, or his relationships with friends and family.[431] As Abraham Lincoln once said about Ulysses Grant's penchant for alcohol: "Find out what he drinks and give it to the other generals."[432]

Son Bob says perhaps it was all the whiskey that caused the cancer, although all the spicy food Howard loved could have irritated his esophagus and stomach lining as well. The irony is that after having rheumatic fever as a child and being told by the doctor that he would always be an invalid, it was not his heart that gave out.[433]

Sick or not, Howard always had one more tune to play, and he and Roy and the boys made yet one more album together, *Roy Acuff...All Time Favorites*, Opryland 101. The album jacket bills it as *Grand Ole Opry, 60th Anniversary Album*. Howard's fiddling seems more subdued, but it has a definite presence and that robust tone is still there.

Howard's health, however, continued to deteriorate, and in June, 1987, at the 16th annual Grand Master Fiddler Championship held at Opryland, a weak and gaunt-looking Howdy Forrester was presented with the Master Fiddler Trophy, honoring his lifetime influence and achievements. Howard was thrilled with the award and took the microphone long enough to say: "Herald Goodman told me, 'Don't believe what people say about you,' but after hearing all of the testimonials today, I really want to believe some of this."[134] One measure of how ill Howard really was: he didn't have his fiddle with him, and he didn't play for the crowd.

Tennessee Governor Ned McWherter presented him with a citation honoring him for his long years of service to the country music business and the community. At this moment in time, Howard must finally have known that not only was he on that mythical list of greatest fiddlers, but he was up at the top.

That was his farewell, and despite his return to playing at the Opry, Howard's health continued to deteriorate, and the sicker he became, the faster he played tunes, seemingly trying to outrun the specter of death, even as it stalked him. "I've had a wonderful life," he said, "things nobody would dream of. I'd like to live longer, but I'm grateful for what I've had."[435]

Howard had been a lifelong agnostic, and although he wanted to believe in God and in a life hereafter, he just felt it was "too good to be true." On his deathbed, however, he realized he had never been baptized, and Bob's favorite Catholic school teacher, Father Rohling, came and baptized Howard.[436]

On August 31, 1987, Big Howdy Forrester died peacefully at his home in Bellevue, Tennessee. His death certificate was signed by his attending physician, his friend Dr. Perry Harris.[437]

The wake service was held at 7:00 p.m. on Sunday and on Monday, his funeral mass, the Mass of the Resurrection, was held at 11:00 a.m. at St. Joseph's Catholic Church. The mass was a grand affair, with Monsignor George Rohling officiating. Billy Grammer honored Howard by playing Howard's composition, "Memory Waltz," on guitar.

Honorary Pallbearers included many of the greats in country music: Orval V. Rhodes, Roy Acuff, Bill Monroe, Dr. Perry Harris, Billy Grammer, Hubert Gregory, Lewis and Herman Crook, Rudy Meeks, Herb Harris, Dewey Groom, Vernon Solomon, Johnny Gimble, Harry Strobel, plus artists, musicians, and management of the Grand Ole Opry. Active pall bearers were Oswald Kirby,

Charlie Collins, Larry McNeely, H.G. Roberts, Matthew Forrester, "Woody" Paul Chrisman , Ed Lane, and Stephen Forrester.[438]

Howard was survived by Billie, son Bob, and all three of his older brothers: Clayton, Clyde, and Joe, plus assorted grandchildren and other relatives. He was interred at Spring Hill Cemetery in Nashville, where he shares a plot with his wife, Billie, who died of Alzheimer's disease in 1999.

Country music mourned the demise of this fine fiddler. Howard's longtime employer and personal friend, Roy Acuff, said in tribute, "Howard's the finest fiddler I have ever known."

And the local newspaper, *The Tennessean*, gave him a glowing eulogy, saying: "Howdy Forrester was one of the most familiar names in Nashville country music. Mr. Forrester had many friends both inside the industry and on the outside. He will be sadly missed."[439]

His friend Dr. Perry Harris said of him in the *Nashville Banner*: "Howdy has been the most influential fiddler for the past fifty years. I first saw him perform in 1953 in Raleigh, North Carolina, and my interest in his fiddling led me to start the [Grand Master's] festival."[440]

And *Bluegrass Unlimited* magazine mourned his death as well: "Bluegrass and traditional country music has lost another of its premier sidemen."[378]

The day after Howard's death, the Smoky Mountain Boys played "Jesus Will Outshine Them All" as a final tribute to him on the Grand Ole Opry.

Big Howdy Forrester, one of the greatest fiddlers of all time, may have left this earth, but his music lives on in the hearts, minds, and instruments of thousands of fiddlers, pickers, and listeners throughout the land. The tunes he wrote and the ones he learned from others and then improvised upon are still played in fiddle contests, on shows, and at dances around the world, and his recordings are valuable collector's items, a final tribute to the "best of the best."

Rest in peace, Howard. You've earned it.

CHAPTER 9

Town and Country Fiddler

So why is the music of Big Howdy Forrester so important that it merits a book about him? What is it that drives people to spend whole days browsing in music and antique stores, searching through stacks of old vinyl looking for Howdy's records…or spend hours careening madly through cyberspace, trolling for a used copy of Howdy's records—*any* record—in good condition? What is it that makes people who hear his playing start reflexively tapping their toes or swaying to the music, almost from the first note that strikes their ears? Why do the top old-time fiddlers learn Howdy's tunes to play in the fiddle contests? And what is it about his music that makes even classical violinists say, "Now *that* guy can really play!"?

Howdy Forrester (or Howard, as he preferred to be called) was a very humble man, despite the fact that his thirty-six consecutive years as a fiddler with Roy Acuff on the Opry makes him the Grand Old Man of Opry Fiddlers. Add in the rest of the time he was on the Opry, first with Herald Goodman and the Tennessee Valley Boys, then with Bill Monroe (two separate stints), and later with Cowboy Copas, and Howard has about thirty-eight years of time fiddling on the Opry, a historical record that will probably never be duplicated! Yet, he never bragged to anyone about his playing or his time on the Opry, and he felt no need to show off for people or to try to outplay someone else.

As a result of his humility, he did not participate in fiddle contests and did not use a lot of "trick fiddling" (wild theatrics and hokum bowing) in his playing. He felt his music spoke for itself, and, in his case, it certainly did. Howard always felt he was born to fiddle. He said, "It is something that is in you, and if it is, you have to get it out." Howard always maintained that there were two kinds of fiddlers: "show" fiddlers and "great" fiddlers and that they were usually not the same people. "Curly Fox is a terrific *show* fiddler," he would say, "and I have the greatest admiration for his showmanship (not his fiddling). But Bob Wills now—Bob Wills was a *great* fiddler. It's either in you to be a show fiddler or it's not. And I guess it's not in me. Everyone has to be true to themselves."[441]

As a result, Howard didn't do tricks with his music—he just played really great music with all his heart. He was quite disdainful of tunes like "Back Up and Push," tunes which have little melody and just rely on fancy shuffle bowing, rather than good playing, to spark the audience. "Shuffles? That's not fiddlin'," he sniffed. "That's for show." And he refused to play that kind of music, saying, "That's not very interesting."[442]

Notwithstanding that—or perhaps *because* of that—his music did speak for him, and he wound up playing for some of the biggest names in the country music business—Bill Monroe and Roy Acuff—and having a good and long career in the tough music trade. Bob said his dad had as little ego as anyone he had ever known. It didn't bother him to be a sideman. He always said his job with Roy was the best he could ever have. Howard loved Roy Acuff, and they had a great relationship.[443]

Roy often complimented Howard by calling him a "country violinist." And on the lack of ego, Roy said: "I have never heard Howdy make a disparaging remark about anyone."[444] The most severe criticism Howard ever gave to others was: "Now, that's not very interesting" (which he, with his Tennessee twang, pronounced "inersting"). This comment, delivered with his polite southern charm, meant he absolutely *hated* what he had heard![445]

Still, there are many people who, when asked about Howdy Forrester, respond with a blank look and a one-word answer: "Who?" When told that Howard was the sweet fiddle sound with

Roy Acuff and the Smoky Mountain Boys on the Grand Ole Opry for all those years, they nod and say, "Oh, him. I remember him—what a beautiful sound he had" or words to that effect. With such humility and not a lot of current-day name recognition, how did Forrester become such an influential person on the fiddling (and country music) scene?

Howard's long-lived success can be attributed to four qualities, all starting with "i": intonation, intellectual curiosity, innovation, and interrelationships.

Intonation is one of the real keys to great fiddle playing, and while classical players are often critical of intonation in old-time fiddling, Howard shared the classical aesthetic that precise intonation produces maximum resonance of the fiddle's strings.

Howard probably figured that out over the years, but in the beginning, he learned to play by matching the pitches his mother sang or played on the banjo. His mother was a good musician, with a finely-tuned ear. She always insisted on tuning his fiddle for him before he played and, with her keen ear, no doubt insisted on Howard finding exactly the right pitches, not just something that was close. No one, including son Bob, seems to know whether Howard actually had perfect pitch, but certainly he had, at the very least, a well-developed sense of relative pitch, which came from the early sessions with his mother. One of the first things classical players notice, upon being exposed to Howard's recordings, is that he plays perfectly in tune—not necessarily what they were expecting from an old-time fiddler!

One of Howard's big hallmarks was his ability to play all sorts of double stops—in virtually any key and in many variations. They were always perfectly tuned, a result of both his good ears and his long hours working to perfect the double stops. "Close enough" didn't work for him; it had to be perfect.

Since he learned to play essentially by matching pitches, he was always listening—a skill that stood him in good stead all his life. This was one of the reasons he could sit in with almost any band of any genre and play along—he was always listening and could pick up the chord changes, understand where the music was going, and what the style was. This allowed him to fiddle over the top of it and take breaks any time he was asked, in the same style as the music being played.

Intellectual curiosity was another attribute that Howdy Forrester possessed in large measure. He was interested in almost anything and anybody, although he was not a dilettante. He always looked at things carefully to see how and why they worked the way they did. He would look at or listen to something new, ponder it a while, then try it out over and over until he could make it work for him.

He actually figured out on his own how the notes were arranged on the fingerboard of his fiddle and how to make the bow do different kinds of strokes. And he discovered as he moved up the neck of the fiddle that certain positions were fingered just like they were in first position: e.g., in third position, if you play the fingerings for the key of G, you are actually playing in the key of B-flat! This was how he mastered the higher positions so quickly and was able to find the double stops up there so readily.[446] (This also leads me to believe that Howard probably did not have perfect pitch.)

He also watched other people and asked them lots of questions, people like his Great-uncle Bob, who taught him a little technique and lots of Hickman County tunes, many of which Uncle Bob had composed himself. Joe Forrester says that Uncle Bob had an "interesting bow stroke." He would "kinda twist the bow" as it came across the strings, instead of leaving the hair totally flat on the string. What Bob Cates was probably doing was rotating his forearm, which is how classically-trained players pull their bows! Uncle Bob liked a heavy bow and sometimes even used a cello bow to play his fiddle. Howard later preferred heavier bows (although not a cello bow!) and played with a huge sound, undoubtedly a result of Uncle Bob's early influence.

Uncle Bob played lots of separate notes and some shuffles in his tunes. Howard also played lots of separate notes as well; one fiddler called his playing "note-y," although the shuffles eventually gave way to a more elegant, long bow style of playing, which he learned from Arthur Smith, slurring multiple notes on one bow. This allowed for a smoother sound and a different rhythmic pattern to the music.

From James Byrd, Howard learned a better way to hold his bow, one which later stood him in good stead as he tried to emulate the sounds of Fritz Kreisler, which he heard on recordings. From the Youth Orchestra at the State Fair, he learned to hold his fiddle in a better way (with his wrist down), which then allowed him access to all the high notes up on top of the fingerboard.

From Georgia Slim he received an introduction into the fine art of twin fiddling and learned to match his bow strokes precisely with Slim's. In fact, they were so good that in one photo of them, they are side by side, arms wrapped around each other and bowing each other's instrument while still fingering on their own fiddles!

He learned new tunes from anyone who would teach him one, including his wife Billie, who taught him tunes like "Over the Waves."

Howard was quick to spot when someone had something he could use, and he was not the least bit embarrassed to ask them to show him how to do it. He did not have much formal education, but his intellectual curiosity provided him with all the education, both musical and otherwise, he could soak up.

It led him to read books on all sorts of subjects—faraway places, Scotland (his ancestry), the Civil War, current affairs, and especially books about music and musicians, like his idol Fritz Kreisler. And it led him to listen to recordings by people whose sound he liked and try to figure out what they were doing and how they did it.

His early influences, after Uncle Bob, came from recordings by the Georgia fiddler, Clayton McMichen. Howard's style of fiddling hoedowns was modeled on McMichen's playing, which Howard heard on the Skillet Lickers' *Corn Liquor Still in Georgia* recordings. (On the recordings, they were actually making whiskey and playing tunes!)

Imagine Howard's surprise when Slim Rutland joined the Tennessee Valley Boys and played his breakdowns the same way Howard did. Of course, Slim was from Georgia, just like McMichen, so it makes sense that Slim would have been influenced by him. This similarity in styles between Howard and Slim led Slim to the idea of "twin fiddling" with Howard, one on lead, the other on harmony, for which they became famous.[447]

Later influences on Howard's playing came when he went to hear the Nashville Symphony play at the park, but once he heard Fritz Kreisler play on a recording, he liked Kreisler's sound better than any of the other violinists who came to solo with the symphony, and he began emulating Kreisler.

He would often put on a Kreisler recording, and the tears would run down his face as he listened, as he thought it was so beautiful. Pretty soon, out would come his fiddle, and he would try to reproduce what he heard on the recording. Bob Forrester said his dad actually learned to play *Caprice Viennois* from a Kreisler recording! He further opined that if his Dad had come from a family with money, he might have gone to a music conservatory and become a classical violin virtuoso.[448]

Imagine what his improvised cadenzas would have sounded like! Mozart, who was quite a fancy fiddler himself, would have loved him, although old-time fiddling would not have matured (and maybe not even survived) without Forrester.

Les Leverett, long-time WSM photographer, who shot many pictures both at the Opry and other musical events, listened to, watched, and memorialized on film many of Howard's performances. His comment was: "I loved the guy. If he had wanted to, he could have gone on stage as a concert violinist."[449]

Certainly, Howard's moving double stops are something he learned from listening to Fritz Kreisler play. In fact, in a recent experiment I played a recording of a gypsy-style song full of double stops for Dr. B. J. Mitchell, a friend who is quite musical and who loves both classical and old-time fiddle music. "Do you know who that is playing?" I asked her.

"Sure," she responded. "Fritz Kreisler—everyone would recognize those double stops."

I then played a cut from another gypsy-style recording for her. "And who might this be?" I asked with a smile.

"That's Fritz Kreisler again," she said. "There are those unmistakable double stops."

Her face registered total shock when I told her, "Well, actually it's the old-time fiddler Howdy Forrester playing a tune he composed called 'Gypsy Lament.'" Howard had perfected those double stops so they sounded just like Kreisler's![450]

Later in life, Howard read in a biography of Kreisler that he played his double stops in an unorthodox manner. This fact really tickled Howard, since he knew that he himself had learned to play double stops by trial and error, listening carefully to the pitches and not caring so much about which fingers he used. As a result, he was pretty sure that he, too, probably was not employing the "proper" technique![451]

Bob Forrester, although a fairly credible fiddler himself, does not know what was unconventional about his dad's double stops, other than that Howard learned them by trial and error rather than out of a book like Bob did. But in listening to his recordings, several things stand out.

At the end of a phrase, Howard often played a two-open string double stop, e.g., a double stop of open D and open A, as a grace note (very short) before a final double stop in the same chord structure, e. g., D2 (F#) and A3 (high D).

Another unusual aspect of Howard's double stops often occurred as he moved from one double stop to another by means of a slide (portamento). He would "push off" from the double stop he was leaving by giving it a little extra bow pressure just before the slide began. This is evident in many of his waltzes and tunes, such as "Still on the Hill."

Another example of Howard's curiosity paying off is evident in a tune he wrote called "Fiddler's Waltz." The last two parts of this tune are pure Kreisler: The next to the last part is played spiccato (with the bow slightly off the string) and, although the melody is totally different, the tune and the way it is played immediately call to mind Kreisler's own composition, "Schön Rosmarind." The last part of "Fiddler's Waltz" is filled with double stops slid around in a romantic style and sounding exactly like Kreisler again.

It was Howard's intellectual curiosity about Kreisler's style that allowed him to compose and play the "Fiddler's Waltz," a tune that is often played in old-time fiddle contests today.

Howard had a large arsenal of different bow strokes he could employ, most of them learned through experimentation as he listened to recordings and tried to reproduce sounds he heard. A palette of bow strokes gave him many colors he could bring to the music, one of the things that gave his music that elegant sound.

The third thing that led to Howard's success was innovation. Howard was not afraid to take chances, to do things with his music that were outside what others were doing at the time. He took little things his intellectual curiosity led him to along the way and coupled them with his good ear for both intonation and what music "should sound like" to produce tunes and arrangements that were extremely innovative.

Stephen Davis had this to say in the *Devil's Box,* the publication of the Tennessee Valley Old Time Fiddler's Association: "The variations and improvisations that Howdy puts into each tune make each one a 'standout.' Especially well-treated are the high parts. They are clean, precise, and well-executed."[452]

When Howdy Forrester and Georgia Slim Rutland began playing together with the Tennessee Valley Boys, several other bands had what was then called "double fiddles," that is, two fiddles playing the same line, doubling on melody and lead. All this did was to make the sound of the fiddle louder.

Howard and Slim began experimenting with one fiddler playing the melody and the other playing a harmony part. It was very different from what other bands were doing, and Herald Goodman dubbed it "twin fiddling." The young men introduced their new technique on the Grand Ole Opry, and it brought the house down.[453] After a while they took their twin fiddling to new heights and began producing the sound of three and even four fiddles while playing only on two, through the innovative use of double stops. Howard would later become a pioneer in bluegrass twin fiddling, playing twin fiddles with Everett Lilly on a recording with Flatt & Scruggs.

Although Howard is most famous for his playing—"that sweet fiddle sound"—he was a prolific composer of music, as well. BMI's website shows some fifty-four tunes that he either composed or arranged,[454] and the computer file for Howard at Sony/ATV (formerly Acuff-Rose Music Publishing) includes at least eight more.[455]

These are the tunes it is *known* that he wrote because he copyrighted them, but as son Bob has related, Howard used to take some old melody—or just make up a melody—and add parts to it on the spot, play it, and then forget about it, so no one really knows *how* many hundreds of songs Forrester actually wrote. He also added extra parts to tunes he learned from others. As an example, Howard learned to play the tune "Topeka Polka" while he was out in Texas, then added a third part (in the key of E-flat) to it. According to son Bob, his dad did this many, many times.[456]

Howard told Earl Spielman, "I think fiddling should get into movements, almost, like your classical tunes do. To me, when fiddle tunes are played, why they're the most beautiful things in the world when they're played right. And I would like to see fiddlin', if it's going to be played at all, go into deeper and more movements, more tunes and even tempos and so forth. That would be my idea."[457] And he did just that with the tunes he wrote and arranged, adding new parts (sometimes several new parts), changing the key for some of them, changing the tempo for certain parts…as he said, just like classical music.

Forrester's improvisations are unique in that they are interesting, exciting, and yet stay fairly well within the melody of the tune. Howard always said, "If you want to depart that far from the tune with your improvisation, then write your own songs. I wrote my own songs when I wanted to say something." As an example, Howard spent hours crafting "Wild Fiddler's Rag," carefully taping it on a little recorder as it evolved.

Many of his improvisations are like a theme and variations. He would play the melody, then make up endless variations, then finish with the melody again, "completing the circle," as he called it.[458]

He had an encyclopedic memory of tunes, hundreds of them, and he knew them exactly as they were, not just in a half-baked sort of way. He always prided himself on being able to play the *exact* tune. His way of setting up a tune was to play the melody (the real one) first and then go about his improvisations, always returning to the melody to close out the tune. It was his way of making a speech: first you say what your point is, then you back it up with the facts, and then you reiterate your point in closing. His tunes were almost always played in this way, and he sometimes became annoyed when tunes were presented otherwise.[459]

When Howard's Aunt Nell (Uncle William's wife) died, Howard, Billie, and Bob were asked to play some hymns at the funeral—two fiddles and accordion. They were supposed to play two tunes: "What a Friend We Have in Jesus" and "Whispering Hope." They must have rehearsed those tunes five hundred times, but Bob still got "Whispering Hope" mixed up with "The Waltz You Saved for Me." Howard just looked at him: "No, no. What are you *doing?* Look; it goes like this." The tunes always had to be played correctly.[460]

Because he stayed close to the melody of the tune for his improvisations, his flights of fancy were always carefully constructed and in keeping with the tune itself. Although he had as much technique and could play as well as most symphony players, he never did something to a tune "just because he could." If it made good musical sense, he did it. Otherwise, he left it out. There was none of this "add this lick just because I can" that so many fiddlers inject into their playing.

And yet, his improvisations and compositions were never ordinary. One example of something quite different was his penchant for briefly injecting a new tonality into a piece; this is readily apparent in "Wild Fiddler's Rag" and "Memory Waltz," both of which were original compositions of his.

These pieces are written in the key of G major, and in both of them, the chord changes from G to E-flat and then back to G, not exactly a standard chord progression by anyone's standards! And yet it works perfectly in both places, because each of the chords he chose has one tone that is constant between them. He moves from G major (G-B-D, with G as the root) to E-flat major (E-flat-G-B-flat, with G as the middle tone.) He repeats this effect in the "Snowflake Reel," which is in D major (D-F#-A), when he moves to a B-flat chord (B-flat-D-F). This technique quickly became one of his "signatures."

Son Bob said that once his father had worked out an idea in one tune, he was good at moving that idea to another place, another key, or even another tune.[461]

One of the reasons Howard was able to hear—and thus write—these types of key changes was that early on he recognized that each different key possesses its own tonality—each key produces a sound that is uniquely its own on the fiddle. So he taught himself to play in all the various keys, laboriously trying out new notes until he could find them consistently and play them in tune. Along the way, he discovered that certain chords (arpeggios) shared certain tones in common, which made for a smoother transition between them.

One of his favorite keys was B-flat, in which he played and recorded a number of songs, including "High Level Hornpipe" and "Clarinet Polka." (The "Clarinet Polka" actually has a section that goes into the key of E-flat as well.)

Howard even composed tunes in B-flat, like "Doc Harris Hornpipe" and "The Last Waltz," which are on his United Artists album. "The Last Waltz" also includes a chord progression from Bb to G and back to Bb, the same type of tonality change noted earlier.

The key of B-flat was in common use by fiddlers of the nineteenth century, but later American fiddlers usually played only in the open string keys of G, D, A, and E and the neutral key of C. Forrester's fine playing in the key of B-flat brought him a lot of attention from other fiddlers of his time, and many of them raced to catch up with him.

Howard also liked the sound of minor keys and often added minor parts to songs originally written in major keys. He also composed tunes in minor keys—"Doc Harris Hornpipe" moves into G minor and "Gypsy Lament" opens in D minor.

Another of Howard's innovations was his extensive use of double stops, and not just the drones favored by other old-time fiddlers, but actual fingered double stops, which he inserted liberally in many of his tunes and moved around at will through the chord progressions. Examples of this are "Fiddler's Waltz," "Memory Waltz," "Howdy Waltz," and the middle portions of many tunes, such as "Still on the Hill" and "Black & White Rag." "Brown Skinned

Gal" and "Bully of the Town" are other examples, where Howard took a well-known old-time tune and made it his own through the extensive use of double stops.

Many fiddlers "cheat" on double stops—that is, they get only one finger down before they start moving the bow. Then they place the second finger and tune it to the first one. This makes for a slightly messy sound.

Howard, on the other hand, shaped both his fingers to the right spacing and dropped them onto the fingerboard at precisely the same time. He made sure his bow landed evenly on both strings at once, but not until his fingers were securely placed. He worked at this constantly, so the notes sounded precisely together and in tune. This is one of the reasons his playing is regarded as clean and clear.

He was meticulous about his double stops being in tune. He would tell Bob (and probably other fiddlers as well), "If you can't play them, then don't." It really bothered him to hear a fiddler play one of his tunes like "Fiddler's Waltz" and massacre the double stops in the last part.[462]

Howard also discovered harmonics on his fiddle and, loving the extra resonance they brought to a tune, used them liberally, mostly just by a quick slide in and out of the harmonic tone, a kind of "zinger" in the music. From listening to guitar players over the years, he had also discovered "pull offs," and he would often finish a harmonic by pulling the string sideways with his finger (like left-hand pizzicato) as he left the string, which made it ring even louder.

Examples of this include the last note of "Say Old Man," and several places in the high parts of "Grey Eagle Hornpipe" and "Still on the Hill."

Howard also experimented with bowing, using "off the string" (slow spiccato) bowing in "Fiddler's Waltz," using slurs (more than one note on a bow) to slide his double stops around, and adding slurs to his hornpipes and reels to make them more interesting.

He had learned to use a "slur two, slur two" style of bowing from Arthur Smith, who had perfected this bowing and used it a lot.[463] But Howard took it a step further and developed a "slur two, separate two" bowing that he used in fast tunes (some fiddlers call this a single shuffle). On occasion, he would also employ a "slur three, separate one" bowing, now known as a Georgia shuffle. And once in a while he would use Arthur's "slur two, slur two" bowing.

Mixing these alternate bowings in with long strings of separately bowed notes imparted a bouncy, highly danceable quality to his playing, as the slurs changed where the down bow would fall and, hence, where the accented note was. This is not surprising, since he began his fiddling career playing for square dances and his sense of rhythm was highly developed.[464]

Many of the hornpipes and reels he liked to play reflect his Scotch-Irish heritage; he claimed "I've always liked the hornpipes. It was *in* me, I guess you might say, and that's one of my specialties. They're a challenge. You have to strive for execution and tone. They must be played really clean, notes right on the head."[465] And that is how he played them.

He had figured out early on that the very cleanest sound came when his finger first pushed the string down to the fingerboard and *then* his bow started moving. "Fingers first" was his motto, and he worked hard to get his fingers down quickly and squarely before his bow moved onto that note.

In the old country, those hornpipes and reels actually are played somewhat differently than Howard played them. In Ireland and England, the eighth note duplets are played as a dotted eighth note followed by a sixteenth note. In Scotland, they are often played in the opposite manner, with the sixteenth note preceding the eighth note in the group of two, which is called a Scotch snap.

By contrast, Howard played his eighth note duplets *almost* (but not quite) evenly. Fiddler Stacey Phillips contends that Howard held the first note of each pair slightly longer, but *not* long enough to tripletize them[466] (what fiddlers call "swinging the eighth notes"). But after careful listening, I believe he was actually playing both eight notes right on the money, but putting less accent on the second eighth note of each pair, which made it sound like he was slightly shortening the second eighth note. In other words, he was playing his duplets *precisely* as classical musicians do!

One of the fiddlers Howard really admired—although their paths never crossed—was Donnell Clyde "Spade" Cooley. Spade had a dance band in California, and his musical arrangements for the band were so advanced that he was way ahead of his time.[467] He had a rich full sound "far more refined than Bob Wills' hot fiddle band style."[468]

Spade's music was so advanced, it was over the head of most of his audience, but Howard knew and understood exactly what Spade was doing and really respected his innovative style. Howard thought music should be interesting, and he had the greatest respect for musicians who could play it that way and not just put notes out into the room.

Howard loved to challenge himself musically—to figure out new ways of turning a phrase or making the music sound better. It was one of the things that drew him to the reels and hornpipes of his ancestors—they were difficult to play cleanly, and he strove to make them sound like music, instead of just rhythmic figures for dancing.

He loved western swing music, as well, because here he could take all the musical technique he had learned (figured out on his own) and use it to make up complex, swinging breaks, something new and different that required his very best playing. This is one of the reasons he had such great respect for his friend, Johnny Gimble, as Johnny was—and still is—one of the masters of western swing music.

In addition to intonation, intellectual curiosity, and innovation, Howard had a very strong suit in inter-relationships. He had strong ties to his family and his friends, preferring evenings spent with them to almost anything else in life.

These cemented relationships helped him learn about jobs he could get—J. L. Frank sent him to Pee Wee King, and he got a job in the tent show, which led him to Bill Monroe; Curt Poulton helped him get the radio job in Tuscola; Art Davis helped him get back to Tulsa; Georgia Slim helped him get the job at KRLD in Dallas; and countless people he befriended along the way taught him new tunes, new techniques, and new ways of thinking about music. Howard always had time for his friends and family.

His knack for inter-relationships extended far beyond the realm of people, however. Howard could see the relationships between things, between certain skills, between various types of music, between different styles of playing. He was able to use these observations of inter-relationships to enhance and improve his own playing. In this regard, he would have made a good detective, as he was able to take seemingly isolated facts and string them together to make them into something new and special.

As an example, he could take his own unique style of playing and tailor it to fit like a glove with almost any other fiddler's style. No wonder he was in such demand as a twin fiddle partner!

He made twin fiddle albums with Chubby Wise and later with Kenny Baker, did four twin fiddle tracks with Georgia Slim Rutland, twin-fiddled with Tommy Jackson on a square dance album, recorded "In the Pines" with Arthur Smith, played twin fiddle backup with Benny Martin and again with Everett Lilly on Flatt & Scruggs albums, and with Paul Warren on Mac Wiseman/Lester Flatt recordings, and again with Johnny Gimble and Sammy Dodge on a Calhoun Twins' recording.

To be able to fit one's own style with so many other fiddlers' styles is a real tribute to Howard and his great skills of listening and blending in. Very few fiddlers can adapt to so many different styles and still invent a credible, coherent second fiddle part.

And he played all styles of music as well, including western swing with Art Davis and later Georgia Slim, old-time with Roy Acuff, bluegrass with Bill Monroe, classical for his own enjoyment, square dance music for dances in Hickman County and elsewhere, and even rock 'n' roll with his son Bob's band!

One of Howard's Smoky Mountain Boy colleagues, rhythm guitarist Charlie Collins, called him "the genius of fiddle players, one of the country's greatest fiddlers." Collins has taught himself to fiddle and is planning to make a tribute album to Howdy Forrester; that is how much he admired him.[469]

Howard also saw how inter-related fiddling and classical music truly are—how the folk tunes of long ago had found their way into the classical compositions of famous composers such as Beethoven, Dvorak, and even Mozart, and how the innovations of classical music—the double stops; the fast string crossings with an open string note between each note of a descending scale line

(Handel and Mozart were both known for this); the improvised cadenzas in concertos, the harmonics, both natural and fingered—could be integrated into fiddling to make it something really special.

Some fiddlers, especially those who cannot read music, have a bias against classically-trained players and accuse them of not playing from the heart. Having listened to Fritz Kreisler and other classical masters play, Howard did not feel that way, which left him open to embrace what the classical players knew and to learn from them.

Because Roy Acuff felt as Howard did about classical music, there was some cooperation between the country music people and the classical people, as represented by the Nashville Symphony. A stripped down Symphony actually played at the Grand Master Fiddler Championship on numerous occasions, under the moniker Nashville Symphonette.

In 1974, Porter Wagoner emceed a show while the judges were busy tallying the Grand Master contest scores. The Wagonmasters (Wagoner's own band) played some numbers, followed by Roy Acuff singing "Great Speckled Bird." Then Howard played his own composition, "Doc Harris Hornpipe," on the show, with the Symphonette serving as his backup band. When the violins began "chopping" the chords behind Howard, the crowd went wild with applause.

Porter told the crowd: "Howdy Forrester is one of the finest fiddle players in America today; he's a great man as well...this really shows the versatality [sic] of the fiddle."[470]

Howard took everything he heard and saw, determined if and how it might fit into the fiddling genre, practiced and experimented with it, and then integrated it seamlessly into his playing and made it his own. That is what makes his own playing unique.

Howard saw the relationships between the "little things" in music and the overall presentation of the tune. He worked long hours on such (seemingly mundane) things as drawing a continuous, big, beautiful sound from one end of the bow to the other.

He always said tone was the most important thing. "There's nothing wrong with playing a beautiful, unadorned melody well—

many melodies can stand on their own if your tone is good, so just play the melody and don't try to do things you haven't mastered."[471]

And he practiced string crossings over and over until they were extremely smooth. This took the roughness out of his playing and added a certain elegance. He used a kind of "round bowing" style where his bow movements matched the curve of his classically-carved bridge.

Howard started his musical career playing for square dances, but after playing the same dance tunes over and over, the music lacked any intellectual challenge for him. So he began to make changes in the music, which altered the rhythmic structure of his part while still maintaining the strong two-beat so necessary for dancing. At the beginning of a section of a hoedown, he would often add an anticipation note—that is, he would play the starting note early, on the last beat of the preceding bar and tie it over to the first actual beat of the section. To provide further emphasis for this "off-the-beat" note, he would use a fourth finger double stop along with the open string opening note and would slide into the double stop. He does this repeatedly in "Grey Eagle Hornpipe" and "Durang's Hornpipe."

He also liked to play with the rhythm of a tune, using different bowings, which would move the accent off the beat. And he used rhythmic figures several times in succession, but moved them to different places in a measure so the accented beats made them sound different. One example of this is the "C" part of the "Memory Waltz." And sometimes he would change the composition of rhythmic figures, playing four notes the first time and three notes the next. This imparted a very bouncy quality to a tune; one great example of this is the "A" part of "Willow Springs." He also used a rest to make a "pregnant pause" at the start of a measure, coming in on the second beat of the bar instead of the first one. The "Howdy Waltz," one of his original compositions, makes great use of this device.

He experimented with the beginning and endings of tunes, as he observed that people really remembered the first few notes and the last few notes he played. He made sure that he didn't start a tune until he was ready, so that the first few notes would sparkle just like the rest of the tune. And he planned his endings carefully, so his tunes would be remembered as good music. He never trailed off or just quit playing at the end of a tune.

Howard was mindful of the "seams" in the music, as well, and worked to make them as smooth as possible, writing great little turnaround licks (like in the "A" part of "Ragtime Annie") and focused transitions to lead the listener to the next part of the tune. He often used double stop sequences to execute a key change between sections of a tune. He had a keen attention to detail, without losing the big picture of the tune he was playing.

And he learned to turn a phrase, not just put notes out into a room. His music always "went somewhere," building in excitement and pizzazz and carrying the listener along with it. Audiences would often start clapping in mid-tune; they were so caught up in the music.

Howard had powerful hands with well-developed fingers. As he matured and put on weight, he gained fleshy pads on his finger tips. This allowed him to play with a light, gypsy touch, which gave him a sweet tone despite his powerful bow strokes. A light touch also allowed him to play really fast notes (like triplets in a hornpipe) cleanly, and it made it easier for him to shift in and out of higher positions and to perform those smooth portamento slides for which he was famous.

Howard worked hard to master all the higher positions on his fiddle. He thought tunes that were just chorus-verse format were not very interesting, so he often added a high part, either moving the melody up an octave or making up a new melody in a high register. Both required him to acquire and maintain a real fluency in third through fifth positions.

And he practiced every day. Even though he was one of the big stars of the Opry, he felt he could—and must—continually improve his playing, keep making his music more interesting to the listeners, and keep challenging himself musically so that he never "lost his edge."[472]

Because of all the many ways in which he "pushed the envelope," Howdy Forrester has become the *bridge* fiddler, spanning the gap between the shuffling hoedown style of the old-time fiddlers and the more modern Texas contest style fiddling practiced today. The Texas Old Time Fiddlers Association is quick to credit Howdy Forrester with helping develop that Texas style during the time he was in Dallas and later upon his return to Nashville:

> Virtually all the fiddle tunes that were played on the radio by fiddlers such as Rutland [Georgia Slim] and Forrester, were emulated by such Texas fiddlers as Benny Thomasson, Lewis Franklin, Major Franklin, and Orville Burns just to mention a few.... Many Texas fiddlers are unwilling to admit that these professional musicians had any effect on the style. In fact, some have gone so far as to say that fiddlers such as Forrester and others, would show up at the contests and "learn some of the licks" from the contest fiddlers. This was hardly the case...the groups simply did not have the time to allow their fiddler to haunt a contest unless, perhaps, they were hired to entertain at one.[473]

And John Rumble, the Country Music Association's historian, had this to say:

> His military hitch over, Howdy went back to KRLD from 1946–49, teaming with "Georgia Slim" Rutland. There they joined Benny Thomasson, Red Franklin, and others in perfecting what came to be called the Texas fiddle style, an intricate, exciting style emphasizing continuous melodic variations through long bow strokes, double stops and varied accents.[474]

It is not surprising that Forrester had an impact on Texas style fiddling. He played nearly every type of music there was—southeastern old-time, western swing, bluegrass, string band, and even some rock 'n' roll with his son Bob. He also "played at" classical music and listened to lots of it, even though he couldn't read it off the page. In his own way, he had an impact on *all* fiddling, not just Texas-style, an impact that has helped to keep old-time fiddling alive in this country.

Most children of today do not learn to fiddle as their ancestors did, sitting on the porch and painstakingly learning one tune at a time from grandpa. They are the "instant everything" generation, and that applies to music as well. They have neither the discipline, nor the time, to spend four or more hours learning one tune by rote. They want to learn to play quickly and easily.

The Suzuki method of teaching violin was tailor-made for these children, and they master "Twinkle, Twinkle Little Star" very quickly and soon learn to read music. Once they can read, they go to the local music store and buy whole books of fiddle tunes, which they can then play through at their leisure. They can learn the rudiments of a tune in ten minutes or so, just by playing it off the music four or five times. And since most books of fiddle transcriptions include the guitar backup chords, they can learn to improvise off the chord changes easily.

Suzuki was a big proponent of "listening," and so the students listen to CDs of the songs in their book, even as they are learning to play them. As they branch into fiddling, they can readily hear the chord changes as they have learned to listen.

Suzuki also believed in structured practice, telling his students they must play each of the tunes in their lesson at least ten times a day. Howard was also a strong proponent of practice. He believed in working out every portion of a tune before you played it publicly, so that there were no slip-ups. And he always said that everyone—even classical violinists—must practice every day to stay on top of the music.

Most violin teachers insist on perfectly tuned instruments and children who play in tune, often taping a child's violin for correct finger placement in the early keys they learn. So children are trained to recognize precise intonation, and when they are exposed to the music of someone like Howdy Forrester, they recognize him as being "one of them."

This is the model for the future of fiddling—take Suzuki-trained violinists and teach them to fiddle. From the moment they are exposed to fiddle music, almost all the children love the strong driving rhythms, and soon their Bach Minuets and Handel Gavottes become very danceable, their bow arms become much stronger, and their rhythm much steadier. They also become more excited about working on their tone, once they have heard that big, bold Forrester sound.

Howard always posited "If you are going to play the fiddle, then get the wood out of it," meaning draw out the biggest, most beautiful sound that was in there.[475] Children like and understand that phrase "Get the wood out," and it definitely motivates them to work on tone production. It is from these children that the fiddlers of tomorrow will come, and it will be the music of Howdy Forrester that leads them along.

Howard's music is, as Bob Forrester put it, "very dense. You can copy some fiddlers readily, but daddy's fiddling is not easily accessible." He packs a lot of improvisation into one small tune and, unless a fiddler has an outstanding ear and lots of technique, it is almost impossible to play Howard's tunes exactly as he played them. He often used to say to Bob, "I know younger fiddlers will come along and some will trim me [beat me], but I'm gonna make it as hard as I can for them,"[476] and he certainly did so.

In his heart, he was competitive, but the most important thing to him was that his music was interesting. He studied his own playing and consistently worked to make it more interesting. West Virginia fiddler Blaine Sprouse said of Howdy: "I like his ability to write these tunes that are so monstrously hard to execute. He has written some of the technically hardest tunes for a fiddle player to play. They're good tunes."[477]

Howard worked diligently and continuously at writing those hard tunes. He went for a walk nearly every morning, taking with him an ornately-carved cane he had acquired in Mexico. Neighbors thought he used the cane as a defense against errant dogs, but that is not the case. As Howard walked along, he was trying out fiddle tunes in his mind, and he used the cane to work out the fingerboard challenges.[478]

These days, however, more fiddlers have been classically trained and understand thoroughly the theory behind the music. This fact, coupled with the advent of technology, which allows fiddlers to slow down the playback of old long play records without altering the pitch, means more of Howard's songs will be transposed and played in a manner more like he played them. This bodes well for a new generation of fiddlers, who will keep the old-time music alive and continue down the path Forrester has laid out for them.

I often imagine Big Howdy Forrester sitting up in heaven, playing twin fiddles with Chubby and Slim and Arthur and all the other angels, and occasionally stopping to listen to us mortals fiddling away down here on earth. I am sure he is clapping his hands in glee and cheering for us, watching to see if we know something he needs to learn.

"Let the music play on."

Appendix

Original Compositions and Arrangements
by Howdy Forrester

A. From the BMI Catalog

SONG TITLE	BMI WORK #
1. "Apple Blossom Polka"*	51538
2. "Beaumont Rag"	95494
3. "Black & White Rag"	120067
4. "Blackberry Blossom"	121994
5. "Brilliancy"*	151194
6. "Brown Skin Gal"	155509
7. "Brown Skinned Gal"	155524
8. "Build a Little Boat"	158228
9. "Bully of the Town"	159014
10. "Cathy With the Raven Black Hair"*	191208
11. "Chasin the Squirrel"	201366
12. "Cindy"	214867
13. "Clarinet Polka"	217937
14. "Cluckin' Hen"*	222425
15. "Cruel Willie"	260499
16. "Doc Harris Hornpipe"*	313328
17. "Dog in the Ryestraw"	314576
18. "Durang's Hornpipe"	350040
19. "Durang's Hornpipe"	350075
20. "Eighth of January"	358919
21. "Fiddler's Waltz"	413563

22. "Fiddlin' Trombone"   413689
23. "Grandmammy Look at Uncle Sam"*   505015
24. "Grey Eagle"   509734
25. "Grey Eagle Hornpipe"   506226
26. "Hollow Poplar"   577194
27. "Howdy in Hickman County"*   595549
28. "Howdy Polka"*   595559
29. "Howdy Waltz"*   595563
30. "Indian Creek"   721338
31. "Last Waltz"*   835264
32. "Leather Britches"   844191
33. "Memory Waltz"*   978424
34. "Old Grey Bonnet"   1107904
35. "Over the Waves"   1143610
36. "Pretty Polly Ann"   1202539
37. "Red Apple Rag"   1236055
38. "Red Haired Boy"   1236464
39. "Run Johnny Run"   1275969
40. "Rutland's Reel"*   1278934
41. "Rye Bread"*   1278986
42. "Sally Goodin"   1284209
43. "Say Old Man"   1295174
44. "Se-Cesh"   1301981
45. "St. Anne's Reel"   1399576
46. "Still On The Hill"*@   1411402
47. "Strictly Forrester"*   1420961
48. "Topeka Polka"   1534280
49. "Town and Country Fiddler"*   1537745
50. "Trombone Rag"   1546158
51. "Trot Along My Honey"   1546565
52. "Uncle Bob"*   1569937
53. "The Weeping Heart"*   1623857
54. "Wild Fiddlers Rag"*   1672930

* denotes a totally original Forrester composition

@ the second and third parts are original Forrester composition

In addition, Acuff-Rose Music (now SONY ATV) shows the following original compositions and arrangements by Forrester which are not included in the BMI listing:

SONG TITLE	ACUFF-ROSE WORK #
55. "Dallas Polka"	SG036973
56. "High Level Hornpipe"	SG036952
57. "LaRagona Polka"	SG036958
58. "Ragtime Annie"	SG036937
59. "Sally Johnson"	SG036932
60. "Staccato"	SG036867

Further, according to son Bob Forrester, Howard also composed "Springtime Polka" and "Gypsy Lament," which do not appear on either list of copyrighted works, but which were recorded by Howard. The following additional arrangements are on records Forrester cut, but do not show up in BMI/ASCAP/Acuff-Rose or any other file listings of Howdy Forrester tunes or arrangements:

"Blue Danube, The"
"Don't Let Your Deal Go Down"
"Evening Shades"
"Golden Eagle Hornpipe"
"I Love You Because"
"Ida Red"
"Legend in My Time"
"Memphis Blues"
"Slippin' Around"
"Willow Springs"

Howard was known for making up tunes—and/or additional parts to existing tunes—on the spot, so unless the tape recorder was running at the time, many of these tunes did not get transcribed or copyrighted.

CLUCKIN' HEN

By
Howard Forrester

THE LAST WALTZ

By
Howard Forrester

(The Last Waltz – 2)

CATHY WITH THE RAVEN BLACK EYES

By
Howard Forrester

(Cathy with the Raven Black Eyes – 2)

PRETTY POLLY ANN

By
Howard Forrester

DOC HARRIS HORNPIPE

By
Howard Forrester

THE WEEPING HEART

By
Howard Forrester

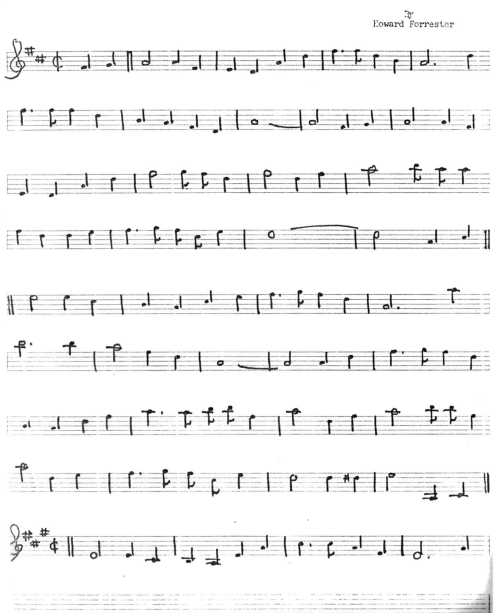

(The Weeping Heart – 2)

HOWDY IN HICKMAN COUNTY

By
Howard Forrester

MEMORY WALTZ

By
Howard Forrester

(Memory Waltz – 2)

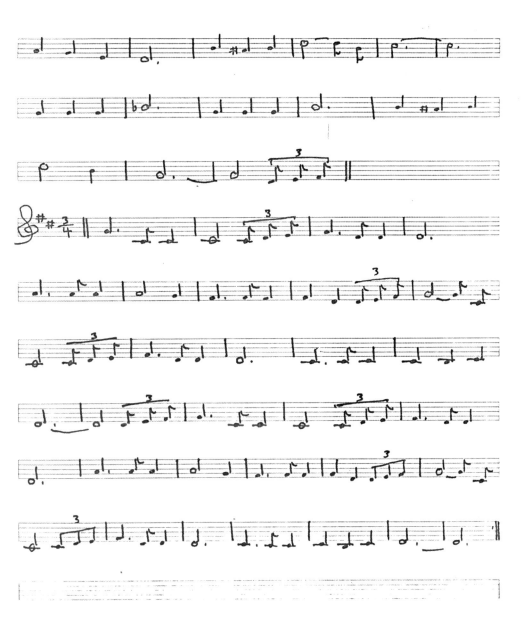

TOWN AND COUNTRY FIDDLER

By
Howard Forrester

WILD FIDDLERS RAG

By
Howard Forrester

(Wild Fiddlers Rag – 2)

APPLE BLOSSOM POLKA

By
Howard Forrester

(Apple Blossom Polka – 2)

GRANDMAMMY LOOK AT UNCLE SAM

By
Howard Forrester

Howdy Waltz

Howdy Forrester

Howdy Waltz

Strictly Forrester

Howdy Forrester

Still on the Hill

Howdy Forrester

Still on the Hill

Howdy Polka

Howdy Forrester

Howdy Polka

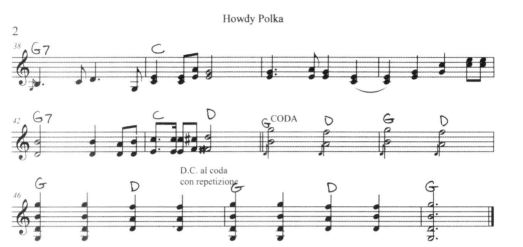

Old Grey Bonnet

Arr. Howdy Forrester

Old Grey Bonnet

Topeka Polka

Howdy Forrester

Fiddler's Waltz

Howdy Forrester

Fiddler's Waltz

Rutland's Reel

Howdy Forrester

D.S. al fine
senza repetizione

Gypsy Lament

Howdy Forrester

Gypsy Lament

Willow Springs

Howdy Forrester

D.C. al fine

The Forrester Clan c. 1907—Odom, Hezekiah, Lucinda (Bet), Albert, Willie, Stephen (Howdy's father), and Hickman. Music ran in this family.

At home in Hickman County— Joe Forrester (L) and Howdy Forrester (R). c. 1929

Howdy Forrester, Joe Forrester, and cousins Floyd and Hattie Ruth Pruitt, on Pretty Creek in Hickman County, Tennessee. c. 1933.

The Tennessee Valley Boys on the Grand Ole Opry: Howdy Forrester on fiddle, Joe Forrester on bass. c. 1938. Photo courtesy of Bob Forrester.

Red and Chuck Penn, Billie Forrester, Howdy, and Joe "Lespedeza" Forrester, Wichita Falls, Texas, 1940.

Wedding day for Howdy Forrester and Wilene (Billie) Russell, June 1940.

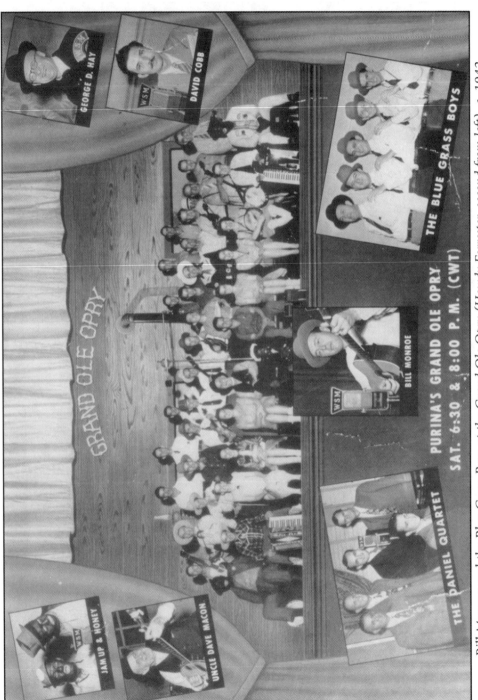

Bill Monroe and the Blue Grass Boys at the Grand Ole Opry (Howdy Forrester, second from left). c. 1942.

Emmie Forrester (Howard's mother), Howard, and Billie Forrester, 1945.

Howdy and Joe Forrester on radio station KRLD, Dallas, Texas, 1946.

Howdy Forrester in Dallas, Texas, 1946.

Texas Roundup—Dub Hendricks, Howdy Forrester, Georgia Slim Rutland, Dewey Groom, and Joe Forrester. Dallas, Texas, 1947.

Howdy Forrester with son Robert Allen (Bob), 1947.

The Smoky Mountain Boys at Dunbar Cave in Clarksville, Tennessee, 1952.

The New Jug Bang with Curly Rhodes, and Howdy Forrester on fiddle. Dunbar Cave, 1952.

Howdy Forrester on USO tour in Alaska, 1954.

Hubert Gregory, Howdy, Vito Pelletieri, and Brother Oswald (Pete Kirby). c. 1968.

*Emmie Totty Forrester
(Howard's mother). Photo
courtesy of Clyde Forrester.*

*Chubby Wise, Danny Ross, and
Howdy Forrester in Texas,
October 1972.*

*Howdy Forrester with classical
violinist Eugene Fodor. c. 1973.*

Howdy Forrester and grandson Matthew Forrester at Renfro Valley Festival, June 1973.

Roy Acuff's "balancing act" at Fan Fair, June 1974. Photo: Les Leverett, WSM Photographer.

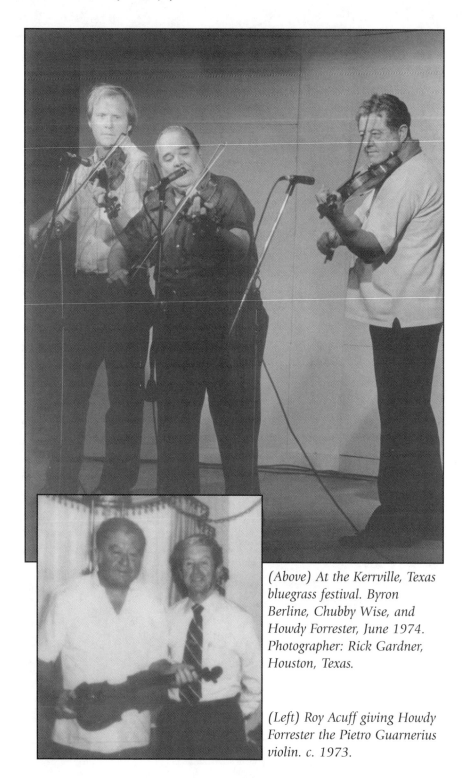

(Above) At the Kerrville, Texas bluegrass festival. Byron Berline, Chubby Wise, and Howdy Forrester, June 1974. Photographer: Rick Gardner, Houston, Texas.

(Left) Roy Acuff giving Howdy Forrester the Pietro Guarnerius violin. c. 1973.

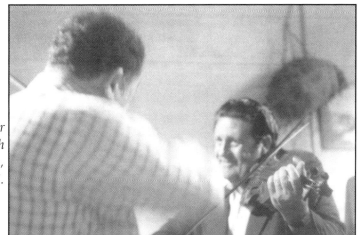

Howdy Forrester jamming with Benny Martin, 1975.

Perfect form, Howdy Forrester, 1970s.

Charlie Daniels, Wayne Rogers, Charlie Collins, and Howdy, in Roy Acuff's dressing room at the Opry, August 1976. Photo: Les Leverett, WSM Photographer.

Smoky Mountain Boys Show in Pittsburgh, Pennsylvania, September 1977. Howdy Forrester, Onie Wheeler, Roy Acuff, Jimmie Riddle, Gene Martin.

Kirk McGee and Howdy Forrester, Nashville, Tennessee. c. 1977.

Howdy Forrester and "Woody Paul" Chrisman of the band Riders in the Sky, March 1978.

Dr. Perry Harris, Honey Wild (of Jamup and Honey) and Howdy Forrester in Roy Acuff's dressing room at the Opry, March 1979. Photo: Les Leverett, WSM Photographer.

Senator Robert Byrd and Howdy playing twin fiddles backstage at the Opry, March 1979. Photo: Les Leverett, WSM Photographer.

Howdy Forrester with fellow Smoky Mountain Boys Charlie Collins and Brother Oswald (Pete Kirby) backstage at the Opry.

Edna Woods (front), Roy Acuff, Howdy Forrester, Larry McNeely, Charlie Collins, Brother Oswald, in Roy's dressing room at the Opry. c. 1980.

Roy Acuff watches Howdy and Bob Forrester play, 1981.

Country Music Association Awards Show at Opryland; Howdy on left, March 1981. Photo: Les Leverett, WSM Photographer.

Jerry Strobel, Opry Manager (L) and Porter Waggoner (R) present Howdy with the Master Fiddler Trophy honoring a lifetime of achievement. Fan Fair, Nashville, Tennessee, June 1987.

Howdy Forrester in repose, 1982. Photo: Jimmie Riddle.

Howdy and Billie Forrester's final resting place, Spring Hill Cemetery, Nashville, Tennessee. April 2004.

HOWARD W.
MAR. 31. 1922
AUG. 1. 1987

WILENE R.
DEC. 20. 1922
NOV. 17. 1999

FORRESTER

Author Gayel Pitchford playing Howdy Forrester's fiddle "The Mustang" with Joe Forrester on backup guitar. Nashville, Tennessee, April 2004.

About the Author

Author Gayel Pitchford is a contest award-winning old-time fiddler and concertmaster of the Tehachapi Community Orchestra. She is Fiddlin' Red Hattie in the old-time fiddle band Fiddlin' Red Hattie and the Friends of Hattie Band, which plays for parties, shows, and dances in southern California.

Pitchford has a Bachelor of Arts degree in American studies from California State University—Los Angeles and a Master of Arts degree from the University of Redlands. After a long career in the corporate world (with music always as her avocation), she took a very early retirement and moved to Tehachapi, California, where music is now her vocation. She teaches all her violin, viola, cello, and bass students to fiddle.

She is State Director for District 3 of the California State Old Time Fiddlers Association, a member of the American String Teachers Association (ASTA), and first violin in the string quartet Four with a Score. Her love of Forrester's music inspired her to write this long overdue book about his enormous contributions to country music.

Endnotes

Chapter 1

1. Joe Forrester, Interview at Nashville, TN, April 2004.
2. Clyde Forrester, Interview at Nashville, TN, April 2004.
3. Op. Cit., Joe Forrester.
4. Op. Cit., Clyde Forrester.
5. Perry Harris and Howard Roberts, "Howard 'Big Howdy' Forrester," *Devil's Box XXV,* June 1, 1974.
6. Visit to Hickman County, TN, by Gayel Pitchford, December 2004.
7. Op. Cit., Clyde Forrester.
8. Birth Certificate of Howard Wilson Forrester.
9. Op. Cit., Clyde Forrester.
10. Op. Cit., Joe Forrester.
11. Schlappi, Elizabeth, *Roy Acuff, the Smoky Mountain Boy,* Pelican Publishing Co., Gretna, LA, 1978, p. 93.
12. Logan, Tex, "Big Howdy! Howdy Forrester, Fiddler," *Muleskinner News,* September 1973, 13.
13. Op. Cit., Joe Forrester.
14. Spielman, Earl V., *Interview with Howdy Forrester,* page 2, December 12, 1968, Southern Folklife Collection Artist Names Files #30005, courtesy of Southern Folklife Collection, Manuscripts Department, Wilson Library at University of North Carolina—Chapel Hill.
15. Joe Forrester, Interview at Nashville, TN, December 2004.
16. Op. Cit., Spielman, *Forrester,* 2.
17. Op. Cit., Schlappi, 94, and Op. Cit., Joe Forrester.
18. Op. Cit., Joe Forrester, 4/04.
19. Bob Forrester, Interview at Nashville, TN, April 2004.
20. Op. Cit., Clyde Forrester, 4/04.
21. Op. Cit., Joe Forrester, 4/04.
22. Op. Cit., Bob Forrester, 4/04.
23. Op. Cit., Logan, 12.
24. Op. Cit., Clyde Forrester, 4/04.
25. Op. Cit., Bob Forrester, 4/04.
26. Op. Cit., Joe Forrester, 4/04.
27. Op. Cit., Perry Harris and Howard Roberts, 8; Joe Forrester actually recalls the man's name as being George McClanahan.
28. Ibid.
29. Op. Cit., Bob Forrester, 4/04.
30. Op. Cit., Spielman, *Forrester,* 4.
31. Ibid.
32. Joe Forrester, Interview at Nashville, TN, December 2005.
33. Buddy Spicher, "An Interview with Big Howdy Forrester," *Devil's Box,* Vol. XXI, No. 4, Winter, 1987.
34. Op. Cit., Bob Forrester, 4/04.
35. Op. Cit., Clyde Forrester, 4/04.

Chapter 2

36. Op. Cit., Joe Forrester, 4/04.
37. Eighth-grade notebook of Howard Forrester, courtesy of Bob Forrester.

[38] Op. Cit., Clyde Forrester, 4/04 and 12/04.

[39] Phone conversation between Gayel Pitchford and Charlie Collins, 12/04.

[40] Op. Cit., Joe Forrester, 4/04.

[41] E-mail of 6/11/04 to Gayel Pitchford from Paul Rawls of Isaac Litton HS Alumni Association.

[42] Op. Cit., Joe Forrester, 12/04.

[43] Op. Cit., Bob Forrester, 12/04.

[44] Country Music Foundation Oral History Project, †interview with Howdy Forrester, Interviewer Doug Green, Nashville, TN, September 26, 1974, and Op. Cit., Joe Forrester, 12/04.

[45] Op. Cit., Joe Forrester, 12/04, and Op. Cit., Doug Green.

[46] Op. Cit., Bob Forrester.

[47] Op. Cit., Spielman, *Forrester*, 3.

[48] Ibid.

[49] Ibid.

[50] Ledger Book of Joe Forrester, April 2, 1938–December 16, 1938.

[51] Charles Wolfe, *The Devil's Box, Masters of Southern Fiddling*, Country Music Foundation and Vanderbilt University Press, Nashville, TN, 1997, 130.

[52] Op. Cit., Joe Forrester, 4/04.

[53] Ibid.

[54] Ibid.

[55] Ibid.

[56] Op. Cit., Bob Forrester, 4/04.

[57] Op. Cit., Joe Forrester.

[58] Op. Cit., Ledger Book.

[59] Acuff, Roy, with Neely, William, *Roy Acuff's Nashville: The Life and Good Times of Country Music*, Perigee Books (The Putnam Publishing Company), NY, 1983, -89.

[60] Country Music Hall of Fame Staff, "The Vagabonds," *Encyclopedia of Country Music*, Oxford University Press, NY, 1983, 561–562.

[61] Op. Cit., Joe Forrester, 4/04.

[62] Op. Cit., Ledger.

[63] Ibid.

[64] Op. Cit., Joe Forrester, 4/04.

[65] Op. Cit., Ledger.

[66] Ibid.

[67] Op. Cit., Bob Forrester, 4/04.

[68] Op. Cit., Joe Forrester, 4/04.

[69] Russell, Tony, *Country Music Records, A Discography, 1921–1942*, Oxford University Press, 2004, 375 and 842.

[70] Phone Interview with Fiddler Ron Eldridge, 12/05.

[71] Op. Cit., Ledger.

[72] Ibid.

[73] Op. Cit., Spielman, *Forrester*, 7, and Op. Cit., Logan, 13.

[74] Ibid.

[75] Ibid.

[76] Ibid.

[77] Publicity Flyer, 12/15/38, courtesy of the Country Music Foundation Library.

[78] Op. Cit., Joe Forrester, 4/04.

[79] Op. Cit., Ledger.

[80] Ibid.

[81] Op. Cit., Joe Forrester, 4/04.

Chapter 3

[82] Op. Cit., Joe Forrester, 12/04.

[83] Letter to Emmie and Clyde Forrester from Howard and Joe Forrester, 3/22/39, courtesy of Joe Forrester.

[84] Op. Cit., Logan, p. 14.

[85] Op. Cit., *Encyclopedia of Country Music*, 491.

[86] Op. Cit., Bob Forrester, 4/04.

[87] Henry, Murphy, *Come Prepared to Stay: Bring Fiddle,* (The Story of Sally Ann Forrester, the Original Bluegrass Girl), M.A. Thesis, George Mason University, VA, 1999, 31—32.

[88] Op. Cit., Joe Forrester, 4/04.

[89] *KVOO Lariat*, Vol. I, No,. 1, of 6/17/39, Tulsa, Oklahoma.

[90] Op. Cit., Joe Forrester, 4/04.

[91] Op. Cit., Murphy Henry, 24.

[92] Post-card from Emmie Forrester to Joe and Howard Forrester, courtesy of Joe Forrester.

[93] Second Ledger of Joe Forrester, October 1939–May 1940.

[94] Ibid.

[95] Ibid.

[96] Ibid.

[97] Spielman, Earl, "An Interview with Georgia Slim Rutland," *Devil's Box*, Vol. 20, No. 3, Fall 1986, 12—14.

[98] Op. Cit., Joe Forrester, 4/04.

[99] Op. Cit., Murphy Henry, 14.

[100] Op. Cit., Bob Forrester, 4/04.

[101] Op. Cit., Joe Forrester, 4/04.

[102] Op. Cit., Second Ledger.

[103] Op. Cit., Joe Forrester, 4/04.

[104] Music and words from Publicity Brochure, Georgia Slim Rutland and the Texas Roundup Radio Stage Show, courtesy of Country Music Foundation Library.

[105] Op. Cit., Joe Forrester, 12/04.

[106] Op. Cit., Second Ledger.

[107] Op. Cit., Murphy Henry, 36.

[108] Op. Cit., Second Ledger.

[109] Op. Cit., Joe Forrester, 4/04.

Chapter 4

[110] Op. Cit., Murphy Henry, 36–37.

[111] Letter from Howard Forrester to Billie Russell, 3/7/40, courtesy of Joe Forrester.

[112] Op. Cit., Second Ledger.

[113] Letter from Howard Forrester to Billie Russell, 3/28/40, courtesy of Joe Forrester.

[114] Op. Cit., Joe Forrester, 4/04.

[115] Op. Cit., Second Ledger.

[116] Post-card from Howard Forrester to Wilene Russell, 4/2/40, courtesy of Joe Forrester.

[117] Op. Cit., Second Ledger.

[118] Letter from Howard Forrester to Wilene Russell, 5/18/40, courtesy of Joe Forrester.

[119] Op. Cit., Bob Forrester, 4/04.

[120] Telegram from Howard Forrester to Wilene Russell, 5/23/40, courtesy of Joe Forrester.

[121] Telegram from Howard Forrester to Wilene Russell, 5/31/40, courtesy of Joe Forrester.

[122] Op. Cit., Murphy Henry, 41.

[123] Op. Cit., Joe Forrester and Bob Forrester, 12/04.

[124] Op. Cit., Murphy Henry, 36.

[125] Op. Cit., Joe Forrester, 4/04.

[126] Ibid.

[127] Ibid.

[128] Op. Cit., Joe Forrester, 4/04.

[129] Op. Cit., Doug Green, 6.

[130] Op. Cit., 7.

[131] Op. Cit., Bob Forrester, 4/04.

Chapter 5

[132] Op. Cit., Clyde Forrester, 4/04.

[133] Ibid.

[134] Op. Cit., Buddy Spicher, 4–5.

[135] Op. Cit., Logan, 16.

[136] Ibid.

[137] Postcards from Howard Forrester to Emmie Forrester and Billie Russell Forrester, courtesy of Bob Forrester.

[138] Op. Cit., Murphy Henry, 45.

[139] Op. Cit., Clyde Forrester, 4/04.

[140] Op. Cit., Murphy Henry, 45.

[141] Smith, Richard D., *Can't You Hear Me Callin?* (DaCapo Press, Cambridge, MA, 2000) 74.

[142] Draft Notice of Howard Forrester, courtesy of Joe Forrester.

[143] Interview of Tom Ewing by Gayel Pitchford at the Country Music Foundation Library, 4/04.

[144] Noles, Randy, *Orange Blossom Boys*, Centerstream Publishing, Anaheim Hills, CA, 2002, 192.

[145] Op. Cit., Bob Forrester, 4/04.

[146] W-2's for Howard Forrester and Billie Forrester for 1943, courtesy of Country Music Foundation Library.

[147] Op. Cit., Joe Forrester, 4/04.

148 Op. Cit., Murphy Henry, 48.

149 Ibid., 73.

150 Op. Cit., Clyde Forrester, 4/04.

151 Op. Cit., 75.

152 Op. Cit., Joe Forrester, 4/04.

153 Op. Cit., Bob Forrester, 4/04.

154 DD-214 (Discharge Papers from the US Navy) of Howard Forrester.

155 Op. Cit., Joe Forrester, 4/04; Joe recalls his guitar being a Martin D-16, but Martin did not make that model until much later.

156 Op. Cit. DD-214.

157 Op. Cit., Clyde Forrester, 4/04.

158 Letter from Howard Forrester to Billie Forrester, 5/7/45.

159 Letter from Howard Forrester to Billie Forrester, 6/1/45.

160 Op. Cit., Joe Forrester, 4/04, and Op. Cit., Doug Green, 11.

161 Op. Cit., Clyde Forrester, 4/04.

162 Letter from Clayton Forrester to Billie Forrester, 1/23/44.

163 Op. Cit., Clyde Forrester, 4/04.

164 Letters from Howard Forrester to Billie Forrester and Emmie Forrester, 1944—45, courtesy of Bob Forrester.

165 Op. Cit., Murphy Henry, 56—57.

166 Telegram from Howard Forrester to Emmie Forrester, 11/13/45, courtesy of Joe Forrester.

167 Telegram from Howard Forrester to Billie Forrester, 11/19/45, courtesy of Joe Forrester.

168 Op. Cit., DD-214.

169 Op. Cit., Joe Forrester, 4/04.

170 Op. Cit., DD-214.

171 Op. Cit., Clyde Forrester, 4/04.

172 Op. Cit., Joe Forrester, 4/04.

173 Ibid.

174 Op. Cit., Bob Forrester, 4/04.

175 Op. Cit., Joe Forester, 12/04.

176 Op. Cit., Joe Forrester, 4/04.

177 Ibid.

178 Op. Cit., Doug Green.

Chapter 6

179 Op. Cit., Murphy Henry, 87.

180 Op. Cit., Joe Forrester, 12/04 and Op. Cit., Murphy Henry, 88.

181 *Bluegrass Unlimited*, Vol. 37 No. 2, August 2002, "Joe Forrester: Forgotten Bluegrass Boy, by Murphy Henry , 49.

182 KTUL Newsletter, date unknown, courtesy of Country Music Foundation Library.

183 Op. Cit., Bob Forrester, 12/05.

184 Op. Cit., Joe Forrester, 4/04.

185 Promotional Brochure from the KRLD Roundup.

186 Op. Cit. Joe Forrester, 4/04.

187 Recordings taken from Radio KRLD, 1946, and put on CDs, courtesy of Bob Forrester.

188 Ibid.

189 Op. Cit., Joe Forrester, 12/05.

190 Op. Cit., Bob Forrester, 4/04.

191 Op. Cit., Logan, 15.

192 Op. Cit., Joe Forrester, 4/04.

193 Op. Cit., KRLD CDs.

194 Op. Cit., Joe Forrester, 4/04.

195 Op. Cit., Bob Forrester, 4/04.

196 Ibid.

197 Letter from Dave Macon to Howard and Billie Forrester dated 8/46, courtesy of Country Music Foundation Library.

198 Letter from Howard Forrester to Emmie Forrester, using Edgefield address.

199 Letter from Honey Wilds to Howard Forrester dated 12/46, courtesy of CMF Library.

200 Phone interview with Bob Forrester, 8/05.

201 Op. Cit., Bob Forrester, 4/04.

202 Promotional Flyer No. 1 for Texas Roundup, courtesy of CMF Library.

203 Promotional Flyer No. 2 for Texas Roundup, courtesy of CMF Library.

204 *Crockett Democrat*, Vol. 7, No. 31 of 6/19/47, 1, "All-Out Welcome to Fiddlers and Guests," courtesy of CMF Library.

205 Texas Roundup Publicity Flyer, courtesy of CMF Library.

206 Op. Cit., Joe Forrester, 4/04.

207 Op. Cit., Joe Forrester, 4/04 and 12/04.

208 Op. Cit., Bob Forrester, 12/04.

209 Op. Cit., Murphy Henry, 93.

210 Op. Cit. Joe Forrester, 4/04.

211 Ibid.

212 Promotional Flyer—Eagletown Dance, courtesy of CMF Library.

213 Op. Cit., Joe Forrester, and Op. Cit., Bob Forrester 4/04.

214 Op. Cit., Joe Forrester, 4/04.

215 Interview of Ossie White by Gayel Pitchford, 3/04.

216 *Contest Fiddling*, Mel Bay Publications, Inc., Pacifica, MO, 1983, 30, Interview of Benny Thomasson by Stacey Phillips.

217 *Hank Thompson & the Brazos Valley Boys* boxed CD set, jacket and liner notes.

218 Op. Cit., Joe Forrester, 4/04.

Chapter 7

219 Op. Cit., Clyde Forrester, 4/04.

220 Op. Cit., Joe Forrester, 4/04.

221 Op. Cit., Bob Forrester, 4/04.

222 Ibid.

223 Op. Cit., Joe Forrester, 4/04.

224 Op. Cit., Bob Forrester, 4/04.

225 Op. Cit., Clyde Forrester, 4/04.

226 Op. Cit., Bob Forrester, 4/04.

227 *Nashville Banner*, 4/20/50, 18, "Hippodrome Rocks and Reels to Tune of Old-Fashioned Square Dance," courtesy of CMF Library.

228 Publicity Flyer, "WSM Grand Ole Opry Presenting Radio Stars in Person," courtesy of CMF Library.

229 Op. Cit., Bob Forrester, 4/04.

230 Op. Cit., *The Encyclopedia of Country Music*, "Cowboy Copas," by Jonathan Guyot Smith, 110.

231 Op. Cit., Logan, 16.

232 Promotional Flyer for Old-Fashioned Square Dance and Barbecue in Only, TN, courtesy of CMF Library.

233 Op. Cit., Clyde Forrester, 4/04.

234 Op. Cit., Schlappi, 93.

235 Op. Cit., Schlappi, 139.

236 Op. Cit., Bob Forrester, 4/04.

237 Rosenberg, Neil V., e-mail of 10/4/06 to Robert Cogswell.

238 Ibid.

239 *Flat & Scruggs: The Golden Years*, Rounder Records CDSS 05/A22614, 1992, and *Flat & Scruggs: Don't Get Above Your Raisin'*, Rounder Records CDSS 08/A22695, 1992; re-issued in 1991 as a Bear Family boxed CD set *Flatt & Scruggs: 1948–1959*, BCD 15472. (Originally issued as Columbia sides 20886, 20915, 21002, and 21043 in 1951.

240 Videos of Grand Ole Opry segments, courtesy of Bob Forrester.

241 Op. Cit., Schlappi, 94.

242 Op. Cit., Bob Forrester, 12/04.

243 Phone interview with SMB Charlie Collins by Gayel Pitchford, 12/04.

244 Ibid.

245 Op. Cit., Schlappi, 127–128; Op. Cit., Doug Green, 12.

246 Op. Cit., Charlie Collins.

247 Op. Cit., Murphy Henry, 100.

248 Op. Cit., Elizabeth Schlappi, 240.

249 Certificate from Department of Defense, courtesy of Bob Forrester.

250 Op. Cit., Bob Forrester, 12/04.

251 Op. Cit., Schlappi, 103.

252 Op. Cit., Bob Forrester, 12/04.

253 *Royal Crown Cola Shows Vols. 1–5* CDs, music and jacket liners, 2001, RME Enterprises.

254 Ibid.

255 *The Roy Acuff Show Collection: the Great 48*, CD, 2006.

256 Op. Cit., Bob Forrester, 4/04.

257 Op. Cit., Schlappi, 241.

258 *Pickin' & Singin' News* of 1/15/55, courtesy of CMF Library.

259 Certificate of Membership—Royal Order of Polar Bears, courtesy of CMF Library.

260 Certificate of Membership—Order of the Arctic Realm, courtesy of CMF Library.

261 Twork, Danny, Unpublished Interview with Howdy Forrester of 2/84, 1, courtesy of Bob Forrester.

262 Op. Cit., Schlappi, 103.

263 Op. Cit., Doug Green, 24.

264 Op. Cit., Schlappi, 36.

265 Op. Cit., Clyde Forrester, 4/04 and 12/04.

266 Souvenir Program, Liberty Bicentennial Observation, Liberty, TX, 4/18–21/56.

267 Op. Cit., Bob Forrester, 4/04 and 12/04.

268 Op. Cit., Schlappi, 110.

269 Ibid, 132.

270 Ibid., 139.

271 Op. Cit., Buddy Spicher.

272 *Tennessean*, "Royalty in Exclusive Rose Contract" of 8/11/57, courtesy of Bob Forrester.

273 *The Stanley Brothers and the Clinch Mountain Boys—The Complete Mercury Recordings* CDs—songs and liner notes.

274 Op. Cit., Spielman, *Forrester*, 10.

275 *Fancy Fiddlin' Country Style* LP, MGM E-4035, songs and liner notes and Op. Cit., Bob Forrester, 4/04.

276 Op. Cit., Buddy Spicher, 12.

277 *Roy Acuff's Open House*, videotapes of eight shows, courtesy of Bob Forrester.

278 Op. Cit., Schlappi, 243–245.

279 Op. Cit., Bob Forrester, 4/04.

280 Op. Cit., *Roy Acuff's Open House*, and Op. Cit., Bob Forrester, 8/05.

281 Op. Cit., Schlappi, 245.

282 Op. Cit., Bob Forrester, 4/04.

283 Op. Cit., Schlappi, 245.

284 Letter from W. D. Kilpatrick of Acuff-Rose Artists to Howdy Forrester, 3/28/60, courtesy of CMF Library.

285 *Nashville Banner*, "Round the Clock" by Harry Draper, 3/28/60.

286 Op. Cit., Bob Forrester, 4/04.

287 Op. Cit., Schlappi, 134.

288 Ibid.

289 Op. Cit., Schlappi, 245–246.

290 Op. Cit., Bob Forrester, 12/04.

291 Op. Cit., Schlappi, 245–246.

292 Certificate of Esteem, USAREUR, courtesy of Bob Forrester.

293 Op. Cit., Bob Forrester, 4/04.

294 Op. Cit., Clyde Forrester, 4/04, and Op. Cit., Joe Forrester, 4/04.

295 Picture of Howdy Forrester and Dewey Groom at the Longhorn Ballroom, courtesy of Bob Forrester.

296 Op. Cit., Schlappi, 246.

297 Op. Cit., Schlappi, 246, and Op. Cit., Bob Forrester, 4/04; Schlappi says Benny Martin was the fiddler on this Smoky Mountain Boy trip; Bob Forrester contends it was his father, Howard, who went on the trip.

298 Op. Cit., Bob Forrester, 4/04.

299 Ibid.

300 Ibid.

301 Ibid.

302 "Grand Ole Opry Spectacular 2-record set, Starday SLP 242 songs and jacket notes.

303 *Big Howdy: Fiddlin' Country Style*, UAL 3295, songs and liner notes.

304 Op. Cit., Buddy Spicher, 12.

305 Op. Cit. Bob Forrester, 12/05.

306 Op. Cit., Bob Forrester, 4/04.

307 Ibid.

308 Ibid.

309 Ibid.

310 Op. Cit., Joe Forrester, 4/04.

311 Op. Cit., Bob Forrester, 4/04.

312 Ibid.

313 Ibid.

314 *The World Is His Stage* LP, Hickory LPM-114, songs and liner notes.

315 Schlappi, 111.

316 Op. Cit., Schlappi, 246–247.

[317] Op. Cit., Bob Forrester, 4/04 and *allroadsleadtobranson.com.*

[318] Ibid.

Chapter 8

[319] Ibid.

[320] Op. Cit., Schlappi, 95.

[321] Letter from Peggy Lamb of SONY/ATV (formerly Acuff-Rose Music) to Gayel Pitchford, 8/21/03.

[322] Op. Cit., Doug Green, 32.

[323] Phone interview with Jean Thomas by Gayel Pitchford, Nashville, TN, 12/04.

[324] Op. Cit., Bob Forrester, 12/04.

[325] Op. Cit., Schlappi, 247.

[326] Op. Cit., Schlappi, 66 and Op. Cit., Bob Forrester, 12/04.

[327] Op. Cit., Schlappi, 95 and 248.

[328] News clip, 9/65, author unknown.

[329] Op. Cit., Bob Forrester, 4/04.

[330] Ibid.

[331] Ibid.

[332] *Simply Roy Acuff* LP, Hilltop JS-6028, songs and liner notes.

[333] Op. Cit., Bob Forrester, 12/05.

[334] Op. Cit., Schlappi, 95.

[335] "Howdy Forrester Turned Booker," *Billboard,* 2/3/68.

[336] *Famous Opry Favorites* LP, Hickory LPS-139, songs and liner notes.

[337] Op. Cit., Bob Forrester, 8/05.

[338] Op. Cit., Clyde Forrester, 4/04.

[339] Op. Cit., Spielman, 5.

[340] Op. Cit., Bob Forrester, 4/04.

[341] Op. Cit., Bob Forrester, 8/05.

[342] Ibid.

[343] E-mail from Johnny Gimble to Gayel Pitchford, 10/8/03.

[344] Tape of Thanksgiving Jam Session at Forresters, courtesy of Bob Forrester.

[345] Audio tape from November 7, 1972 of Howdy Forrester and Johnny Gimble jamming, courtesy of Bob Forrester.

[346] Op. Cit., Joe Forrester, 12/04.

[347] Op. Cit., Bob Forrester, 12/05.

[348] Audio tape of 1971 jam session in Roy Acuff's dressing room at Grand Ole Opry, featuring Howdy Forrester and Johnny Gimble.

[349] Phone conversation between Les Leverett and Gayel Pitchford, 12/05.

[350] Op. Cit., Les Leverett.

[351] *I Saw the Light* LP, Hickory LPS-158, songs and liner notes.

[352] Op. Cit., Bob Forrester, 12/04.

[353] Op. Cit., Bob Forrester, 4/04.

[354] *Ralph Stanley and the Clinch Mountain Boys: the Complete Mercury Recordings,* re-released on CD in 2003, songs and liner notes.

[355] Op. Cit., Joe Forrester, 4/04.

[356] Op. Cit., Bob Forrester, 4/04.

[357] Op. Cit., Ron Eldridge, 12/05.

[358] Op. Cit., Doug Green, 37.

[359] Op. Cit., Bob Forrester, 4/04.

[360] Op. Cit., Ron Eldridge, 12/05.

[361] Ibid.

[362] Ibid.

[363] Op. Cit. Joe Forrester, 4/04.

[364] Op. Cit., Bob Forrester, 4/04.

[365] Ibid.

[366] Op. Cit., Charlie Collins.

[367] Op. Cit., Bob Forrester, 4/04 and Op. Cit., Schlappi, 92.

[368] E-mail from George Gruhn of Gruhn Guitars, Nashville, TN, to Gayel Pitchford, 6/04.

[369] Op. Cit., Bob Forrester, 4/04.

[370] Ibid.

[371] Promotional flyer for the fiddling class "Fiddlers on Fiddling," 7/73, courtesy of CMF Library.

[372] Op. Cit., Bob Forrester, 8/05.

[373] Op. Cit., Bob Forrester, 4/04.

[374] *Howdy's Fiddle and Howdy, Too!,* Stoneway Records, STY-127, LP, 1973, songs and liner notes.

[375] Op. Cit., Doug Green, 37.

[376] Photos, e-mails, and letter of 1/2/04 from Photographer Rick Gardner of Houston, Texas, to Gayel Pitchford.

377 Op. Cit., Joe Forrester, 4/04.

378 *Big Howdy*, Stoneway Records, STY-136, LP, 1974, songs and liner notes.

379 Op. Cit., Bob Forrester, 4/04.

380 Op. Cit., Doug Green.

381 Op. Cit., Perry Harris and H. G. Roberts.

382 Op. Cit., Bob Forrester, 4/04; Listing of Howdy Forrester's Compositions from BMI Website.

383 *Fiddler Magazine*, Vol. 12, No. 1, Spring of 2005, 19–20, "Fiddle Music of the Civil War" by Jim Wood.

384 Op. Cit., Bob Forrester, 4/04.

385 Op. Cit., Bob Forrester, 8/05.

386 Op. Cit., Bob Forrester, 4/04.

387 Certificate of Performance dated 6/14/75 from Country Music Foundation.

388 Op. Cit., Bob Forrester, 4/04.

389 Op. Cit., Bob Forrester, 8/05.

390 *Devil's Box* of 6/1/74, Newsletter No. XXV, 40, record review by Dave Garelick.

391 Barry R. Willis, *America's Music—Bluegrass*, Pine Valley Music, Franktown, CO, 1989.

392 Op. Cit., Bob Forrester, 12/04.

393 *Leather Britches*, Stoneway, STY-150, 1975,and *Fiddle Tradition*, STY-149, 1975 LPs, songs and liner notes.

394 Op. Cit., Bob Forrester, 4/04.

395 Op. Cit., Bob Forrester, 8/05.

396 *Fiddle Tradition*, Stoneway, STY-149, 1975 LP, songs and liner notes.

397 Op. Cit., Bob Forrester, 12/05, and *Sincerely Yours* LP, Stoneway Records, songs and liner notes.

398 Op. Cit., Bob Forrester, 4/04.

399 Op. Cit., Randy Noles, 57.

400 *Smoky Mountain Memories* LP, Hickory H3G-4517, *That's Country* LP, Hickory H3G-4521, and *Wabash Cannonball* LP, Hilltop JS-6162, songs and liner notes.

401 *Howdy Forrester—Stylish Fiddling*, Stoneway, STY-168, LP, 1976, songs and liner notes.

402 Op. Cit., Clyde Forrester, 4/04.

403 Op. Cit., Bob Forrester, 4/04.

404 Ibid.

405 Op. Cit., Ron Eldridge, 12/05.

406 Op. Cit., Ossie White.

407 *Bluegrass Unlimited*, March 1976.

408 *Bluegrass Unlimited*, February 2006, "Thirty Years Ago: This Month" by Tom Ewing.

409 Op. Cit., Joe Forrester, and Op. Cit., *Bluegrass Unlimited*, August 2002, 50.

410 Letter from Jo Walker at Country Music Association to Howdy Forrester, dated 2/16/78, courtesy of CMF Library.

411 *Bluegrass Unlimited*, "General Store," January 1978.

412 Letter from Senator Robert Byrd to Howdy Forrester, 3/16/79, courtesy of Clyde Forrester.

413 Op. Cit., Bob Forrester, 4/04.

414 Ibid.

415 Ibid., and Op. Cit., Murphy Henry, 101.

416 Op. Cit., Bob Forrester, 4/04.

417 Op. Cit., Ron Eldridge, 12/05.

418 Ibid.

419 *Bluegrass Unlimited*, September 1987, "Obituary: Howard 'Big Howdy' Forrester, 1922–1987."

420 Op. Cit., Bob Forrester, 4/04.

421 Op. Cit., Murphy Henry, 104.

422 *Red Apple Rag* LP, County Sales, 1983, songs and liner notes.

423 Op. Cit., Bob Forrester, 12/04.

424 Op. Cit., Bob Forrester, 4/04.

425 Op. Cit., Bob Forrester, 4/04 and 12/04, and *Devil's Box*, 1981–1996.

426 Framed copy of check for $10k from Roy Acuff to Howdy Forrester, courtesy of Bob Forrester.

427 Op. Cit., Bob Forrester, 4/04.

428 Op. Cit., Bob Forrester, 8/05.

429 Video of Forrester family party dated 2/87, courtesy of Bob Forrester.

430 Op. Cit., Bob Forrester, 4/04.

431 Op. Cit., Bob Forrester, 8/05.

432 Citation unknown.

433 Op. Cit., Bob, Joe, and Clyde Forrester 4/04.

434 Pictures of Fan Fair of 6/87 (Courtesy of Bob Forrester); Op. Cit., Bob Forrester, 4/04.

435 Op. Cit., Bob Forrester, 4/04.

436 Ibid.

437 Death Certificate of Howard Forrester, 8/31/87.

438 Spring Hill Mortuary Funeral Memorial Book, courtesy of Bob Forrester.

439 *Tennessean*, 8/6/87, "Mr. Howdy Forrester, Fiddler."

440 *Nashville Banner*, 6/12/87, "Grand Master Fiddler to Top Off Fan Fair Fun" by Pat Embry.

Chapter 9

441 Op. Cit., Bob Forrester, 4/04.

442 Ibid.

443 Ibid.

444 Ibid.

445 Ibid.

446 Ibid.

447 Op. Cit., Joe Forrester, 12/05.

448 Ibid.

449 Op. Cit., Les Leverett, 12/05.

450 Experiment conducted by Gayel Pitchford with Dr. B. J. Mitchell, 8/04.

451 Op. Cit., Bob Forrester, 4/04.

452 *Devil's Box Newsletter XXV* of 6/1/74, 41.

453 *Bluegrass Unlimited*, April 1985, "Georgia Slim Rutland, a Fiddler's Fiddler," by Janice McDonald, 23.

454 BMI Listing of Howdy Forrester Compositions and Arrangements (taken from their website).

455 Op. Cit., Peggy Lamb.

456 Op. Cit., Bob Forrester, 12/04.

457 Op. Cit., Spielman, *Forrester*, 10.

458 Op. Cit., Bob Forrester, 4/04.

459 Ibid.

460 Ibid.

461 Op. Cit., Bob Forrester, 8/05.

462 Ibid.

463 Op. Cit., Spielman, 5.

464 Op. Cit., Joe Forrester, 12/04.

465 Op. Cit., Green, 12.

466 *Strings* Magazine, Vol. 5, May–June 1991, "Fancy Fiddlin' Country Style", Stacey Phillips, 38–41.

467 Op. Cit., Bob Forrester, 8/05.

468 Op. Cit., *The Encyclopedia of Country Music*, "Spade Cooley," by Johnny Whiteside, 109.

469 Op. Cit., Charlie Collins.

470 Audiotape of 1974 Grand Master Fiddler Contest, courtesy of Bob Forrester.

471 Op. Cit., Bob Forrester, 8/05.

472 Op. Cit., Bob Forrester, 12/04 and Op. Cit., Joe Forrester, 12/04.

473 Texas Old Time Fiddlers' Association Website at texasoldtimefiddlers.org .

474 Op. Cit., *The Encyclopedia of Country Music*, "Howdy Forrester" by John Rumble, 178.

475 Op. Cit., Bob Forrester, 4/04.

476 Ibid.

477 Op. Cit., Barry Willis, 361.

478 Op. Cit., Bob Forrester, 8/05.

Bibliography

1. Books

Acuff, Roy with Neely, William, *Roy Acuff's Nashville: The Life and Good Times of Country Music*, Putnam Publishing Company, New York, 1983.

Apel, Willi, *Harvard Dictionary of Music*, 2d ed., Belknap Press of Harvard College, Cambridge, MA, 1972.

Country Music Hall of Fame Staff, *The Encyclopedia of Country Music*, Oxford University Press, 1998.

Hemphill, Paul, *The Nashville Sound: Bright Lights and Country Music*, Simon & Schuster, 1970.

Malone, Bill C., *Country Music, U.S.A.*, 2d ed., University of Texas Press, Austin, TX, 1968, 1985, 2002.

McCloud, Barry, *Definitive Country, the Ultimate Encyclopedia of Country Music & its Performers*, Berkley Publishing Group, New York, 1995.

Morton, David, with Wolfe, Charles K., *DeFord Bailey: A Black Star in Early Country Music*, University of Tennessee Press, Knoxville, 1991.

Noles, Randy, *Orange Blossom Boys*, Centerstream Publishing, Anaheim Hills, CA, 2002.

Phillips, Stacy, *Contest Fiddling*, Mel Bay Publications, Inc., Pacifica, MO, 1983.

Russell, Tony, *Country Music Records, A Discography, 1921–1942*, Oxford University Press, 2004.

Schlappi, Elizabeth, *Roy Acuff, the Smoky Mountain Boy*, Pelican Publishing Company, Gretna, LA, 1978.

Shelton, Robert, and Goldblatt, Burt, *The Country Music Story*, Castle Books, Seacaucus, NJ, 1966.

Smith, Richard D., *Can't You Hear Me Callin'—The Life of Bill Monroe*, DaCapo Press, Cambridge, MA, 2001.

Wesbrooks, Wilbur, with McLean, Barbara, and Grafton, Sandra, *Everybody's Cousin*, Manor Books, NY, 1979.

Willis, Barry R., *America's Music—Bluegrass*, Pine Valley Music, Franktown, CO, 1989.

221

Wolfe, Charles K., *A Good-Natured Riot—the Birth of the Grand Ole Ory*, Country Music Foundation and Vanderbilt University Press, Nashville, TN, 1999.

Wolfe, Charles K., and Akenson, James E., ed., *Country Music 2001 Annual*, ed., University Press of Kentucky, Lexington, KY, 2001.

Wolfe, Charles K., *Tennessee Strings*, University of Tennessee Press, Knoxville, TN, 1977.

Wolfe, Charles, *The Devil's Box: Masters of Southern Fiddling*, Country Music Foundation and Vanderbilt University Press, Nashville, 1997.

2. Commercial Recordings and Liner Notes

Howdy Forrester Solo Fiddling

MGM E4035 (also on CUB 8008), *Fancy Fiddlin'—Country Style*, 1962.

Stoneway—STY-127, *Howdy's Fiddle and Howdy, Too!*, 1973.

Stoneway—STY-136, *Big Howdy*, produced by R. M. Stone, 1974.

Stoneway—STY-150, *Leather Britches*, produced by R. M. Stone, 1975.

Stoneway—STY-168, *Howdy Forrester, Stylish Fiddling*, 1976.

United Artists UA 329, *Big Howdy—Fiddlin' Country Style*, produced by Tommy Jackson, 1963.

Howdy Forrester Twin Fiddling

County Sales, *Red Apple Rag*, County 784, (with Kenny Baker), 1983.

Kanawha 601, County Sales, *Twin Fiddling—Country Style*, (with Robert "Georgia Slim" Rutland), 1947, re-issued as Tri-Agle-Far Records, *Twin Fiddling, Texas Style: Georgia Slim and Howdy Forrester*, 2006.

Stoneway—STY-149, *Fiddle Tradition* (with Chubby Wise), 1975.

Compilation Albums on Which Forrester Plays

Deluxe DCD 7823, Highland Music Company, *30 Greatest Fiddlers' Hits* (CD), 1987, 2 cuts ("Still on the Hill" was formerly released on Starday—246, *Country Music Cannonball*).

Stoneway, STY-148, *Fiddle Hoedown*, produced by R. M. Stone, re-publication of two Forrester solo cuts: "Brown Skin Gal" and "Clarinet Polka."

Recordings of Forrester with Roy Acuff and the Smoky Mountain Boys

Capitol DT-2103, *The Great Roy Acuff*, 1964.

Capitol DT-2276, *Voice of Country Music*, 1965.

Columbia CS-1034, *Greatest Hits*, 1970.

Elektra 9E-302, *Roy Acuff Greatest Hits, Vol. 1*, 1978.

Elektra E1-60012, *Roy Acuff Back in the Country*, 1981.

Hickory LPM-101, *Once More It's Roy Acuff*, 1959.

Hickory LPS-109, *Roy Acuff—King of Country Music*, 1962.

Hickory LPM-113, *Star of the Grand Ole Opry*, 1963.

Hickory LPM-114, *Roy Acuff and his Smoky Boys: The World Is His Stage*, 1963.

Hickory LPS-115, *American Folk Songs*, 1963.

Hickory LPS-117, *Hand Clapping Gospel Songs*, 1964.

Hickory LPS-119, *Country Music Hall of Fame*, 1964.

Hickory LPS-125, *Great Train Songs*, 1965.

Hickory LPS-134, *Roy Acuff Sings Hank Williams*, 1966.

Hickory LPS-139, *Famous Opry Favorites*, 1967.

Hickory LPS-145, *Roy Acuff, A Living Legend*, 1968.

Hilltop JS-6090, *Sunshine Special*, 1970.

RME, Inc., *Roy Acuff and the Smoky Mountain Boys, Vol. 1–5*, Royal Crown Cola Shows, re-released on CD, 2001 (no CD number).

The Roy Acuff Show Collection: The Great 48, 2006, no CD number available. This is a collection of Acuff show segments with many tunes played by Howdy Forrester, including ones not released on any of Howdy's commercial recordings.

Other Recordings on Which Forrester Plays

Bear Family Records—*Kitty Wells—The Golden Years (1949–1957)* Forrester twin fiddles with Ray Crisp on two tunes.

Bluebird Records, 20 sides including "Tell Me" and "That'll Do Now, That'll Do"—BB B-8033; "The Old Mountain Man" and "Is Your Name Written There?"—B-8065; "Tennessee Swing" and "Banjo Rag"—B-7868; "The Great Shining Light" and "New Lamplighting Time in the Valley"—B-7999; "The Lamplighter's Dream" and "Dad's Little Boy"—B-7935; "I've Had a Big Time Today" and "Give Me Old-Time Music"—B-7982; "The Farmer's Daughter" and "Gypsy's Warning"—B-7893; "In the Pines" and "Why Should I Wonder?"—B-7943; "When the Roses Grow Around the Cabin Door" and "I'm Lonesome, I Guess"—B-8009; "Hesitating Blues"— B-8101; and one Montgomery Ward only release: "Girl of My Dreams"—MW M-7689. One cut, "In the Pines," was re-issued in 2002 on the CD *Fiddlin' Arthur Smith and his Dixieliners* and another cut Tennessee Swing was re-issued in 2003 on the CD *Farewell Blues—Hot String Bands, 1936—1941*.

Columbia KC-34035, *Sonny James: 200 Years of Country Music*, 1976; Forrester plays on "Blue Moon of Kentucky."

County Records, *Flatt & Scruggs: Foggy Mountain Jamboree*, 1996 (previously released as a Columbia side in 1951–52: "Earl's Breakdown"—20886).

Decca DL7-8950 and later MCA-162, *Square Dances Without Calls*, produced by Tommy Jackson. Forrester is the unpublished lead fiddle on "Snowflake Reel," "Clarinet Polka," and "Jesse Polka."

MCA Records, *Bean Blossom*, MCA 2-8002, 1973.

Mercury Records, *The Stanley Brothers & the Clinch Mountain Boys: The Complete Mercury Recordings*, Mercury B0000534-02, released on CD in 2003 (Originally released as: Mercury LP20884 and Merc-Starday 71258.

RCA APLI-0309, *Over the Hills to the Poorhouse* (Lester Flatt and Mac Wiseman), 1973— Howard twin fiddles with Paul Warren.

RCA 4547, *Lester & Mac,* (Flatt & Wiseman), 1971; Howard twin fiddles with Paul Warren.

Rounder Records Corp., CDSS 08/A22695, *Flatt & Scruggs: Don't Get Above Your Raisin',* 1992 (originally released as Columbia sides recorded in 1951–52: "'Tis Sweet to be Remembered"—20886; "My Darling's Last Good Bye"—21002; "Get in Line Brother"—20915; and "I'm Gonna Settle Down"—21043).

Rounder CDSS 05/A22614, *Flatt & Scruggs: The Golden Years,* 1992 (Originally released as Columbia sides in 1951–52: "Earl's Breakdown"—20886 and "Brother, I'm Getting Ready to Go"—20915).

Starday Records, SLP-228, *The Original Talking Blues Man: Robert Lunn,* 1957; Howard solos on Fiddlin' Trombone and also plays with the Jug and Washboard Band

STOP LP#10001, *Calhoun Twins—Jet Set in the Caribbean,* produced by Shot Jackson, Forrester is the uncredited fiddle.

Radio KRLD, *Texas Roundup Gang from KRLD,* 2 CDs taken off the air, 1946 (courtesy of Bob Forrester).

3. Newspaper and Magazine Articles

Billboard, Vol. 77, of 10/30/65, "Howdy Forrester Recalls Grand Old Days," p. 68–69.

Billboard, of 2/3/68, "Howdy Forrester Turned Booker", p. AR-8.

Billboard, Vol. 99, of 8/22/87, "Lifelines: Deaths—Howdy Forrester," p. 96.

Bluegrass Unlimited, 1976, advertisement for Lester Flatt's 4th Annual Mt. Pilot Festival.

Bluegrass Unlimited, "General Store," January 1978.

Bluegrass Unlimited, August 1978, "The Odyssey of Arthur Smith," by Charles Wolfe, p. 50–55.

Bluegrass Unlimited, November 1979, "Robert Byrd: Fiddler in the Senate," by Charles Wolfe, p. 28–31.

Bluegrass Unlimited, April 1985, "Georgia Slim Rutland, A Fiddler's Fiddler," by Janice McDonald, p. 22–25.

Bluegrass Unlimited, September 1987, "Howard 'Big Howdy' Forrester," p. 72–79.

Bluegrass Unlimited, September 1988, "Notes & Queries," by Walter V. Saunders, p. 7–8.

Bluegrass Unlimited, Vol. 37, No. 2, August 2002, "Joe Forrester: Forgotten Bluegrass Boy," M. Henry, p. 44.

Crockett Democrat, Crockett, TX, Vol. 7, No. 31, of 6/19/47, "All-Out Welcome to Greet Fiddlers and Guests," p. 1 (courtesy of CMF Library).

Devil's Box, published by Tennessee Valley Old Time Fiddlers, Association, Madison, AL (All song transcriptions by John Hartford).

Issues: Newsletter 25 of 6/1/74, " Howard 'Big Howdy' Forrester," by Perry Harris and H. G. Roberts, plus *Trot Along*, p. 1–14 and Cover Photo.

Vol. 15, No. 4, Winter 1981, *Brilliancy*, p. 69.

Vol. 16, No. 3, Fall 1982, *High-Level Hornpipe*, p. 53–54.

Vol. 17, No. 3, Fall 1983, *Nancy Roland*, p. 32.

Vol. 19, No. 2, Summer 1985, *Memory Waltz*, p. 23.

Vol. 20, No. 3, Fall 1986, *Doc Harris Hornpipe*, p. 25 (transcribed by Frank Maloy) and "An Interview with Georgia Slim (Bob Rutland)" by Earl Spielman, p. 5–14.

Vol. 21, No. 4, Winter 1987, Cover Photo and "An Interview with Big Howdy Forrester," by Buddy Spicher, p. 3–15.

Vol. 22, No. 1, Spring 1988, *Hollow Poplar, Old Hollow Poplar* (from Uncle Bob), *Dugler with a Shoofly On* (from Uncle Bob), p. 39–41.

Vol. 22, No. 2, Summer 1988, *Home-made Sugar and a Puncheon Floor* (from Uncle Bob), *Se-Cesh, Stump-Tailed Dog* (from Uncle Bob), and *Hawk Got a Chicken* (from Uncle Bob), p. 47–48.

Vol. 22, No. 3, Fall 1988, *Sells Bros. Circus Rag, Polly Put the Kettle On, Twinkle, Twinkle Little Star*, and *Ladies in the Ballroom*, p. 20–21.

Vol. 22, No. 4, Winter 1988, *Lost Indian, Cotton-Eyed Joe, Goin' Up Town*, and *Bitter Creek*, p. 50–51.

Vol. 23, No. 1, Spring 1989, *Possum Up a Gum Stump, Balance All* (from Uncle Bob), *Ruffled Drawers (New Five Cents), Tumblin' Creek Liza Jane*, p. 22–23.

Vol. 23, No. 2, Summer 1989, *Billy in the Low Ground*, p. 50–53.

Vol. 24, No. 3, Fall 1990, *Greenback Dollar* and *Fourteen Days in Georgia*, p. 39.

Vol. 26, No. 1, Spring 1992, *Peter Went A-Fishin'* and *Georgia Railroad*, p. 40 .

Vol. 28, No. 3, Fall 1994, *Dog in the Rye Straw*, p. 41–42.

Vol. 30, No. 2, Summer 1996, *Trot Along*, p. 46.

Unknown Issue called "Fiddler's Dream," No. 18 in the Fiddling Archives Series, "Fiddler's Dream: The Legend of Arthur Smith," by Charles Wolfe, p. 26–83.

Fiddler Magazine, Vol. 12, No. 1, Spring 2005, "Fiddle Music of the Civil War" by Jim Wood, p. 18–20.

KVOO Lariat, Vol. 1, No. 1, Tulsa, OK, 6/17/39.

Mandolin World News, Vol. V, No. 14, *Town & Country Fiddler*.

Muleskinner News, Sept. 1973, "Big Howdy! Howdy Forrester, Fiddler," p. 12–17.

Nashville Banner, of 4/20/50, "Hippodrome Rocks and Reels to Tune of Old-Fashioned Square Dance," p. 18.

Nashville Banner, of 3/10/60, "'Round the Clock," Harry Draper.

Nashville Banner, 1964, "Occidents Happen in Orient-ated," by Red O'Donnell.

Nashville Banner, 12/8/84, "Back on Opry," Associated Press.

Nashville Banner, of 6/12/87, "Grand Master Fiddler to Top Off Fun Fair" (courtesy of CMF Library).

Pickin' & Singin' News, Vol. 2, No. 25, of 1/15/55, "Acuff Company Captures Alaska."

Strings Magazine, Vol. 5, May–June 1991, "Fancy Fiddlin' Country Style," Stacey Phillips, p. 38–41.

Tennessean, of 8/11/57, "Royalty in Exclusive Rose Concert."

Tennessean, of 8/2/87, "Obituary—Forrester, Howard Wilson (Big Howdy)" and "Opry fiddler Forrester, 65, dies; rites set," p. 4-B.

Tennessean, of 8/6/87, "Mr. Howdy Forrester, fiddler."

Variety, Vol. 328 of 8/12/87, "Obituaries, Howdy Forrester," p. 113.

4. Documents

—Birth Certificate of Howard Forrester, 3/31/22

—Marriage License of Howard Forrester, 6/29/40

—Death Certificate of Howard Forrester, 8/01/87

—Draft Notice of Howard Forrester

—DD-214, Notice of Discharge, Howard Forrester

—IRS Form W-2 from W. S. Monroe to Howard Forrester, 1943

—IRS Form W-2 from National Life & Accident Insurance to Howard Forrester, 1943

—IRS Form W-2 from W. S. Monroe to Wilene Forrester, 1943

—Flyer from Course: Fiddlers on Fiddling, dated 7/73

—Certificate—Order of the Arctic Realm, dated 12/54

—Certificate—Royal Order of the Polar Bear Club, dated 12/54

—Certificate—Family Reunion of Country Music, dated 6/14/75

—Certificate of Esteem from US Army, Europe, dated 12/14/60

—Certificate of Esteem for Patriotic Service, from Dept. of Defense, 1953

—Souvenir Program—Liberty Bicentennial Observation, Liberty, TX, dated 4/18–21/56

—Program—The Texas Roundup Presents Souvenir Folder, 1947

—Program—Georgia Slim Rutland and the Texas Roundup Radio Stage Show

—Radio Station KRLD, Dallas, TX, Music Clearance Logs for March 22, April 25, 26, and 28, May 5 and 7, 1949

—Black Book (Ledger) of Joe Forrester, dated April–December, 1938

—Red Book (Ledger) of Joe Forrester, dated October 1939–May 1940

—Spring Hill Mortuary Funeral Memorial Book, 1987 (courtesy of Bob Forrester)

—Framed copy of check for $10,000 from Roy Acuff to Howdy Forrester, 8/85

—BMI file of Howdy Forrester's copyrighted compositions and arrangements

5. Letters and Cards

—Postcard from Howard and Joe Forrester to Emmie Forrester, 3/22/39

—Postcard from Emmie Forrester to Howard and Joe Forrester, 5/10/39

—Letter from Howard Forrester to Wilene Russell, 3/7/40

—Letter from Wilene Russell to Howard Forrester, 3/28/40

—Postcard from Howard Forrester to Wilene Russell, 4/2/40

—Letter from Howard Forrester to Wilene Russell, 5/18/40

—Letter from Howard Forrester to Wilene Russell, 5/23/40

—Telegram from Howard Forrester to Wilene Russell, 5/31/40

—Postcard from Joe Forrester to Howard Forrester at KTSA, San Antonio, TX, 11/17/41

—Postcard from Joe Forrester to Howard and Billie Forrester, 2/19/42

—Postcard from Clyde Forrester to Billie Forrester, 4/17/43

—Postcard from Billie Forrester (in Boston) to Emmie Forrester, 5/43

—Letter from Howard Forrester to Billie Forrester, 5/15/43

—Letter from Howard Forrester to Emmie Forrester, 9/1/43

—Letter from Howard Forrester to Billie Forrester, 9/4/43

—V-Mail Letter from Clayton Forrester to Billie Forrester, dated 1/23/44

—Letter from Howard Forrester to Billie Forrester, 5/7/45

—Letter from Howard Forrester to Billie Forrester, 6/1/45

—Telegram from Howard Forrester to Emmie Forrester, 11/13/45

—Telegram from Howard Forrester to Billie Forrester, 11/19/45

—Letter to Howard Forrester from Uncle Dave Macon, 8/46

—Letter from Howard Forrester to Emmie Forrester, using Edgefield address

—Letter from Honey Wilds to Howdy Forrester, dated 12/31/46

—Letter Contract from Sally Ann Forrester to Tommy Scott, 11/27/47

—Letter from Acuff-Rose to Howdy Forrester, dated 3/28/60

—Letter from CMA to Howdy Forrester, dated 2/16/78

—Letter from Senator Robert Byrd to Howdy Forrester, dated 3/16/79 (courtesy of Clyde Forrester)

—Letter from Peggy Lamb at Sony/ATV (formerly Acuff-Rose Music Publishing to Gayel Pitchford, dated 8/21/03

—Letter from Photographer Rick Gardner to Gayel Pitchford, dated 1/2/04

—Letters from Clyde Forrester to Gayel Pitchford, dated 4/24/04 and 812/04

—Letters from Joe Forrester to Gayel Pitchford, dated 8/10/04, 8/30/04, 12/8/04, 3/15/05, and 6/9/05

—Letters from Bob Forrester to Gayel Pitchford, dated 9/1/04 and 12/1/04

6. Manuscripts

—*Come Prepared to Stay: Bring Fiddle (The Story of Sally Ann Forrester, the Original Bluegrass Girl)*, unpublished Master's Thesis of Murphy Henry, George Mason University, Fairfax, VA, 1999.

—*Country Music Foundation Oral History: Howdy Forrester,* Doug Green, 9/26/74

—Interview of Howdy Forrester Compilation, Danny Twork, 2/24/84, courtesy of Bob Forrester.

—Interview of Howdy Forrester by Earl Spielman, Southern Folklife Collection Artist Names File #30005, Southern Folklife Collection, Manuscripts Department, Wilson Library at UNC Chapel Hill, 1968.

7. Interviews

Robert (Bob) Forrester, 4/04, 12/04 and 12/05, at Nashville, TN, plus numerous phone conversations.

Clyde Forrester, at Nashville, TN, 4/04 and 12/04.

Joe Forrester, at Nashville TN, 4/04, 12/04 and 12/05, plus numerous phone conversations.

Roscoe and Ossie White, 3/04 at Oroville, CA, and 9/04 at Tehachapi, CA

Tom Ewing, 4/04 at Nashville, TN.

Charlie Collins, 12/04 and 12/05 at Nashville, TN.

Jean Thomas, 12/04 at Nashville, TN.

Robert Cogswell, 12/05 at Nashville, TN.

Les Leverett, 12/05 by phone.

Ron Eldridge, 1/06 by phone.

8. Photographs

Country Music Foundation Library

Bob Forrester

Clyde Forrester

Joe Forrester

Steve Forrester

Rick Gardner

Les Leverett, WSM Photographer

Isaac Litton High School Yearbook

Gene Lowinger

Dr. B. J. Mitchell

9. E-mails

Mike Armistead at RME, Inc.

Robert Cogswell

Stewart Evans

Rick Gardner

Fiddler Johnny Gimble

George Gruhn

Murphy Henry

Barbara Hoffman at Nashville Symphony

Dawn Oberg, Denny Adcock, and Alan Stoker at CMF Library

Fiddler Stacy Phillips

Paul Rawls

Eddie Stubbs

Anton Ullrich

Charles K. Wolfe

10. Visits

Opryland Museum, Roy Acuff Exhibit, 4/04

Public Library of Nashville and Davidson County, 4/04

Country Music Foundation Library, 4/04 and 12/04

Kansas State University Library, Emporia, KS, 7/03

Garland County Library, Hot Springs, AK, 7/03

Hickman County, TN (Vernon, Centerville, Pretty Creek, Bucksnort, Forrester family homestead), 12/04

11. Videotapes

—*The Ryman, Mother Church of Country Music,* Nashville Public Television, 2004

—Roy Acuff's Open House—*3 shows (from Bob Forrester collection)*

—Roy Acuff's Open House—*5 shows (from Bob Forrester collection)*

—Howdy Forrester, family and friends at Clyde Forrester's house, party, 2/15/87 (from Bob Forrester collection)

—Roy Acuff & Smoky Mountain Boys, 1957, and 20/20 video clip from 12/15/89 (from Bob Forrester collection)

—Trip to Scotland by Howdy Forrester, family and friends, 1974, 8 mm movie transferred to video (from Bob Forrester collection)

—Nashville Symphonette Tribute to Howdy Forrester at the National Grand Master Fiddle Contest, 6/11/89 (from Bob Forrester collection)

—*Hall of Fame Special* at the House of Cash, Nashville, TN

12. Audio Tapes—as yet unpublished (courtesy of Bob Forrester)

—1970 Jam Session in Roy Acuff's Dressing Room, Howdy Forrester, Johnny Gimble, and other Opry stars

—July 25, 1971—Jam Session, Howdy Forrester and Johnny Gimble

—November 5, 1972 Jam Session, Howdy Forrester, Johnny Gimble, and family and friends in Hickman County

—Grand Master Fiddle Contest—Porter Wagoner show, 1974

—Thanksgiving 1971, Jam Session

—"One of our best parties (with John [Gimble] on mandolin)", undated

13. Websites

Allroadsleadtobranson.com

Countrymusichalloffame.com

Doodah.net/bgb

Earlscruggs.com

Grandmasterfiddlechampionship.com

Luma-electronic.cz

Music.lycos.com

Nwbn.freeserve.co.uk

Texasoldtimefiddlers.org

Theiceberg.com

Tomrutledge.com

Unitylodge.ca/nashville

Vh1.com

Wnpt.net/ryman

14. Publicity Flyers, courtesy of Country Music Hall of Fame Library

—Corsicana Junior Chamber of Commerce presents Hal Horton and his Texas Roundup

—WSM Grand Ole Opry Presenting Radio Stars in Person (Sally Ann Forrester) on May 25 at Opelika Old Ball Park

—WSM Grand Ole Opry Presents Herald Goodman and Tennessee Valley Boys, December 15, 1938, Maxie, VA

—Old Fashioned Square Dance & Barbeque in Only, TN

—Howdy Forrester and Texas Roundup heard on KRLD and Cornbread Matinee (Promo Flyer #1)

—DANCE: Howdy Forrester and Texas Roundup at Crystal Springs Ballroom, May 4 (Promo Flyer #2)

—DANCE: Howdy Forrester and Texas Roundup at Eagletown, OK, March 5

—KTUL Newsletter, date unknown

15. Experiments

Doublestop experiment, Gayel Pitchford and Dr. BJ Mitchell, 8/04

Index

Give the Gift of

FIDDLER OF THE OPRY
The Howdy Forrester Story
to Your Friends and Colleagues

❑ **YES**, I want _____ copies of *Fiddler of the Opry* at $26.95 each, plus $4.00 shipping per book (California residents please add $1.95 sales tax per book). Canadian orders must be accompanied by a postal money order in US funds. Allow 15 days for delivery.

My check or money order for $_____ is enclosed.

Name _____

Organization _____

Address _____

City/State/Zip _____

Phone_____ E-mail _____

Please make your check payable and return to:
Viewpoint Press
PMB 400, 785 Tucker Road #G
Tehachapi, California 93561